RESTORING SCOTLAND'S CASTLES

RESTORING SCOTLAND'S CASTLES

An account of the restoration or rebuilding of eleven tower houses,
based on the presentations made at a conference held in Glasgow
at the Henry Wood Hall, Woodside,
organised by the Strathclyde Group of
the Architectural Heritage Society of Scotland.

Editor: Robert Clow

Published by
John Smith and Son (Glasgow) Ltd.,
Glasgow University Bookshop,
University Avenue,
Glasgow G12 8PP.

MM

First published in AD 2000

Copyright © 2000 Robert Clow on behalf of the individual contributors.

ISBN 0-900673-26-5

Typeset in Berkeley Old Style, 11 pt on 14 pt.
Made and printed in Scotland by
The James McVicar Printing Works
Colour Printers and Publishers
97 Dykehead Street, Queenslie Industrial Estate, Glasgow G33 4AQ
Telephone: 0141 774 5132   Fax: 0141 744 4440

for Katrina and Elinor

The Royal Commission on Ancient and Historical Monuments has kindly given permission to reproduce the illustrations of the following castles: Aiket, Aldie, Ballindalloch, Barcaldine, Brora, Dean, Kellie (near Arbroath), Nunraw and Tioram. For this, and for the helpful assistance of the Commission's staff, grateful acknowledgement is made.

Contents and Contributors

Foreword
Dr W. A. Brogden, Chairman AHSS, 1990-91 vii

Acknowledgements
Michael C Davis..xi

List of Subscribers xiii

The Adaptation and Restoration of Tower Houses:
an Historical Review from the Reign of Charles II to the Present
Professor David Walker..1

Midhope Castle - consolidation for the Hopetoun Estate
Bill Cadell, Architect..31

Muckrach Castle - for occupation
Ian Begg, Architect 43

Tilquhillie Castle - the architect's work
France Smoor, Architect 55

Tilquhillie Castle - the owner's approach
Dr John Coyne, owner 67

Aiket Castle - for owner occupation
Robert Clow, owner 87

Alloa Tower - for public access
Andrew Millar, Director of the Alloa Preservation Trust..111

Fawside Castle - for owner occupation
Tom Craig, owner..123

Mains Castle - for owner occupation
Mike Rowan, owner..145

Rusco Tower - for owner occupation
Graham Carson, owner..161

Tillycairn, Hatton Castle and Forter Castle - the work
Ian Cumming, builder and mastermason 177

Castle Tioram and the Restoration Debate: conclusion
Michael C Davis, Architectural Historian 193

Foreward

The castles of Scotland, especially those that are smaller, have exercised a phenomenal attraction to many couples (usually young and not very rich) in the thirty years or so between 1960 and 1990. Few have been as fortunate as the late Maurice and Geraldine Simpson who lived at Muchalls, near Aberdeen, the early 17th century marine villa of the Leys family, which was habitable when they acquired it in the late 1960s, so no major work required to be undertaken. More characteristic was the experience of the Tennants of Balfluig, in the late 1950s, and the Ellingtons at Towie Barclay, ten years later, where very significant rebuilding had to be undertaken, as the castles were uninhabitable.

Whatever caused such extraordinary interest and affection to persuade these individuals, and many others, to mortgage themselves far beyond prudence, committing themselves and their young families to years of rebuilding, with little to guide them other than the buildings themselves? It is partly because the castles were so numerous, so neglected and so much bound up with Scotland's landscape, and with Scottish history. Partly, it is also due to Nigel Tranter, who had written about them in a most accessible and, at the same time, exciting way. He doubtless fostered and fed additional interest, as did the reprinting of MacGibbon and Ross's Domestic and Castellated Architecture of Scotland, which is still available from good bookshops.

The very romance of a ruin, and the uncertainty - the very many uncertainties - of just what these buildings had been, how they had been used, furnished, finished and decorated, and how they fitted into their environment and times, made them ever more appealing as objects of study and rebuilding.

In 1991 the Architectural Heritage Society of Scotland held a very lively conference in Glasgow. Organised by the Society's Strathclyde Group, ten speakers with experience of making tower houses habitable again came together to share their stories and Professor David Walker, then the Government's Chief Inspector of Buildings, set the current spate of restorations into its historical perspective. These presentations, reworked for publication, largely form the contents of this book and still give some sense of the joyous celebration of the day itself - a typical Strathclyde mixture of scholarly seminar and a rather grown-up children's picnic party!

It may never be possible to write a definitive guide on how to go about restoring tower houses, or castles, but without the experience these case studies reveal, and many others similar to them, we should still be very significantly in the dark. Most of the lessons we needed have come from the buildings themselves. Although many mistakes may have been made and although many questions remain to be answered, so much has been learned by these keenly committed restorers and rebuilders through their engagement with the castles. Their works are so many experiments and, through these, the tower house has begun to reveal itself - or perhaps, more accurately, their selves.

As David Walker shows in his magisterial but characteristically genial overview and historical introduction, the tower house, having been the universal landed proprietor's house type, was abandoned from the mid 17th century in favour of the preferred modern, low-built mansion house of usually two or three floors. These, in turn, were refined into the one or two storey regular houses, whether cottage, farmhouse, or manse, which so many of us now inhabit. Having been thus abandoned, the tower house began its slow decay but, being so very robust, that decay took centuries to accomplish, and in the meantime it began to acquire the romance of decay. Robert Adam perhaps was responsible for our preoccupation with how most appropriately to respond to these venerable old buildings.

The various responses to that concern are brilliantly conveyed in Professor Walker's paper, which, having formed the introduction to the day's proceedings, has been considerably expanded. He puts the work addressed by the Conference into the context of three or more centuries of development and takes the reader more specifically through the 19th and 20th centuries. Professor Walker is also able to put the point of view of the scholar, as authority, and to demonstrate how authority has had to try, sometimes from a scanty knowledge base, to curb the innocent exuberance of keen castle restorers, whose knowledge base might have been even scantier, if more enthusiastic.

William Cadell, with many years respected experience, introduces the architect's approach - a judicious mixture of archaeology, accumulated knowledge from old buildings, and more modern ideas of what late 20th century habitations ought to comprise. Ian Begg, also a respected architect of considerable experience, makes a kind of bridge between Walker and Cadell and the enthusiastic owner. He is always alive to the picturesque power of these old buildings, and respectful in his way of them, but it could never be said of him that he is in any way intimidated, as his cheerful use of concrete blockwork, in place of stone, attests.

Of the owner restorers, the most soberly intellectual were possibly the Coynes - perhaps because one of them is a trained scientist. In addition, Tilquhillie was largely intact and its rescue was relatively late. (A similar response to that which the Coynes took had been already exhibited in the late 19th century, by Dr William Kelly, whose proposals compare very favourably with Lorimer's more sensitive work.) The book records the restoration from the architect's point of view (France Smoor) and from the Coynes's experience. Tilquhillie was listened to in the manner of a good medical practitioner listening to a patient, and over time its health was regained.

Robert and Katrina Clow let us see into their hearts, with Robert's account of undertaking the design and contracting work themselves, at Aiket Castle. All the problems (remember bridging loans and mortgages at 15% per annum?) and most of the joys of rebuilding old tower houses were recounted, as were the lessons learnt along the way, or not learnt, as the case may be. The Clows were equally dismissive of 18th century work at Aiket, as were the Coynes of the 19th century additions at Tilquhillie.

Alloa Tower is unusual. It is much bigger than all the other castles considered. Its architectural history is known to us from good documentary sources, and it is, and always was, a building of European importance. But its survival was a close run thing. As late as ten or fifteen years ago its importance was not fully recognised, and in its early 18th century heyday it came within a hair's breadth of being made by the (then) Earl of Mar into a baroque palace. In the event, his remarkable inventiveness as an architect is confined to the transformation of the interior into a series of magnificent spaces, served by a truly grand semicircular stair. Andrew Millar and his colleagues undertook an excellent and sympathetic, minimalist restoration, using best current conservation practice, with the advantage of public finance behind such a project - an option not open to private owners.

Fawside - a huge undertaking - was rebuilt by an engineer working closely with a young architect. It possessed a relatively sound tower, but a much less viable wing and the financial implications of this, and Tom Craig's skillful handling of his bankers, became apparent as work progressed.

Those who felt they might sleep for a few minutes, after a luxurious picnic lunch, were quickly to be disappointed, thanks to the hilarious Tales of a Travelling Stonemason - Alastair Urquhart, the master mason from Aboyne, who had worked with both Ian Begg and Ian Cumming on a number of projects, recounted his experiences in the profession, during an extremely funny, illustrated presentation that had everyone rocking with laughter and left, wide awake, for Mike Rowan to give the next paper.

Mains Castle was a sound if roofless (and floorless) building - and the carefully thought out and enthusiastic replacement of these essentials, and all other woodwork, was the major act in rebuilding, undertaken by Mike Rowan, an immensely practical man, and his friends. When required so to do, a structural engineer designs a roof, using his or her scientific knowledge, which also secures professional indemnity insurance, but the engineering stories that tower house rebuilders tell are as legion and entertaining as their Historic Scotland stories. In Mains Castle's case the professional proposal for an over designed roof scheme was abandoned in favour of the owner's ideas, which turned out to be the same as that of a contemporary building. The occasional embarrassments, which follow the obligation to open houses that have been publicly grant-aided, are entertainingly related by Graham Carson of Rusco.

The last but one chapter introduces a testimony from neither keen owner, nor architect. Ian Cumming is a young builder who has specialised in working on tower houses. He is no less keen than any of the other owners, but his excitement comes from the actual problem at hand. I have often seen him puzzle over the geometrical improbabilities of the roof and, in consequence, the loft rooms at Tillycairn are an example of his deliberations. His is a kind of knowledge that architects can rarely acquire, or which owners can hardly accommodate, but it is a most valuable kind of insight into how old buildings actually work, after three centuries of alteration, neglect and reconstruction.

These experiments, eleven case histories in all, give us an extraordinary insight into an important architectural and cultural problem, and they allow - or rather, will allow – us to see the problem more fully and powerfully in a few years' time when they become history, from a variety of committed points of view. At no other time has such a thing been possible, and this series of papers will provide a legacy for students of Scottish architecture, as well as a most entertaining read in the shorter term.

The final paper in this book raises some of the issues that failed to be discussed at the Conference, but were hotly debated at the Civic Reception which followed. Michael Davis summarised the day's proceedings, but rather than repeat what you, gentle reader, have already read, he concludes this volume with views on the restoration debate, brought again into focus by the recent proposal to restore Castle Tioram

In concluding, may I record appreciation of the manner in which the day's proceedings were genially and amusingly conducted by Katrina Clow and add my thanks to the lecturers and authors for giving freely of their experience and time, both at the seminar and, thereafter, in seeing the proposed publication to its conclusion.

W.A. Brogden, PhD., FRIAS.,
Chairman, AHSS, 1990-91.
Aberdeen, July, 1999.

Acknowledgements

Thanks are due to Katrina Clow for chairing the Conference with her customary ebullient enthusiasm, and to the then AHSS (Strathclyde Group) committee members - especially Audrey Gardner, Tom Gardner, Robert McCallum, Margaret McCallum, Bill Nevill, Ruth Nevill and Adam Swan - for their work in making the day go smoothly and easily. With considerable skill Adam Swan recorded the spoken word on an antique Grundig tape recorder and, with even greater patience, Elinor Macfarlane transcribed the ten cassettes, laughter and all, which formed the basis for most speakers' final papers. Our grateful thanks also go to Glasgow City Council for providing the Civic Reception in the City Chambers on the evening of the Conference, as so many delegates came from the north, the east and from London. It was kindly hosted by Councillor Pat Chalmers in her capacity as Convenor of Planning.

It was Robert Clow who organised and publicised what was planned as a modest Strathclyde Group's event. When it looked as though there were to be more than four hundred attenders, the powers that be in Edinburgh subsumed it into the 1991 Architectural Heritage Society of Scotland's National Conference. Keeping its original title, Restoring Scotland's Castles, it was from this series of illustrated presentations that all but two of the papers printed here were drawn. Against what seemed like increasingly long odds, Robert has subsequently battled with the speakers to get them to produce written accounts of their talks, which would become the publication that was originally promised. I suspect that, in at least one or two cases, the restorers took less time to restore their buildings than to write about them! He also encouraged me to update the reader on a current issue which has a bearing on the discussions in the City Chambers reception that followed the Conference, rather than merely repeat my words of summary and thanks, given at the time. This, on the restoration debate and Castle Tioram, is published as the last contribution. Thanks are also due to Alistair Urquhart for a rollicking account of a stonemason's experiences, that kept everyone awake after their lunch.

The task of producing this book would have been infinitely more onerous without the type and illustration-setting skills of Alan Key and the enthusiasms of Brian Sharp of James McVicar Colour Printers and Publishers, the book's printer.

Neither the Conference nor this book could have come about without the freely given contributions of the authors. We are indebted to Professor David Walker for a scholarly introduction to the history of restoration and the restorers have candidly - perhaps once or twice a tad too candidly - supplied a real insight into their restorations, ruminations, methods and motivations. They have given freely of their time, their enthusiasm and their experience and, we hope, not too freely of their views! Their work represents, in many ways, a snapshot in time.

Inclusion of an account of a particular restoration does not carry with it any suggestion of approval (or otherwise) of its restoration techniques, or of the owner's philosophy. Nor were, or are, the talks and subsequent papers intended to represent the views of the AHSS, as one or two members close to the AHSS Council mistakenly thought they might so do. Indeed, it might be difficult for the AHSS to have a corporate view on the restoration of tower houses! Rather, the papers display a selection of restorations of different types of towers, for different sorts of owners, by different methods, with differing results, which tell it like it is or, at least, as those involved in the restoration or rebuilding see it.

This book may inspire enthusiasm. I hope it will also inspire enjoyment, appreciation and respect for the architecture of the past.

Michael C Davis

List of Subscribers

A

Gordon Adam, Esqr., Blairlogie Castle, Stirlingshire.
Iris and Harry Adams, Paisley.
R. W. Alexander, Esqr., Barnweil, Ayrshire.
Sheila Maureen Troy Allan & Family, Ayr.
Robin Allison, Esqr., Merchiston, Edinburgh.
Elizabeth Haldane Anderson, Wishaw.
Louise Annand MacFarquhar, Glasgow.
Earl of Annandale and Hartfell, Raehills.
David Ker Armstrong, Esqr., West Kilbride.
John Armstrong, Esqr., Edinburgh.
Jim Arnold, Esqr., New Lanark.
ARP Lorimer, Architects, Ayr

B

David W. Baird, Esqr.
William Balfour Esqr., Edinburgh.
John N. L. Banister, Esqr.
Dr. Malcolm Bangor-Jones, Dundee.
D. and M. Barber, Cloverhill Farm, Ayr.
E. O. Barnett, Esqr., Kirkhill Castle, Colmonell, Ayrshire.
Mark Barrie, Esqr., The Coach House, Uddingston.
Mrs Anne Baxter, House of Aquahorthies, Aberdeenshire.
Neil Baxter Associates, Glasgow.
Dr Gilbert T. Bell, Erskine, Renfrewshire.
Andrew R. Betchley, Esqr., Edinburgh.
The Bett Family, Glasgow and Kilmarnock.
Julian Birchall, Esqr., Rumelzier, Peeblesshire.
Dr Graham Blackburn, Carriden House, West Lothian.
Keir Bloomer, Esqr., Dunblane.
Michael and Carolyn Blyth, Low Borland, Ayrshire.
Alan and Sheila Borthwick, Mains of Aiket, Dunlop.
John R. E. Borron, Esqr., Near Sawrey, Cumbria.
Frank and Shirley Bracewell, Drymen.
Robert Bradford and Ronnie Cann, Holestone Lodge, Muckhart.

Ian Brash Associates Ltd., Architects, Fa'side Castle.
R. and J. Brinnand, Bristol.
Hugh M. Brodie, Esqr., Farnborough, Kent.
W. A. Brogden, Esqr.
John Wetten Brown, Esqr., Architect, Glasgow.
Ken Brown, Esqr., KLM Partnership, Hailes Avenue, Edinburgh.
Ludovic Brown-Lindsay of Colstoun, Esqr., Colstoun, East Lothian.
Nick Brown, Esqr., Conservation Section Architect, Moray.
V. U. Brown, Esqr., Shalloch Park, Doonfoot, Ayr.
Dr. George G. Browning, Glasgow.
Ian B. D. Bryce, Esqr., FSA Scot., Ferryhill, Aberdeen.
Janey Buchan, Glasgow.
Bernard Burgin, Esqr., Solsgirth, Kinross-shire.
Dr. Jack Burt, FSA Scot., Dunfermline, Fife.
Johnny Bute, Bute.
Mrs. Bridget Butter.

C

Patrick Cadell, Esqr., Edinburgh.
Mrs. W. F. Cairns Smith, Troon.
Sir Ilay Campbell, Bt., Crarae, Argyll.
James W. Campbell, Esqr., Inshock, Nairnshire.
Niall A. Campbell, Esqr., Rowallan Castle, Kilmaurs.
Dr. Helen Cargill Thompson, Glasgow
Carricks, Architects, Alloway Place, Ayr.
Mrs. Valerie Casely, Aberdeen.
Chiene and Tait, CA.
Kenneth Chapelle, Esqr., St. Vincent Crescent, Glasgow.
David and Fiona Chapman, Yetts O' Muckhart.
Michael J. Chapman, Esqr., Lochyhill, Moray.
Clackmannanshire Heritage Trust (formerly Alloa Tower BPT).
Ralph and Susie Cleworth, Yetts O' Muckhart.

Castles of Scotland Preservation Trust, Hamilton House, Prestonpans.
Gordon A. Clark, Esqr., 'Cladach', Ainslie Road, Girvan.
Mr. and Mrs. Andrew Clow, Bury, Lancashire.
Dr. and Mrs. Bill Clow, Haverfordwest, Daffyd.
Dr. David James Clow, Brentwood, Essex.
Dr. Douglas Clow and Rebecca L. Jones, Buckinghamshire.
Mr. G. I. M. Clow and Mrs. C.L. Clow, Beeston, Notts.
Peter Clucas, Esqr., Architect, Broughton in Furness, Cumbria.
Alistair W. R. Cochrane, Esqr., Calsheenig, Prestwick.
Sir Howard Colvin, St. John's College, Oxford.
L. Corbett, Esqr., for Clackmannanshire Field Studies Society.
Alison Cowey, Feddens, Cardross.
Pat Cownie, D. A., 4 Braid Court, Kilwinning, Ayrshire.
Dr. John and Mrs Kay Coyne, Tilquhillie Castle.
Tom and Claire Craig, Edinburgh.
Nola Crewe, M.A., LL.B, FSA Scot., St Monance Castle, Fife.
Cameron and Sarah Crook, The Hague, The Netherlands.
Mary and Eric Curtis, Laglingarten, Argyll.

D
Earl of Dalkeith.
Dr. and Mrs Peter Dallas Ross, Strathview, Blairgowrie.
Ian and Marie Dalglish, East Netherhill, Dunlop.
E. A. M. Davidson, Easdale Island, Argyll.
Michael C. Davis, Esqr., Partickhill, Glasgow.
Gary Dawson, Esqr., Paisley, Renfrewshire.
Sir Ian and Lady Denholm.
David Lee Donachie of Ireby, Astley, Lancashire.
Mr. and Mrs. T. H. P. Donald, East Tannacrieff, Fenwick.

Gavin and Mary Douglas, Arizona, USA.
Gawain and Jenny Douglas, Arizona, USA.
Patricia Douglas, Tantallon, Killearn.
Patrick Dromgoole, Esqr., Penkill Castle, Girvan.
Katrina Drummond, Teignmouth, Devon.
Peter Drummond, Esqr., Kilmarnock.
Findlay Dunachie, Esqr., Glasgow.
John Dunbar, Esqr., Carlops, Scottish Borders.
Morrison Dunbar, Esqr., Glasgow.
Robert J. Dunlop, Esqr., Appin, Argyll.
Stewart Dykes, Esqr., Aberlour, Fife.

E
Earl of Elgin, Broomhall.
Dr Elton A. Eckstrand, Florida, U.S.A.
Sir Archibald Edmonstone.
Mr. and Mrs. Edward D. Enright, Murroes Castle, Kellas.
Angus Erskine, Esq., Edinburgh.
Christine, Lady Erskine-Hill, Harelea, Lanarkshire.

F
Fenton Toner, Ltd., North Berwick, East Lothian.
Hubert W. W. Fenwick, Esqr., Pittenweem, Fife.
Robert Ferguson, Esqr., Architect, Dalgarven, Kilwinning.
Robert Ferguson, Esqr., Whitecroft, Paisley.
Russell Ferguson, Esqr., Windyhaugh, Troon.
Mr. and Mrs. John Findlay.
Michael Finnie, Esqr., East Burra, Shetland.
Charles Fish, Esqr., Thatcham, Berkshire.
Dirk Fitzhugh, Esq., Beesdau House, Tettenhall Wood.
Peter Robert Fleming, Esqr., Sarasota, Florida.
Peter and Heather Fleming-Brown, Glasgow.
Dr. Andrew G. Fraser, Edinburgh.
Col. S. Furness, Netherbyres, Eyemouth.

G
Mrs. M. M. Garden, 15 Cleghorn Road, Lanark.
Tom and Audrey Gardner, Hyndland, Glasgow.

Daniel Gaskell, Esqr., Auchenbrack, Tynron, Dumfriesshire.
A. Gavin, Esqr., Dalmellington, Ayrshire.
Reinold Gayre, Esqr., Minard Castle, Argyll.
John and Margaret Gerrard, Glasgow.
S. C. Gibbs, Esqr., Dougarie, Isle of Arran.
David Gibson, Esqr., Edinburgh.
Dr J. A. Gibson, Scottish Natural History Library.
David M. Glover, Esqr., Cladville, Argyll.
Professor Andor Gomme, Cheshire.
Sheriff and Mrs. Neil Gow of Auchenfail, Ayrshire.
J. M. D. Graham, Esqr., Clairmont, Winton Drive, Glasgow.
Alexander Grant, Esqr., Inverquharity Castle, Angus.
Simon Green, Esqr., Canongate, Edinburgh.
Martyn Gregory Esqr.
Sir Angus and Lady Grossart, Pitcullo Castle, Fife.
John Groves, Esqr., Lundie Castle, Edzell, Angus.
Nicholas Groves-Raines, Esqr., Liberton House, Edinburgh.

H

Lady Hagart-Alexander of Ballochmyle.
Mrs John Haldane, East Wing, Blair, Dalry, Ayrshire.
Dr. Viola Hallman, Killochan Castle, Ayrshire.
David Hamilton, Esqr., Wormit, Fife.
P. J. Hardie, Esqr., Kames Castle, Isle of Bute.
William Hardie, Esqr., New Lanark.
Alastair Harper, Esqr., Glasgow.
Eric Hart and Ian Kirk, Auchendean, Strathspey.
I. Hay, Esqr., Bearsden.
Bob Heath, Esqr., Architect, Alderston, by Haddington.
Drs. Lindsay and Janet Henderson, Strathspey.
Mrs. M. M. Henderson, Prestwick.
Alastair Hendry, Esqr., Ayr.
J. M. Hendry, Esqr., Glasgow.
Nicholas and Zillah Heffer, Caudeval, France.
Lorraine Hesketh-Campbell, Haddo House, Aberdeenshire.
G. Michael Hitchon, Esqr., Ayr.

Kirsteen Holmes, Drumhead, Cardross.
Mrs Sheila Honeyman, Hyndland, Glasgow.
Earl of Hopetoun, Philipstoun House, West Lothian.
George and Doreen Horn, Glasgow.
Dr. Martin G. Horner, Kilmaurs, Ayrshire.
Jean Houghton, London.
Linda Howie, BSc., Darmalloch, Cumnock.
Miles Horsey, Esqr., Edinburgh.
James Hume, Esqr., Auchendoon, Hollybush.
John and Hazel Hunter, Ochiltree Castle, Linlithgow.
J. R. Hutton.
Johatan Irving Hyslop of Dunans, Argyll.

I

Elizabeth Ingleby, Crarae, Argyll.
Sir Malcolm Innes of Edingight, KCVO.
Major Francis Irvine, DL., of Straloch.

J

Andrea Jack, Cardross.
Brian Jamieson, Esqr., Glasgow.
Jim and Krystyna Johnson, 'Crocket's Land', Edinburgh.
Penny and John Johnston, Rhu Arden, Helensburgh.

K

W. J. Keillor, Esqr., Broughty Ferry, Dundee.
Mr. and Mrs. E. T. C. Kennedy, Millhouse of Aiket, Dunlop.
Alan and Joyce Kennedy, Forest Moor, Wigtonshire.
Alastair C. Kennedy, M.D., Vero Beach, Florida, USA.
Susanne M. Kennedy, Paisley, Renfrewshire.
Freda Kennett, Elliston, Howwood, Renfrewshire.
Angus G. Kerr, Esqr., FRIAS, West Kilbride.
Peter R. Kerr, Esqr., Bishopton, Renfrewshire.
Piers Kettlewell, Esqr., Barrhead, Glasgow.
Louise Kilburn, Bath.
Dr. D. A. King, Crail, Fife.
James Kingswell, Esqr., Wallington, Surrey.
T. E. Kinsey, Esqr., Glasgow.

Robert D. Kirkwood, Esqr., Witches Linn, Ardrossan.
William John Kirkwood, Fairlie Castle, North Ayrshire.
Dr. B. I. Knott-Sharpe, Bearsden.

L

Magnus Laird, Esqr., Nisbet, Berwickshire.
Kenneth Lamb, Esqr., Alloway, Ayrshire.
Brian Lambie, Esqr., Biggar.
Hazel Lammie, Whithorn, Wigtonshire.
G. M. S. Lauder-Frost, Esqr., FSA Scot., Mordington, Berwick.
Peter Lavery, Esqr., Bearsden, Glasgow.
William Layhe, Esqr., Alloway, Ayrshire.
Grant E. Lees, Esqr., Benrig, Galashiels.
Lady Lindsey, Gilminscroft, Sorn.
Dr. Maurice Lindsay.
David Lingard, Esqr., Bothwell.
M. Lobanov-Rostovsky, Esqr., Aikenhead House, Glasgow.
Dane Love, Esqr., Lochnoran House, Auchinleck.
Patrick Lorimer, Esqr., Gemilston, Ayrshire.
Robin Lorimer, Esq., Architect.
Anne M. S. Loudon, Langside, Glasgow.
Lumsden of Cushnie, Hamilton House, Prestonpans.
David Lunan, Esqr.
R. and V. Lupton, Ayr.

M

E. Brian McCabe, Esqr., Glasgow.
Robert Duncan McCallum, Esqr., Milngavie.
Mrs. Alexina Macduff, Kilmacolm.
J. and P. McEwen, Auchanachie, Huntly.
Fiona McFadyen, Inchmarlo, Kincardineshire
Elinor Macfarlane, Craigpark, Glasgow.
Gordon McFarlane, Esqr., Burnbrae, Kinross-shire.
Lord Macfarlane of Bearsden.
Brian McGarrigle, Esqr., Glasgow.
Jack McGavigan, Esqr., Kirktonhill, Dumbarton.
Iain A Maciver of Strathendry.

Fiona V. MacKelvie, Glasgow.
Alice A Mackenzie, MBE., Lenzie.
Ian Maclagan, Esqr., LL.B., FSA Scot., Rothesay.
Mr. and Mrs. R. H. McLaren, Crinan Ferry, Argyll.
Robert Maclaren, Esqr., Glenearn, Perth.
Allan Maclean of Dochgarroch, Glen Urquhart, Inverness.
Anna Campbell Maclean, MA., LL.B., Edinburgh.
Sir Lachlan Maclean, Bt., Duart Castle.
Ronald McLean, Esqr., Glasgow.
Mrs. Dianne McLellan, Kircudbright.
Dr. Christine Macleod.
John MacLeod of MacLeod, Dunvegan Castle.
William T. McLeod, Esqr.
Scott MacMillan of Rathdoon, Co. Wicklow, Ireland.
Alison J. McMeekin, Tayport, Fife.
John McMurtrie, Esqr., Balbithan House, Aberdeenshire.
Graham McNicol, Esqr., Arbirlot, Angus.
Robert McWilliam, Esq., Moorfield Ave., Kilmarnock.
Ian and Kim Mains, Fenwick.
Tim Manderson, Esqr., Northants.
Niall Manning, Esqr., Dun Ard, Fintry.
Earl of Mar and Kellie, Alloa.
S. W. Marlow, Esqr., QGM., Forgandenny, Perth.
Harley Marshall, Esqr., OBE., JP., Broadlie, Dalry.
Helen Robertson Martin, Birmingham.
Dr. Calum Massarella, Toronto, Canada.
Mike Masterton, Esqr., St. Andrews Close, London.
Dr. Mark Matheson, Milton Keynes.
Helen Matthews, Irvine, Ayrshire.
Alastair M. T. Maxwell-Irving, BSc., FSA Scot., Telford House, Blairlogie.
J. R. Maxwell Macdonald of Largie.
Dame Jean Maxwell-Scott, DCVO.
Paul Mellon Centre for Studies in British Art, London.
Philip Mercer, Esqr., Hillslap Tower, Roxburghshire.

Matthew Merrick, Esqr., Darnley Street, Pollokshields.
Mary Miers, Ross-shire.
Andrew and Yvonne Millar, Symington, by Biggar.
Mrs. J. W. Miller, Rutherglen, Glasgow.
Margaret S. Miller, Prestwick, Ayrshire
Denys Mitchell.
Ian G. Mitchell, Esqr., QC., North Queensferry, Fife.
Eric Mobey, Esqr., Fairlie House, Kilmarnock.
Hunter Moran, Esqr., Stonemason, Tranent.
Earl of Moray, Darnaway Castle, Moray.
Bruce Morgan, Esqr., Larch Cottage, Grantown on Spey
A. Campbell Morris, Esqr., Bourtree Park, Ayr.
Raymond Morris of Balgonie & Eddergoll.
Stuart Morris of Balgonie & Eddergoll, Yr.
Dorothy Morton, Cailzie, Ruskie, Port of Menteith.
Mrs John Mott, Ayr.
Frank M. Murray, Esqr., 'Kirkfauld', Kilmaurs.
Tom Muirhead, Esqr., Eskbank, Midlothian.

N

Bill and Ruth Nevill, Moray.
William and Dorothy Newlands of Lauriston, Lauriston Castle, Kincardineshire.
Mrs. Anne E. Nimmo, Edinburgh.
D. D. E. W. Nicolson, Esqr., Norton Hall, Pebworth, Warks.
Sir Iain Noble of Ardkingas and Eilean Iarmain, Bt., Skye.
Dr. Raymond Noble, Ayr.
James B. Nodwell, Esqr., Woodlanside, Dumfries.
Laura Norris, Edinburgh.

O

Dr. M. O'Gorman, Thornhill, Stirlingshire.
Paul O'Hare, Esqr., Hamilton.
Bill Osborne, Esqr., Alloa.
Harry Owens, Esqr., Garthbank, Perth.

P

Brian A. Park, Esqr., Stirling.
Ian Parsons, Esqr., Architect, Edinburgh.

Anthony du Gard Pasley, Esqr., Roseburn, Moffat.
David R. Paton, Esqr., Grandhome, Aberdeen.
R. Grant Paton, Esqr., Eynsham, Oxfordshire.
Mrs. Pearl Paul, Milngavie.
Robert Pender, Esqr., Nether Gree, Ayrshire.
Sheila M. Penny, Ayr.
Baron & Lady of Prestoungrange.
Neil Pirrit, Esqr., MBE, Hatton Gardens, Glasgow.
Phil Plevey, Esqr., Craigietocher Tower, Turriff.
The Pollock Hammond Partnership, Linlithgow.
Glen L. Pride, Esqr., St. Andrews.
Mrs S. Purdie, Kilmarnock.

Q

Mrs Margaret Quarm, Annick Lodge, by Irvine.

R

John Ratcliffe, Esqr., Morkeu, Aberdeen.
Brian Reed, Esqr., Watton, East Yorkshire.
F. and P. Reeves, Broomhill, Glasgow.
Ernst and Clara Reimann, Greenock.
R.I.A.S., Edinburgh.
R.I.B.A. Library, Portland Place, London.
Marcus Ridsdill Smith, Esqr., Lyndale House, Isle of Skye.
Kit Rigg, Esqr., Maryfield, Terregles, Dumfries.
The Robert Gordon University Library, Aberdeen.
Gordon Roberts, Esqr., Innellan, Argyll.
Bruce Robertson, Esqr., Cannonmills, Edinburgh.
Mrs. Giles Robertson, Edinburgh.
Mrs. Joan Robertson, Cromalt, Helensburgh.
Neal Robertson, Esqr., Auchtermuchty, Fife.
Mr. and Mrs. Peter Robertson, Noddsdale, Largs.
Ronnie Robertson, Esqr., Elgin.
Mrs Ruth A. Robertson, Rose Cottage, Fenwick.
Stewart and Meryl Robertson, Dunmore House, Argyll.
Thomas Findlay Robertson, 'Lintknowe', Darvel.
Dr. Anthony B. Robertson-Pearce, Stockholm, Sweden.
Ian Rodger, Esqr., Anstruther, Fife.
Robert W. K. C. Rogerson, OBE.

Alastair and Elkine Rolland, Glasgow.

George Rollo, Esqr., B.ARCH., BSC., Anzia.

Mike Rowan, Esqr., Bank Street, Stirling.

Royal Commission on the Ancient and Historic Monuments of Scotland.

Ted Ruddock, Esqr., 20 Lennox Street, Edinburgh.

Christopher Ruffle, Esqr., Dairsie Castle, Fife.

Nigel and Heather Rush, Killinghurst, Surrey.

George R. Russell, Esqr., Linlithgow.

S

Norman Scarfe, Esqr., MBE., FSA., Woodbridge, Suffolk.

Keith Schellenberg, Esqr., Killean, Kintyre.

Nicholas Udny Schellenberg of Knockhall, Newburgh.

A. and A. Scott, Corwar House, Ayrshire.

Michael Scott, Esqr., Edinburgh.

Scottish Civic Trust, Buildings at Risk.

Allan D. Sim, Esqr., Garscadden, Glasgow.

Fiona Sinclair and David Page, Gatehead, Formakin.

Niven Sinclair, Esq., Noss Head, Caithness.

Sinclair-Girnigo Castle Task Force.

Dr. Fraser Smith, Highburgh Road, Glasgow.

Harry Smith, Esqr. MBE., New Lanark and Lanark.

John Smith & Son, Booksellers, Glasgow University.

John Buchanan Smith, Esqr., FSA Scot.

Ronald P. A. Smith, Linlithgow.

David Somervell, Esqr., Holly House, Montrose.

Drew and Nancy Sommerville, Bearsden.

Rev. Alan Sorensen, Greenock.

Simpson & Brown, Architects, Edinburgh

Lord Steel of Aikwood, Aikwood Tower, Selkirk.

Mrs. Mary S. Steel.

Angus Stewart, Esq.

Cecilia H. Stewart, Falkland Street, Glasgow.

Gordon Stewart, Esq., Crerar & Partners, Architects, Edinburgh.

Robert C. Stewart, Esqr.

Ron Stewart, Esqr., Buckie, Banffshire.

Mrs Susie Stewart, Crofthead House, Neilston.

Alan Stockdale, Esqr, Burnsall, North Yorkshire.

P. Stockwell, Esqr., Balcomie, Crail, Fife.

Alex. Strachan, Esqr.,

Roddy and Fiona Strachan, Benholm Castle.

Strathclyde Building Preservation Trust, Glasgow.

John Stuart, Esqr., Glasgow.

Leith and Rachel Stuart, Blackhall Manor, Renfrewshire.

Richard Stuart of Yeochrie, California and Banffshire.

Joseph Sutherland, Esq., Aberdeen.

Adam M. Swan, Esqr.,

T

Jean L. Tait, Uddingston.

Ailsa Tanner, Helensburgh.

Charles Taylor, Esqr., Dalkeith.

Scott Taylor, Esqr., Kilbarchan, Renfrewshire.

Alan and Pamela Templeton, Grange Lodge, Ayrshire.

Mark Tennant of Balfluig, Balfluig Castle, Aberdeenshire.

Mr. and Mrs. D. A. Thin, Fountainhall, Edinburgh.

James Thin, Booksellers, South Bridge, Edinburgh.

Lady Venetia Longstreth Thompson, London W6.

Craig Thomson, Esqr., Thomson Dawes, Architects, Kilmarnock.

Mike Thomson, Esqr., Elgin, Morayshire.

Rosemary Thomson.

W. N. Thomson & Co., Edinburgh, Lothian.

Benjamin Tindall, Esqr., Hermits & Termits, Edinburgh.

Sebastian Tombs, Esqr., RIAS.

Dennis Turner, Esqr., Reigate.

U

Raynor Unwin, Esqr., Little Missenden, Bucks.

V

The Vivat Trust, London.

W

Dr. Anne Walker, Royal Terrace, Glasgow.

Bruce D. J. Walker, Knock Castle, Largs, Ayrshire.

Fiona Walker, Newark Castle, Ayr.
Professor Frank A. Walker, Kilmacolm.
J. A. Wardrop, Esq., DL., Paisley.
N. M. Waring, Esqr., Windsor, Berks.
Ian Watson, Esqr., Balfour Tower, Durris, Banchory.
Jim and Pat Watson, Sandhurst, Ayr.
Tom and Betty Watson, Hillside, Pool of Muckhart.
Dr. D. A. L. Watt, Lochaline, Morven.
Donald G. A. Webster, Esqr.
Graham Webster, Esqr., High Williamshaw, Ayrshire.
Dr. Margaret Weir, Castle of Fiddes.
Earl of Wemyss and March, Gosford House and Redhouse Castle, East Lothian.
R. B. White, Esqr., Newark Drive, Glasgow.
John Wilby, Esqr., Dalzell House, Motherwell.
I. D. Williams, Esqr., Morningside, Edinburgh.
Liz and Peter Whiteside, Hong Kong.
The Hon. Patrick Whitford of Barholm, Barholm Castle.
Mr. and Mrs. Whitley, Oban, Argyll.
J. W. Whittall, Esqr., Fetternear, Aberdeenshire.

Karen G. Wilson, Carlin Craig, Glasgow.
Helen and David Muir Wood, St Edmunds, Milngavie.
Lady Wood, Hughenden Court, Glasgow.
Iain J. Wotherspoon, Esqr., Hillhead, Glasgow.
Bruce Patrick Wright Esqr., Plane Castle, Stirlingshire.
David Patrick Wright, Esqr., Plane Castle, Stirlingshire.
John Patrick Wright, Esqr., Plane Castle, Stirlingshire.
Neil A. Patrick Wright, Esqr., Plane Castle, Stirlingshire.

Y

Mrs R. M. Yeomans, Ashcraig, Ayrshire.
James David Young, Esqr., FLA., Marlborough, Wiltshire.
Moira J. Young, Glasgow.
Bobby Younger, Esq., Old Leckie, Gargunnock.
Helen Younger, Old Leckie, Gargunnock.

Fig. 1
*Murthly Castle, view from the east.
(MacGibbon & Ross).*

The Adaptation and Restoration of Tower Houses: An Historical Review from the Reign of Charles II to the Present

BY PROFESSOR DAVID WALKER

Until the Restoration of Charles II to the throne in 1660, the tower house had been the universal landed proprietor's house type in Scotland. Although few were built after that date, it was to remain so for at least another half century as few estates could finance their replacement. Even where the tower house was a massive vaulted structure which did not easily lend itself to reconstruction, it was almost invariably cheaper to extend and adapt unless there was some fairly catastrophic structural defect. Ideas as to how changing expectations of accommodation and comfort could or should be met, and how the aspirations of the proprietor might be expressed in architectural terms, varied from generation to generation and have continued to do so down to the present century.

Even within generations there have been differences of view. Although the majority of late seventeenth and early to mid eighteenth century gentry aspired to a fashionably modern classical house, wherever the money could be found, there always has been a school of thought which valued the tower house as a powerful symbol of ancient lineage. Thus Charles II and his architect, Sir William Bruce, not merely retained James V's tower in their rebuilding of Holyrood but actually duplicated it, honouring that monarch's intention, when they might equally have chosen to reface it, if not rebuild it, as a classical pavilion. A generation later the 11th Earl of Mar planned the further aggrandisement of his huge tower house at Alloa as the central architectural glory of a vast French Baroque formal garden layout, and yet again in the next generation the 4th Duke of Gordon retained a single tower as the dominant element of the otherwise complete rebuilding of Gordon Castle designed by John Baxter between 1769 and 1782.

In the great majority of cases the reasons for retention were practical as well as economic. Quite often the existing tower house, especially if it was a big Z-plan house, still provided most of the accommodation the family required. Mid to late Georgian modernisations of the larger tower houses tend to follow much the same patterns. In some of the more ambitious cases a new central entrance might be formed through the vaulted chambers of the ground floor, and the back of the house deepened on plan to accommodate a big stair as formerly to be seen at Castle Menzies and at Castle Fraser, and as still to be seen at Careston and at Brodie where a reduction in the number of turrets also formed part of the project. Another common and less expensive solution, well exemplified at Pilrig, was the modernisation of the longest frontage with a central doorpiece at first floor level approached by an external stair, (Fig. 2), the old main door becoming the servants' entrance. At Murthly (Fig. 1, opposite), the smart new Gibbsian first

Fig. 2 – Pilrig House. (MacGibbon & Ross).

An Historical Review – David Walker

floor entrance hall and corridor inserted into the courtyard elevation represented a different and more ambitious new-build response to the problem of providing a more spacious entrance and improved circulation at a house already large enough for the family's needs.

More radical changes were made at Blair Castle, re-planned with a big new stairhall by James Winter in 1747-58 for the 2nd Duke of Atholl. As an architectural expression of more settled times, the siege-damaged towers were cut down and the turrets eliminated to produce an irregular Georgian vernacular pile of uniform height with piended roofs. A similar treatment was adopted by James McLeran as late as 1787-89 at Brahan which survived in its plain Georgianised state until its demolition after the Second World War.

More often the tower house was a smaller one which fell short of what the family required. These were usually extended longitudinally. On the more fashion-conscious estates this tended to be done in a near-symmetrical fashion to produce an effect similar to that of new-built late Stuart houses such as Panmure and The Hirsel, Sir William Bruce's enlargement of Balcaskie in 1668-76 as a small version of John Mylne's Panmure (1666) being a particularly good example. At Craighall, Fife, in 1697, Bruce infilled the court of an early seventeenth century U-plan house and gave it a fashionable pedimented front, a solution adopted in many subsequent modernisations elsewhere. William Adam's enlargement of Brunstane from an L-plan to a U-plan for Lord Milton in 1735 is a late version of the Balcaskie-type solution, though without a central stair, that convenience being envisaged as a later stage in which the forecourt was to have been infilled to produce a square-plan house, as at Craighall.

More formal versions of the same treatment are, or were, to be seen in Sir William Bruce and Alexander Edward's proposals for the pedimented enlargement of Kinnaird Castle in 1698; at Edward's similar enlargement of Brechin Castle in 1698 and 1704; and at the plainer late Stuart reconstruction of Dudhope Castle, Dundee, where the fifteenth century tower house shown in Slezer's view was removed to create a near-symmetrical east front. Similar in principle, but probably achieved without demolition, was the enlargement c. 1700 of the early seventeenth century L-plan house of Balgone where the main jamb was extended and its octagonal stair tower duplicated to produce a fine symmetrical front, a pair of detached pavilions being provided to give a formal grandeur to the layout as a whole. Other exceptional symmetrical solutions, all with forecourts flanked by wings or pavilions, were the reconstruction of the existing house at Drumlanrig as part of a Holyrood-inspired courtyard layout by James Smith between 1680 and 1690, echoing the style of the proposals thought to be by William Wallace of half a century earlier, and the same architect's proposed formalisation of Traquair as a symmetrical frontage, in the idiom of the late sixteenth century. The latter solution was subsequently achieved by William Adam at Taymouth in the 1740s, a very late instance of the Holyroodhouse-Alloa principle of honouring the past by symmetrical duplication. In the particular context of Breadalbane a more relaxed classical solution was perhaps not then thought appropriate.

On the smaller estates the old house was more usually extended to provide the requisite accommodation in a plain vernacular idiom, without any thought of symmetry, as at Kemnay, Ashintully and Old Leckie, or at right angles, as at Old Dalquharran, (Fig. 3), Blair (Ayrshire) and Craighouse, Edinburgh. Particularly

Fig. 3
Dalquharran (MacGibbon & Ross).

interesting examples of longitudinal enlargement were the new wings at Bedlay and Fernie, both provided with outdated round towers to maintain the character of the original tower house, and that at Carnousie where, as late as 1740, William Adam more than doubled the size of the house in the simple idiom of the original Z-plan tower.

In many cases the tower house was either too ancient or offered rather too limited accommodation to form a satisfactory basis for such straightforward enlargement. It also tended to be too daunting a mass of masonry to remove. Reactions to the problem varied from one estate to another. At Amisfield in 1631, only 30 years after the old tower was remodelled, a completely new house was built close by, on the south side of its now vanished court. At Kinneil, c. 1677, (Fig. 4), the ancient tower was gutted, symmetrically rewindowed, re-roofed with a balustraded parapet in place of the old crenellations and augmented by towers to produce an up-to-date late Stuart mansion; and at Hatton (West Lothian) in the 1660s a new mansion was wrapped round three sides of the ancient tower, an exercise repeated by Robert Adam and James Nisbet in their castellated house at Wedderburn as late as 1771-75. More usual was the solution adopted at Kelburn in 1692, or at Ardmillan in the 1730s, where the old tower simply became a useful annexe to the rear of a large new symmetrically planned house. Rather different was Abergeldie, where the old tower, restyled with a Venetian dormer, was given greater prominence as the dominant asymmetrical element in a composition which otherwise comprised a plain but symmetrical U-plan house.

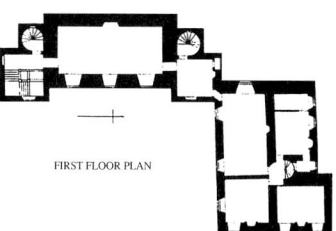

Fig. 4
Kinneil plans and east elevation. The stumps of the original vault on the ground floor of the central block are just traceable in the gutted building.
(MacGibbon & Ross).

An Historical Review – David Walker

Fig. 5
Castle Grant. View from south-east (MacGibbon & Ross).

Unsophisticated though Abergeldie was, it inaugurated a type of composition which was to have a considerable vogue later.

Similar in general principle to Ardmillan was John Adam's work at Castle Grant in 1765 (Fig. 5), where one side of the court was rebuilt as a huge and austere new mansion to which the old, considerably reduced in height on the Blair Castle model, now formed a spacious rear wing and garden court. In a number of instances, as at John Adam's similar but smaller new house at Craig (Auchindoir) in 1767, and at Benholm as originally built in the 1760s, perhaps also by him, completely new houses were constructed leaving the ancient towers as freestanding monuments to the past, their *rôle* now being fairly low-level service accommodation. But more commonly the new house was built on a completely new site. The old house might then be remodelled or reduced as a dower house, as at Old Kippenross, or become a picturesque object or ruin in the landscape, as at Hill of Tarvit, Hopetoun, Auchinleck and Dalquharran; or it might become farm servants' accommodation in association with a steading built from the materials of its barmkin and ancillary buildings, a common fate where desertion followed changing patterns of land ownership.

In a great many instances the layout of the garden made the site of the old house the best location for the new. There are many examples of attempts to incorporate ancient fabric into what was in effect a completely new house with slight irregularities, as at Foulis, where it took the Munros more than thirty years (*c.* 1740-1777) to achieve the desired result. Often these irregularities are more evident in the plan, or at some relatively inconspicuous corner, than on the main elevations. One can see the completed process in James Smith's rebuilding of Dalkeith House in 1702-10 for the Duchess of Buccleuch, where one angle proved too troublesome to rebuild to the square; and uncompleted at Touch of 1757-62 and at Pitcairlie of *c.* 1730 where substantial sections of the previous houses remained undigested. Less thorough-going versions of the same exercise are, or were, to be seen throughout the country. In a fair number of instances, as formerly at Ballencrieff, quite a substantial new single pile house was simply backed up on the old, deepening the plan to double pile: in others the old house was incorporated to form one end of a large provincial Georgian pedimented block, sometimes with the pediment between gable ends, as at Arbuthnott (1755) and formerly at Balgowan, Perthshire; and sometimes with a more up-to-date straight eaves line, as formerly at Lauriston (Kincardine). Gargunnock, recast in 1794, is a good example of the devices to which architects and master-masons might be put to regularise the ancient fabric to an appearance of symmetry. At Aiket, one of the subjects of this volume, the top of the house was simply cut down level with a near-central pediment-gable, (Fig. 6), and the windows enlarged, without any extension to the plan.

Fig. 6
*Aiket Castle, post fire.
Copyright: RCAHMS.*

Towards the end of the century the concept of what should be done with a tower house gradually began to change. At Robert Adam's Culzean from 1777, and at Oxenfoord from 1780, the old castles gradually disappeared almost without trace into the half-Roman, half-Scottish castles which superseded them, Megginch being an interesting example of the uncompleted process. But in Adam's proposals for Cluny a new respect for the geometric qualities of the original is evident, even if the square top stages of the towers were to have been cleared off and replaced by machicolated parapets, perhaps more Italian Mediaeval in inspiration than Scottish. A similar respect for the past is to be seen at Fyvie, where Adam may have been involved. The Gordon Tower, added in 1792, was built with turrets to match the remainder. Something rather similar was achieved in 1797 by a more provincial hand at Leithhall, where the new wing corresponding to the old tower was also given matching turrets, correctly proportioned but dummies bulked out from the walls with no corresponding spaces within.

The 1780s and 1790s saw the first hints of the concept of the tower house as a romantic country seat. In the 1780s a retired East India Company administrator, George Paterson, re-occupied the colossal fifteenth century tower house of Castle Huntly, Perthshire, which he had bought in 1777. He added only a small single-storey frontal addition to supplement the original accommodation, and provided dummy turrets and a circular prospect house at the parapets. The decision to retain and restore the ancient tower was perhaps a chivalrous gesture to his wife, the Hon. Anne Gray, whose family's principal seat it had been until the early seventeenth century. Similar considerations applied at Mount Alexander (now Dunalastair) in the same county where the Robertsons of Strowan, who had just re-purchased their ancestral lands, actually built one anew in the late 1790s. Sited on top of a hillock for added conviction, this tall crenellated four-storey tower, rather similar in silhouette to Castle Huntly, proved inconvenient and incapable of extension. By 1831 its builder was living elsewhere, and it was eventually replaced on a less restricted site after a life of only some sixty years.

Although gothic forms had survived well into the seventeenth century in ecclesiastical work the Gothic Revival made little headway in Scotland, Adam's more robust castellated being fairly consistently preferred to the Wyatt gothic in vogue south of the Border. But in 1802 decisions were taken on the rebuilding of Scone Palace which set the course of greater domestic architecture in Scotland for the next two decades. The 3rd Earl of Mansfield, then aged twenty-four, first consulted the London architect George Saunders. He proposed the removal of the ancient tower house of the Gowries, rebuilding it in conformity with the Renaissance buildings erected by the 1st Viscount Stormont in the early seventeenth century. However innovatory such a scheme might seem now, more than a quarter of a century earlier than William Henry Playfair's pioneer work in the Scots Jacobean idiom at Grange and Prestongrange, in principle it was essentially similar to the later eighteenth century enlargements and re-orderings undertaken at a number of English Jacobean houses, even if on a rather larger

An Historical Review – David Walker

scale. Had it been built, the course of Scottish country house design might have passed straight from Adam castellated to Scots neo-Jacobean. But in that same year Saunders was superseded by William Atkinson, a pupil of James Wyatt, who rebuilt Scone as a fashionably up-to-date English gothic revival house in 1803-10. Atkinson's rebuilding of Drimmie as Rossie Priory followed in 1807-15, and his remodelling and enlargement of the ancient house of Biel in 1814-18, both in the same vein. Similar English gothicisations of ancient Scottish houses took place at Duns, recast and enlarged by James Gillespie Graham between 1818 and 1822, at Johnstone Castle about the same date, and elsewhere.

In 1814 when the London architect William Wilkins was commissioned to build a new house at Dalmeny, the old castle of Barnbougle, which had occupied so much of Robert Adam's attention in his later years, was left as a picturesque ruin some distance away in the park. Wilkins was a much more serious revivalist than Atkinson, bringing to his neo-Tudor revival work the same intensity of scholarship as he applied to his Grecian. Called upon in about 1819 to modernise the great Z-plan tower house at Castle Fraser rather than build anew, Wilkins's response to Scottish antiquity was somewhat different. The tower and turret tops were to be cut off and crenellated as in Robert Adam's proposals for Cluny and the remainder Tudorised, an exercise actually carried out by John Smith at Cluny as late as 1836. Whether Wilkins had assumed from Fraser's big circular tower and keep-like square tower that there was a mediaeval castle under the seventeenth century harl, as an English architect unfamiliar with Scottish castles might well have done at that date, or whether he was simply making it fashionably English, is unrecorded. A far finer exercise of the same kind would have been Charles Barry's neo-Norman reconstruction of Drummond Castle, designed for Lord Willoughby d'Eresby in 1828 and clearly intended to outclass Thomas Hopper's new-build castles at Gosford in Ireland and at Penrhyn in Wales. Barry's scheme was, of course, intended to be for what would, in effect, have been a completely new castle, without any pretence at restoring the existing fabric to its original state.

Whatever may have been in Wilkins's mind, or that of his clients, his proposals for Castle Fraser serve to underline the fact that in the first two-and-a-half decades of the century the corbelled and crenellated parapets of fifteenth and early sixteenth century tower houses were readily appreciated as being of the same family as those of English mediaeval castles, which had been admired for their picturesque qualities in the landscape since at least the mid eighteenth century; and that, despite the best efforts of topographers such as Clerk of Eldin, Grose, Cordiner, Pennant and Nattes in bringing out their picturesque qualities in etchings and engravings, the pepperpot turrets and high dormer-headed roofs of the late sixteenth and early seventeenth centuries remained not merely old-fashioned but unfashionable. The proposals for Castle Fraser and the executed recasting of Cluny, the prime examples of the genre, were by no means unique. At Glamis, where the north-western of the two clasping wings had been demolished, the high crowstep gabled roofs of the surviving southern wing were cut down to lead flats and crenellated, the north-western wing being rebuilt in conformity with it. The main tower may well have been lucky not to share the same fate. At The Binns in 1812 the main elevation seems to have been symmetrically regularised by demolitions and minor additions, the roofs enclosed within crenellated parapets throughout and the windowheads Tudorised. A plainer exercise in the same vein was Dunvegan, where the high roofs were removed, the wallheads levelled up or down and lead flats within crenellated parapets substituted, giving the whole something of the appearance of an Indian hill fort rather than a great clan stronghold.

But within a very few years such Georgian castellations were themselves unfashionable. The fast-changing attitude as to what should be done with a tower house was nowhere more comprehensively chronicled than in the work of William Burn, a friend of Sir Walter Scott, and from 1820 stylistically a follower of Wilkins' Tudor rather than the smooth castellated of his former master, Sir Robert Smirke. At Saltoun in 1818 Burn absorbed the old house as one corner of the main block of his neo-Tudor palace, much as a mid Georgian architect might have done. But at Dundas Castle, where the fifteenth century tower house of the Dundases still retained its corbelled and crenellated parapets, it was left proudly standing guard behind the new Smirke-like castellated house, although only as uninhabited service accommodation. The sixteenth and seventeenth century buildings, even more picturesque to present-day eyes, were cleared away, as were those at Blairquhan two years later, the decorative elements being discreetly preserved in the service court where they would not embarrass the smart English Tudor of the new house. At Strathendry in 1823 the Dundas Castle arrangement was echoed on a smaller scale but at Riccarton in that same year Burn made the ancient tower the dominant element of his new house, refacing it in correct English Tudor ashlar work to match. It was the first time he had adopted such an arrangement, perhaps from force of circumstances, since the client required some serviceable seventeenth and eighteenth century buildings attached to it to be retained, and it was to be the last occasion on which he thought it necessary to Anglicise the detail. Thereafter tower houses were appreciated for what they were rather than what they might become. At Brodie in 1824, not only was the exterior of the great tower respected as found, but the new Jacobethan house was built in rubble to match, eventually being harled to secure still greater unity. But at Burn's rather similar exercise at Lauriston (Midlothian) for Scott's friend, Tom Allen, in 1827, the rubble of the old house was left exposed for picturesque quality and deliberately contrasted with the smart English Jacobethan ashlar work of the new. Much more importantly the conical turret roofs were restored, whereas at Barrogil, only eight years earlier, he had removed them and substituted Braemar-type crenellations. The picturesque qualities of late sixteenth and early seventeenth century tower houses had at last been fully recognised. By 1829 such conical roofs were features of the Scots Tudor houses Burn built anew, and by the mid to late 1830s English Tudor and Jacobethan were gradually being abandoned, Burn's additions at Stenhouse

An Historical Review – David Walker

(Stirlingshire) in 1836 and at Castle Menzies in 1839 being distinguishable from the original work only by their larger late-Georgian mullioned windows.

Burn's final adoption of pure Scots, undiluted by any Tudor or English Jacobean element, had in fact been anticipated by William Henry Playfair in his equally skilful remodellings of Grange (Edinburgh) and Prestongrange in 1830-31. These were followed by the same architect's tactful up-dating of Craigcrook, 1835, the completely new Barmore (Stonefield), seventeenth century neo-Jacobean with a seemingly old tower, and Bonaly which consisted solely of a new-built tower house, both of 1836; similarly precocious was David Hamilton's Dunlop, built completely anew in the style of *c.* 1620-40 in 1833. Even more pioneering would have been the Dumfries architect Walter Newall's proposal for "a border tower" with a lower wing for Glenlair in 1830, but only the wing (subsequently absorbed into a larger mid-Victorian house) was built. Similar patterns of development can be observed elsewhere in the country, notably at Balmoral where the Aberdeen architect John Smith built a Burn-school Jacobethan house adjacent to the ancient tower in 1832. When Smith's son William was called upon to replace it by a completely new house on another site in 1852-55, the style of the 1832 house was reproduced and a gigantic stack of servants' bedrooms built as a reminiscence of the original tower house. By then Balmoral's English Jacobethan was twenty years out of date in Scotland, although not so far removed from the neo-Jacobean houses still being built by Burn south of the Border.

David Bryce's Guthrie (1848) had already set the pattern for the future development of baronial country house design in Scotland, with its much-altered tower restored to a convincing guess at its early sixteenth century appearance as the dominant element of a large Jacobean house which was now wholly Scottish in character. Thereafter if no ancient tower had survived to form the dominant element of the new house, as at Brown and Wardrop's Udny and their proposed new house at Inverquharity, Bryce and his rivals Brown and Wardrop simply built one anew, the early seventeenth century example at Maybole becoming a favourite prototype, reproduced in enriched form with many variations in scale and detail at The Glen, Fothringham and New Gala - all three by Bryce - and elsewhere. But if the estate could not rise to something on that scale, or if the ancient tower was thought too ruinous to restore, the Georgian house which replaced it might itself be reconstructed as a tower house. A good example is David Bryce's Keiss (1862) where the vernacular mid Georgian house incorporated into it makes the result all the more convincing. Only the presence of the ruin of the original tower nearby reminds us that Keiss was a completely new house rather than an over-restored one. Stirkoke, nearby, similarly gained added interest from the plain mid eighteenth century house skilfully incorporated into it. These remodellings took their cue from what Bryce had already carried out between 1858 and 1861 at Cullen, where the eighteenth century additions were remodelled in conformity with the original house. A more archaeologically based exercise was the remodelling in 1870 of Blair Castle, where Bryce used eighteenth century sketches provided by his client, the 7th Duke of Atholl, to reinstate the castle to something like its pre-1747 condition, Winter's staircase being crenellated and the Georgian entrance hall replaced by a new frontispiece inspired by Fyvie.

In the 1840s and 1850s there was, even if only on a smallish scale, something of a vogue for the Bonaly concept of a tall tower house as a country seat. It was, as Michael Davis has suggested to me, a west coast phenomenon and an Argyllshire one in particular. In 1844 the Edinburgh architect Thomas Brown designed what was in effect a new-built tower house with slim dummy turrets at Kilberry. At about the same date an interesting remodelling of what appears to have been a tall plain three-storey three-bay mansion took place at Dunmore. Not only were the wallheads remodelled with dummy parapets with angle rounds and the roof refashioned to look like a cap house, but a court with a range of laigh biggings with conical-roofed circular angle towers was added, all rather successfully, until the effect was spoiled by early twentieth century additions and alterations. The Kilberry formula was reproduced even more successfully by the Glasgow classicist Charles Wilson at Largie *c.* 1855 and again at Inverawe, and even by Alexander "Greek" Thomson *c.* 1854 at Knockderry, his house being subsequently enlarged in the same spirit by John Honeyman in 1871 and again, much more ambitiously, by William Leiper in 1896. Except for Dunmore all of these were built anew, but *c.* 1860 Thomson's brother-in-law and former partner John Baird II re-roofed Haggs Castle, on the Pollok estate, as the factor's house. It was a somewhat misconceived piece of work in which a canted excrescence and a crazy turret were added to the main elevation, supposedly to heighten its picturesque qualities. Equally unarchaeological, but given real neo-mediaeval fantasy by William Bell Scott's wonderful mural cycle of *The Kingis Quair* on the stair, (Fig. 7), was Alice and Spencer Boyd's slightly earlier reconstruction of their fragmentary tower house at Penkill, in 1857, with the Glasgow civil engineer Alexander George Thomson as their architect. Penkill had been an L-plan house

Fig. 7
Lowest mural on main stair at Penkill. Photo: courtesy Dr. Eckstrand and Patrick Drumgoole.

of which only the jamb remained entire and roofed. A water-colour still within the castle until the recent tragic sale, showed a circular stair tower with a corbelled top stage. This had been in the re-entrant angle but in the reconstruction it was, perhaps deliberately, misinterpreted as a flat-roofed angle tower and given a heavy machicolated and crenellated parapet. Some of the details, such as the metal and glass cantilevered hood over the door, were a reflection of the tastes of the Boyds' circle in London which included G.E. Street as well as the Rossettis and Alma-Tadema. The interior was fitted up with antique carved panels, tapestries and painted decoration and furnished with neo-Caroline furniture designed and carved by Spencer Boyd himself. As Ian Gow has remarked, it was a history-painter's props approach to furnishing, in which an artist such as John Pettie would have found everything he could possibly need. Scott's double portrait of the Boyds on their tower roof well captured the romantic spirit of the enterprise.

The concept of a tower house as a medium-sized gentleman's residence never achieved the same popularity in the east as it did in the west, the most significant new-built instances being Charles Wilson's Lochton, Perthshire, rather similar to his Argyllshire houses, and the antiquarian amateur architect Patrick Allan-Fraser of Hospitalfield's Blackcraig in Strathardle, a tall and very convincing turreted pile, built of field-gathered boulder rubble. More significant to the subject of this paper was Cleish, the first restoration of a roofless tower house as a gentleman's house, without significant additions, designed by William Burn's pupil John Lessels for Harry Young about 1843-44, almost exactly parallel with Kilberry. While the original external appearance was more respected than it was to be at Haggs and Penkill, their work was not an archaeologically correct restoration in modern terms either. In the sorrowful words of Dr Thomas Ross "the walls on the various floors were reduced in thickness, and the ground floor vault in the main portion of the structure was taken out, many of the windows enlarged and . . . a complete change made in the entrance arrangements . . . The ruinous remains of the courtyard were removed and the space was converted into a lawn." The only point it had in common with modern restorations was that it would clearly have been a great deal cheaper to have built a new house. The original entrance arrangements were reinstated a quarter of a century ago by Michael Spens, who cleared away Lessels's porch and handsome balustraded stairway.

A much more respectful refitting, even if still somewhat radical internally, was the reconstruction of the fine tower house of Fordell, which had been replaced as the main residence on the estate by a very smart classical house in the mid eighteenth century. It was still roofed and the architect entrusted with the work, the somewhat obscure Robert Hay, had the good sense to leave the exterior almost exactly as it was, but within, the second floor was taken out to create a galleried baronial hall with a massive chimneypiece far removed from the concept of the original master mason. As at Cleish the changes have been partly reversed by a modern hand, that of Sir Nicholas Fairbairn, who reinstated the second floor as part of his further restoration in 1960-67. Somewhat similar in approach to

David Walker – An Historical Review

the work at Fordell was the Dundee architect James Maclaren's restoration of Kellie Castle, near Arbroath (Fig. 8), from a ruinous though still mainly roofed condition, for the Maules in 1864. The courtyard was retained and, perhaps under the influence of the Maules' immediate neighbour, the amateur architect Patrick Allan-Fraser referred to above, so were the beautiful stone slate roofs. The internal refitting was, however, no more sensitive than what had been done at Fordell. Whatever remained of Alexander McGill's interiors of 1701-05 was cleared away.

Fig. 8
Kellie Castle as re-occupied by the Maules, photographed in the 1950s, when it still had its roofs in Abroath slates. Architect James Maclaren of Dundee. Right: The Courtyard. Photos: copyright: RCAHMS.

In the Borders a much more modest exercise was the restoration of the small and remote square tower of Fatlips in the 1850s as an occasional shooting box for the Earls of Minto. Apparently the work was undertaken by another provincial architect, William Anderson of Galashiels. Like so many other Border towers it had survived complete up to the corbelling of the parapet, which was duly reinstated, together with a cap-house rebuilt completely anew, all rather on the model of Bryce's restoration of that at Guthrie referred to earlier.

Although the north-east was richer in castles than any other area, and with a lively antiquarian interest in them, there were fewer parallels to the restorations and new-built tower houses of west and east central Scotland. Those still in occupation tended to be kept in repair much as the seventeenth and eighteenth centuries had left them, sometimes with the addition of a wing to provide a more generous layout at ground and first floor levels, as at Pitcaple (William Burn, 1831), Kininvie (William Robertson, 1838) and Westhall. The most remarkable instance would have been Balmoral, but in the event the Smiths of Aberdeen were instructed to rebuild completely on a new site as described earlier. Some years

An Historical Review – David Walker

previously, in 1848, the Smiths had refitted Craigston. Apart from the addition of a porch, the exterior was on this occasion wisely respected exactly as it was but the interior was made fashionably late classical, the fine woodwork of the previous interior, and probably also of the family pew at King Edward, being incorporated into shutters and doors in order to produce a rich antiquarian effect. A more sensitive remodeller of old houses was Thomas Mackenzie who befriended Robert William Billings and acted as both supporter and as guide to the north-eastern antiquities included in the latter's Baronial and *Ecclesiastical Antiquities of Scotland* published in 1845-52. Mackenzie's work at the large castles of Ballindalloch (1846) (Fig. 9) and Cawdor (1854), where the wallheads had to be raised in places to achieve the requisite accommodation, were remarkable for their date and more convincing than Bryce's work sometimes was, in that he seems to have been able to persuade his clients not to make too radical

Fig. 9
Ballindalloch Castle, view from the SE. An early photograph (c. 1880) showing the house before the A. & W. Reid enlargement, (since removed). The original tower was subtly heightened in effect with a Huntly entrance tower by Thomas Mackenzie.
Photo: Copyright: RCAHMS.

changes, and, in particular, not to introduce bay windows. A similar conviction in the profile and detailing characterised his harled new-built houses at Dess on Deeside and Dall in Perthshire even if the plan forms were unmistakably early Victorian. Mackenzie's partner and successor James Matthews was less successful in that respect, his reconstructions at Arnage and Inglismaldie, and his additions at Monboddo being as heavy-handed as his new-built houses.

Something of a landmark in the history of tower house restoration was James Maitland Wardrop's reinstatement of Castle Stewart, then still roofed but gutted, for the Earl of Moray in 1869. As in the best present-day restorations the exterior was respected exactly as it was, with minimal repair and no enlargement of the windows. Internally, although there was no attempt at restoration, the work was kept simple without any over-imaginative heightening of the character. And although an enlargement rather than a restoration, the same architect's reconstruction of Nunraw (Fig. 10) in 1866 showed a similar respect for the original work, the first in which the thick-walled small-windowed idiom of the fifteenth and sixteenth centuries was fully understood. Although Rowand

Anderson, then a War Office architect, had to some extent shown the way in his fairly tactful re-roofing and enlargement of the much-ruined tower house at Broughty, as a military fortress, in 1861, Wardrop's detailing at Nunraw was at an altogether more sophisticated level of accomplishment. The same trend was even more evident in the work of his son Hew Montgomerie Wardrop whose carefully crafted rubble-built additions at the Place of Tilliefour in 1884 were at that date a triumph of sympathy with the original fabric, and had a profound effect on Robert Lorimer who acted as his site agent.

Earlier, in 1881, the 5th Earl of Rosebery had commissioned an exceptionally ambitious restoration from Maitland Wardrop. To create a secluded library annexe to his house at Dalmeny, the much-ruined castle of Barnbougle was completely reconstructed as a reasonable guess at what it had been, at least in terms of external appearance, the sheer extent of the rebuilding required being at that date matched only at the Marquess of Bute's Castell Coch in Wales. A subsequent scheme, commissioned from Sydney Mitchell to enlarge it to the scale and style of Linlithgow Palace, remained on paper, despite his wife's Rothschild money. Much less archaeological, and surprisingly so given the client, was the re-roofing and refitting as a more occasional scholarly retreat of the two-towered castle at Mochrum carried out in 1873 by the local architect Richard Park for the 3rd Marquess of Bute, who probably provided sketch designs of what he wanted. Crowstepped gables for which there was no evidence were introduced to enliven the profile: a hall, for which there was again no evidence, was added to link the towers in 1877. Although Bute remained fond of the place, as did the 4th Marquess who extensively remodelled it with Robert Weir Schultz as his architect from 1902, the cavalier disregard of archaeological accuracy was to remain a curious contrast to the 3rd Marquess's enterprises of a few years later even if the result was undeniably picturesque.

Similar in spirit to Maitland Wardrop's work at Castle Stewart was the

Fig. 10
Nunraw House. The new house Maitland Wardrop grafted on to the old, closely following its style. Photo: c. 1910, copyright: RCAHMS.

An Historical Review – David Walker

restoration of two large Highland tower houses, Kilcoy (1890) and Dalcross (1897), respectively the work of two Inverness practices, Ross & Macbeth and the arts-and-craftsman William Laidlaw Carruthers, the latter working in association with another architect, Samuel Grant. In both cases the accommodation was found wholly or largely within the original walls, only a small addition being required at Kilcoy to achieve the requisite space.

Equally ambitious but much less respectful of the original plan and detailing was the re-building of the severely ruined Cairnbulg by the Aberdeen firm of Jenkins & Marr - then more civil engineers than architects - for a restoring purchaser, the Aberdeen shipbuilder John Duthie in 1896-97, the block linking the surviving towers being deepened in plan to provide more generous accommodation.

All of these were sizeable structures which offered as much living space as a medium-sized Victorian country house built anew, but in 1897 a somewhat indifferent Perth architect by the name of Butter re-roofed the small L-plan tower-house of Barcaldine (Fig. 11) for Sir Duncan Campbell who had bought it back

Fig. 11
Barcaldine Castle, as first restored, unharled and window grills still in situ. Photo: c. 1900, courtesy of Edinburgh Public Libraries.

in 1896. It may be regarded as the precursor of the post World War II restorations of smaller towers which could be lived in without much in the way of domestic support. The accommodation was strictly limited to what could be found within the original walls so that, externally at least, the integrity of its early seventeenth century form was unimpaired, but some very Victorian detailing in the more important apartments showed that the comprehensive knowledge of sixteenth and seventeenth century domestic detail made available by MacGibbon & Ross had had only a very limited effect.

Rather similar in character to Carruthers's restoration of Dalcross was Sydney Mitchell's restoration in 1900 of the burned-out shell of Schivas for the Earl and Countess of Aberdeen, subsequently enlarged and much elaborated by Fenton Wyness for Lord Catto. Another Aberdeenshire re-roofing with particular relevance for more recent restorations was that of the very small castle of Birse in

1905 as a shooting box for J.R. Heaven, where the Aberdeen architect George Bennet Mitchell respected the original plan but not its fenestration or detail, subsequently reinstated when Annie, Lady Cowdray, instructed Dr William Kelly to enlarge it in 1930. Similar in scale, but enormously more sophisticated in detail, was the restoration of Wester Kames Tower by that supreme arts-and-craftsman, Robert Weir Schultz, originally a pupil of Rowand Anderson's, for the 3rd Marquess of Bute in 1897. Less than half of it had survived but an intelligent guess was made at what had been lost. Schultz's much more ambitious proposals for the rebuilding of Sanquhar Castle, begun in 1896 and again for Bute, remained largely on paper.

In none of these was there any attempt to reinstate the original internal detailing although Schultz would have done so, given any evidence of it. The first exercise of that kind was the restoration of Kellie Castle, Fife, in 1878 for Professor James Lorimer, the father of Sir Robert. It still had a roof but trees were growing through it and the interior work was in a bad way, although still intact. Despite the work being in the hands of a rather eccentric high Victorian architect, John Currie of Elie, Kellie was a model of conservative restoration even by the standards of a century later, those turrets which had been modified in the eighteenth century being respected as they were. No additions were made and all the interior work was either carefully repaired or reinstated as it had been, the floors being strengthened with worn out rails. It set the standard for his son's rather more elaborate restoration of Earlshall for the bleacher R.W.R. Mackenzie, in the early 1890s, where such interior work as remained was carefully respected and an intelligent guess made at what the remainder had been, a reflection of his years with the younger Wardrop and that most tactful of English Victorian architects, George Frederick Bodley.

At Earlshall, where he had been particularly fortunate in his client, Lorimer made no additions, but at Dunderave (1911) and Balmanno (1916) where greater liberties were taken with the profile, courtyards of subsidiary buildings were added to achieve the expected degree of early twentieth century comfort without compromising the original planning. At Duart (Fig. 12), where Sir John Burnet was constrained within the existing walls (1911-16), compromises proved necessary to achieve a workable house. Although the profile of the castle is much as in mid eighteenth century Board of Ordnance views, and although Dr Thomas Ross and David MacGibbon's son Frederick had given advice on behalf of the newly set up Royal Commission on the Ancient and Historical Monuments of Scotland, the vaults of the courtyard ranges were largely taken out, the wallheads slightly raised and one side of the ancient keep slapped out into a spacious hall window on the courtyard side.

Lorimer's restorations had all been for clients with no previous family connection with the site. Duart differed in inspiration in that it had recently been bought back by an elderly general, Sir Fitzroy MacLean, with the conscious intention of restoring it as the rallying point of his clan. It had a particular symbolic significance for the MacLeans as it had been bought back from the

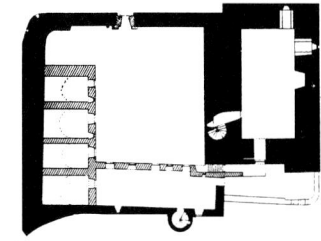

Fig. 12
Plan and NE elevation of Duart Castle. Mull. (MacGibbon & Ross).

An Historical Review – David Walker

Campbells to whom it had been forfeited in lieu of debt. A similar intention lay behind George Mackie Watson's rather more elaborate - and thus less convincingly authentic - reconstruction of the islet castle of Eilean Donan in Loch Duich for Colonel Macrae-Gilstrap, in 1912-32, where a small-arched humpbacked bridge radically changed and falsified the original concept of the place.

Duart and Eilean Donan differed from previous works of historical piety in being conceived as full scale country houses. In most previous works of this kind, not all of them for the original family, there had been no intention to make them permanent residences. Lord Willoughby d'Eresby's low-key (gothic chapel window apart) restoration of Stobhall had been only as a very occasional residence for friends, while his partial rebuilding of the great tower house at Drummond Castle, presumably by G.P. Kennedy, *c.* 1850, had been as an armoury. Murray-Threipland's restoration of Kinnaird Castle in Perthshire, of *c.* 1880, although some distance from his residence at Fingask, had originally also been as an armoury and local museum. All of these were modest exercises compared with the Earl of Moray's second great work of restoration, the re-roofing of his mighty castle at Doune, purely as an ancient monument, in 1883. On this occasion the Earl dropped the Wardrops and commissioned, in a private capacity, Andrew Kerr, the Office of Works architect responsible for the monuments then in state care. For its date the work was a model of conservative restoration with no attempt to reinstate every stone as it was assumed to have been.

Fig. 13
The Old Place of Mochrum.
(MacGibbon & Ross).

Similar in spirit, but more thorough-going, were the purely historic restorations planned and partly executed by the 3rd Marquess of Bute, whose work at the Old Place of Mochrum, (Fig.13), Wester Kames and Sanquhar as occasional residences has been referred to earlier. Rothesay had been the subject of a major early scheme of restoration by William Burges, in 1871, but work was deferred in favour of the reconstruction of Cardiff Castle and Castell Coch in Wales, the latter very similar to the Rothesay proposal. Rothesay remained deferred even although the burning of Mount Stuart in December 1877 had presented the ideal opportunity of undertaking its restoration as a residence, and when work was eventually carried out it was much more modest in extent. At Falkland, where Bute had bought the estate in 1887 because of its associations with the Stuart kings, the main residence remained William Burn's palatial House of Falkland, built in the park in 1839-42, but the surviving chapel range of the old Palace was carefully restored and the gatehouse elaborately fitted up as an occasional residence under the supervision of John Kinross. The rebuilding of the east range, which had been burned out in 1654, was abandoned incomplete at Bute's death in 1900, with the original intention of restoring all as shown in seventeenth century engravings sadly unfulfilled.

Similar in spirit, but more completely realised, was Lord Howard de Walden's restoration of Dean (Fig. 14) at Kilmarnock, a courtyard castle almost comparable in scale with that at Doune, as the Scottish equivalent to Pierrefonds and Castell Coch. It was carried out from 1905 under the supervision of the long-established

Fig. 14
Dean Castle, 1914. Photograph copyright: RCAHMS, showing work on SW elevations in progress for Lord Howard de Walden, (a Scotsman with the family name of Scott-Ellis) under the supervision of Henry Brown of Architects, Ingram & Brown of Kilmarnock, with James S. Richardson, of Edinburgh, as consultant. Dramatic drawing of same elevations by MacGibbon & Ross.

local firm of Ingram & Brown, which had already worked for him on Chirk Castle in Wales, the later stages, being wholly by Prof. James S. Richardson, Principal Inspector of Ancient Monuments, who had been consultant for the early phases. His work has the sensitivity which came from his training with Lorimer; while Railton & Brown's work has something of that same hard-edged contrast of ashlar dressings and rough-hewn rubble as Hippolyte Blanc's restoration of the Great Hall of Edinburgh Castle in 1887-91.

These museum-based Moray, Bute and Howard de Walden enterprises were the precursors of the programme of forming a national reference collection of the archaeological and architectural past which followed the passing of the Ancient Monuments Act of 1900. As it grew, the *rôle* of the private sector faded almost to vanishing point. Lorimer's restoration of Balmanno in 1916, referred to earlier, had been the last to be carried out for private occupation on so magnificent a scale, with more courtyard buildings and a far higher class of neo-Caroline woodwork and plasterwork than it had had originally. Although Lorimer's client, the Glasgow shipowner W.A. Miller, furnished Balmanno and cared for the house and its gardens beautifully, it was symptomatic of the times that the Millers never really moved in and that John A. Holms never finished his new-built Lorimer tower house at Formakin, even although that was primarily the result of horrendous stock exchange losses. At Castle Fraser Lorimer's schemes of 1922-27 were never begun at all, the correspondence closing with a perceptive observation from his client, the Hon. Clive Pearson, which was to be prophetic of the advice The Historic Buildings Council currently gives: "we have endeavoured to fit the castle into what we pretend to be our necessities ..... whereas we ought perhaps to proceed on the basis of fitting ourselves into the castle as she is with the very minimum of disturbance." Perhaps Pearson had seen Barra Castle (Aberdeenshire) (Fig. 15, overleaf) where George Bennet Mitchell, nowhere near so gifted an architect as Lorimer, had fitted the Irvines into it without any alteration, addition or restoration of any kind. It still had, and

An Historical Review – David Walker

indeed has even now, all the magic to be seen in photographs taken before its repair and internal refitting. Even where serious restoration was required, as it was at Fingask after the Georgian and Victorian additions had been demolished in 1926, the inter-war approach tended to be lower key, accepting the building as far as possible as found. Fingask's new owners, the Dundee linen and jute Gilroy family, had initially approached Lorimer but found him "so dictatorial" that they turned to the Dundee practice of J. Donald Mills and Godfrey Shepherd. Their work was not insensitive, but no attempt was made to restore the original main stair which had vanished from the re-entrant angle. William Kininmonth and Basil Spence's restoration of Liberton House in 1936 similarly accepted some of the Georgian modifications as found but it did unpick the later top floor to restore the original crowstepped profile.

Limited in extent and ambition though they were, tower-house restorations such as those at Fingask and Liberton were rare between the wars. The general perception at that period seems to have been that tower houses were no longer suitable for modern living as a result of the greater importance attached to health, sunlight and labour-saving planning. Even before the Great War, in 1904, Lorimer had lost the commission for Fairnilee in attempting to insist on the restoration of the roofless sixteenth century house at the site. It fell to Sir John Burnet to demolish two-thirds of it and roof the remaining end as a generator house and garden pavilion when the new house was built. At Hunterston even Lorimer was obliged to slap a large garage door into the ancient fabric when General Sir Aylmer Hunter-Weston called upon him to repair it as his motor house and chauffeur's quarters in 1913. But by that date even such a utilitarian restoration had become fairly exceptional. The care of ancient castles was now seen by landowners and their agents as more of a national responsibility, as a result of the Act of 1900 referred to earlier, and still more so after the passing of a further Act in 1913 which was the first instrument by which the Office of Works could protect such buildings by scheduling them as ancient monuments in private ownership, rather than by taking them into care. The Office made its first acquisitions under the former Act in 1906. Thereafter, except during the two World Wars, not a year passed without some monument being taken into care, usually under a guardianship agreement with its owners, the peak years being 1932 (eighteen), 1934 and 1953 (both ten), the programme of castle acquisition culminating in one of the greatest, Doune, on a 999-year lease from the Earl of Moray. Altogether just over sixty castles and tower houses have been taken into care, the most recent being Kisimul, of which more below. A fair number of

Fig. 15
Barra Castle. A 1960s photograph of a sympathetic restoration. The outer court was left intact with pavilions on both sides.
Photo: copyright: RCAHMS.

Fig. 16
Ian Lindsay's photograph from the NE, showing Aldie Castle as he found it, in April 1937. Copyright: RCAHMS.

them, such as Huntingtower, Elcho, Affleck, Park, Claypotts and Rowallan, were still roofed when taken into care and in today's terms were capable of being made habitable. Many others, such as Greenknowe, Maclellan's Castle, Huntly and Tolquhon were wholly or largely complete enough to be straightforward candidates for re-roofing.

Mistakes were perhaps made by the Office of Works, and its Principal Inspector James S. Richardson, in the very early days: the stripping out of the fine seventeenth century panelling at Huntingtower in the search for earlier painted work and the rather later removal of the Georgian pavilions which flanked Castle of Park were very different from the approach adopted in recent years, but one can but be grateful for what was achieved, as most of them would otherwise either have been lost or reduced in interest by decay and collapse. The repairs undertaken by the Office of Works were to a much higher standard than the often clumsy consolidation carried out by the larger estates before the First World War, but were almost invariably of the most conservative kind; even in the roofed towers missing floors were not reinstated, which has sometimes made the original planning harder for the public to read than it need have been. Only at Blackness, a state-owned castle which had been converted to a magazine and had lost its upper works, did Richardson venture publicly into the kind of restoration undertaken at Dean Castle.

The founding of The National Trust for Scotland in 1931 and the publication of two important popular books in 1937-38, Sir John Stirling-Maxwell's *Shrines and Homes of Scotland* and George Scott Moncrieff's *The Stones of Scotland* called for a change of heart on the part of the local authorities and the general public alike. As Chairman of the Ancient Monuments Board and one of the founders of The National Trust, Stirling-Maxwell had long recognised that there were budgetary limits to what the Office of Works could achieve. In the introduction to *The Stones* Scott Moncrieff reported the plight of Aldie Castle, (Fig. 16), observing that it was "perfectly situated on the edge of the Cleish Hills" and that "even now it could be turned into the most delightful modern home." The call was answered by Mr Hope Dickson who acquired it and commissioned one of the contributors to the book, Ian G. Lindsay, to restore it. It was then the most

An Historical Review – David Walker

respectful restoration ever done and remains exemplary even today, but the work was interrupted by the Second World War and it was only with some difficulty that it was eventually completely finished in 1957.

Although historic buildings legislation had been introduced in Scotland with the passing of the Town and Country Planning Acts of 1945 and 1948, the immediate post-war years at first seemed to offer even less hope for the tower house than the inter-war years, particularly as it was by then even more evident that the annual maintenance costs of The Ancient Monuments Estate could not go on growing as they had done, and that any future acquisitions would have to be more selective than they had been. A few tower houses had been lost during the war and a good many more, particularly those which had become the nuclei of larger mansions like Nether Pollok, Stenhouse (Stirlingshire), and Macbiehill, disappeared in the spate of demolitions which followed the end of requisitioning, aided and abetted by the unfortunate requirement to levy rates on any house which had a roof, whether occupied or not. The future of those which had long been occupied only by farm servants was equally bleak. Surtax was at record levels and in the "Brave New World" atmosphere of the 1950s and 1960s anything historic was increasingly seen as irrelevant and something which should be cleared out the way: despite cross-party agreement on the legislation in the 1940s, it was an attitude the Government and its agencies did little to discourage. One of the worst instances was British Steel's summary demolition of Old Jerviston which Colvilles had planned to restore prior to nationalisation. Few estates could now afford pensioner buildings and the condition of such houses as Midhope, Flemington and Bonhard deteriorated rapidly, Bonhard being eventually completely demolished. Apart from Michael and Lady Victoria Wemyss's ambitious de-Victorianisation of Wemyss Castle with Stuart Tod as their architect, very little restoration work was undertaken in the post-war years until the setting up of The Historic Buildings Council for Scotland under the Historic Buildings and Ancient Monuments Act of 1953. Even although that body provided the first ever financial inducement to retain historic buildings, there was initially still little enthusiasm for the restoration of tower houses as residences. The earliest grants were to Perth Town Council for the repair of Pitheavlis as local authority housing (1954); to Clackmannan County Council for the restoration of Menstrie Castle, partly as a museum but mainly as part of the housing estate into which it had been incorporated (1957); and to Napier College for the restoration of the surviving tower of Merchiston Castle as part of their new building (1958), a work of piety to the inventor of logarithms which most of us would now see as ill-conceived in terms of what was done.

But in the last of these same years several important developments took place. In 1954 Ian Lindsay demolished Brown & Wardrop's additions at Craichlaw, and modified their restoration of the ancient tower to correspond more closely with what had previously existed. A similar exercise was Druminnor where Miss Margaret Forbes Sempill, initially with Lindsay as her architect, made a courageous attempt to rescue the original house by extricating it from its derelict

Archibald Simpson additions; and The Macneil of Barra, himself an architect, set about the restoration of the Macneil stronghold of Kisimul as a clan seat, very much on the same lines as Sir Fitzroy MacLean's restoration of Duart forty years earlier. Druminnor and Kisimul were both grant-aided by the Minister of Public Buildings and Works - who was then responsible for historic building repair grants in Scotland - on the advice of The Historic Buildings Council. Druminnor was still roofed and was no different from similar cases in England, but Kisimul, although fairly complete to the wallheads, had been roofless for centuries and was the first case of its kind on either side of the Border. But a few years later in the early 1960s the loss of the uniquely important wall-chambered tower house at Elphinstone on purely financial grounds - it had been cracked by subsidence from coal workings - served as a blunt reminder that not everything of first importance could be taken into care and that other solutions would have to be accepted and indeed encouraged by grant-aid if a sufficient representation of Scotland's fifteenth, sixteenth and early seventeenth century domestic architecture were to survive.

That realisation coincided with the dawn of another, in a new era in which domestic help was less available than it had been before the war. It was now recognised that the smaller tower house could be made a compact and manageable living unit, particularly if it was only a weekend house or occasional residence. To a considerable degree The Earl of Perth's reoccupation of the ancient Drummond seat of Stobhall, (Fig. 17), which he had bought back from the Earl of Ancaster, led the way, the Dower House and chapel block being thoroughly repaired at that time. A number of developments in the early 1960s,

Fig. 17
Stobhall and the lower courtyard in the 1880s. Fashion change: the 1781 block on the right survived the mid 19th century restoration only to be demolished as 'modern' in the mid 20th. It has since been rebuilt! (MacGibbon & Ross).

most of them carried out without grant-aid, set the pattern for the future. At Udny, Margaret Udny-Hamilton demolished Maitland Wardrop's work and reduced the castle to the original simple square tower shown in Billings's engraving, an exercise subsequently repeated in 1969 by John Gordon at Abergeldie, a grant-aided case, where the plain mid eighteenth century house, referred to earlier, was demolished after the Royal lease had ended. At

An Historical Review – David Walker

Inchdrewer, which had survived only in a very fragmentary state as a result of a fire in 1713, Robin de la Lanne Mirrlees, who had an ancient family connection with the house, carried out a very convincing rebuilding, aided by an excavation to establish the missing corner of the plan, the only non-authentic element being concrete floors on the Lorimer principle to ensure that the 1713 disaster would not recur. Sadly he never finished it internally although the external result was much admired. All of these were the work of Jock Lamb, a sensitive restorer who had inherited the Bennet Mitchell practice responsible for the restoration of Barra half a century earlier, and in each case there was a family connection with the property. The reconstruction of Garth Castle in Glenlyon as a holiday house differed in that Mr Fry had no such previous connection with the castle. It had in fact been the subject of an earlier attempt at reconstruction by Sir Donald Currie, with Andrew Heiton as his architect, but left incomplete in deference to local opinion eighty years earlier.

Designed initially by a local firm in Aberfeldy, Mr Fry's work was not at all archaeologically-based and would not receive listed building consent now. What had been built of Heiton's cap house was cleared off to form a sun-deck roof and the upper floors treated as one large space with a sleeping gallery, the English architect Leonard Manasseh being brought in to achieve a more presentable result. Although he was consulted too late to change the scheme at Garth, Scottish castles caught Manasseh's interest and it was perhaps unfortunate that his dream of achieving a really archaeological tower house restoration for an English member of the Drummond family was never realised as the intended subject could not be acquired.

Although Garth itself was a failure, at least in historical and architectural terms, the concept caught on. In 1965, perhaps more with Eilean Donan in mind, the roofless island stronghold of Castle Stalker was restored, initially following a sketch scheme by Ian Lindsay. In the same year Captain MacLean Bristol bought back and re-roofed the MacLean stronghold of Breachacha, (Fig. 18), though not with such sophisticated results as the earlier MacLean restoration of Duart; and again in that same year the dilapidated Farnell was repaired, harled and refitted for occupation to designs by Sinclair Gauldie. The years 1966-67 saw the restoration of the still more delapidated Balfluig and Hills. These apparently similar cases revealed an interesting difference in perception on the part of the under-Secretary, through whom The Historic Buildings Council's advice was filtered, and the Minister of Public Building and Works. The recommendation in respect of Hills was accepted as it had corbelled and crenellated parapets and was thus recognisably a castle. At Balfluig, where Jock Lamb had produced a sensitive scheme for its new owner, Mr Mark Tennant, the Council's recommendation was not accepted, as its high-shouldered pitched roof profile did not spell "castle" to English eyes. Perhaps the loss of the pepperpot turret shown by James Giles in his watercolour of it, since reinstated, did not help. Not even the most trenchant writing from Dr W. Douglas Simpson, the redoubtable chairman of The Ancient Monuments Board, would change their minds. It was not until after The

Fig. 18
Breachacha Castle, Coll, from South-West. (MacGibbon & Ross).

David Walker – **An Historical Review**

Secretary of State for Scotland assumed responsibility for The Ancient Monuments Estate and for The Historic Buildings Council for Scotland on 1st July 1966 that the issue was fully resolved. Thereafter recommendations from the Council and their professional advisers in respect of a number of equally simply detailed late sixteenth and seventeenth century houses were accepted without further difficulty. Between 1969-72, these comprised: Kinkell for the sculptor Gerald Ogilvie Laing with the professional assistance of the Wittets of Elgin; Barscobe by John H. Reid and Crichton Lang, as successors to Ian Lindsay, for Sir Hugh Wontner; and Davidston by J.J. Meldrum for an English client - all almost equally delapidated houses. By that date J.J. Meldrum had already become a great force for conservation in the north-east, with his restorations in Portsoy for the Town Council and those for The Banff Preservation Trust, in addition to his personal revolving fund in his own town of Banff. Except for Breachacha, all the tower house restorations of 1966-72 referred to above were for individuals with no previous connection with the property, or at least not a close one, and all except Breachacha and Stalker were grant-aided.

Fig. 19
Pitcullo in the 1880s: the entrance jamb, the only section of the castle to remain entire.
(MacGibbon & Ross).

Kisimul apart, (Fig. 26, p. 28), none of the grant-aided cases referred to above had set any problems of precedent for The Historic Buildings Council. All of them had still had roofs, even if in several instances they had had to be completely replaced. More difficult were the restorations of Pitcullo (Fig. 19) by the architect Roy Spence for himself, and of Inverquharity by W. Murray Jack, with the assistance of Spence, for Mr and Mrs A.C. Grant in 1970-71. (Fig. 20). At Pitcullo a certain amount of masonry as well as the roof was missing, and it proved necessary to demolish a badly built later tower which had separated itself from the original house. At Inverquharity, while the main jamb had survived in an outstanding state of completeness, the jamb had long gone but had to be rebuilt to produce a viable house. In both cases The Council and The Secretary of State accepted the principle of grant-aid because of the outstanding interest of those parts which remained reasonably complete, but in the event at Inverquharity the Grants met all the costs themselves.

These initiated a spate of tower house restorations, re-roofings and rebuildings throughout the mid 1970s which are too numerous to be detailed individually, the most memorable being Marc and Karen Ellington's reoccupation of Towie Barclay (Fig. 21, overleaf) where the upper third of the castle had been lost; Robert Hurd & Partners' courageous restoration of Rossend in the teeth of local authority opposition as owners, thwarted in their plans for demolition; the Remps' re-roofing of Harthill which introduced a very successful restoration architect, William Cowie, to the scene; and Mr and Mrs Wharton's re-occupation of the long deserted Midmar, a house so perfectly preserved as a time capsule of early nineteenth century life in a sixteenth century castle that it would have been better taken into guardianship or National Trust care had it been possible to find the money.

Fig. 20
Inverquharity, from SE drawn by MacGibbon & Ross in the 1880s. The missing jamb on the right was rebuilt in 1970-71. The original tower is a building of exceptionally fine quality, internally.

Grant-aiding re-roofing and reoccupation had thus become ever increasingly to be seen as a supplement, and indeed an alternative, to central government care.

Fig. 21
Left, Towie Barclay, restored. The parapets are mid Victorian. Right, Fig. 22, Leslie Castle, restored timber shutters in lower half of windows. Photos: Robert McCallum.

By the mid 1970s it was apparent that the arrears of maintenance which had built up since the Second World War, together with the necessary consolidation work to post-war additions to The Ancient Monuments Estate, could not be dealt with by The Ancient Monuments Division's direct labour squads alone, and repairs to a number of castles and tower houses had to be put out to contract. Sween, Kilchurn, Dundonald, Balvaird and Spynie Palace inaugurated a major programme of consolidation work which continued through the 1980s to the current programme of work at Lochmaben and Morton. There were thus clearly limits to what more could be taken into the estate and at Midmar and Castle Menzies, the two prime candidates for guardianship among the castles referred to above, The Secretary of State bought their survival fairly cheaply with grants of £56,448 and £59,201 respectively and avoided any commitment to running cost. These had still been roofed, but the restoration of the two roofless towers near the top end of the scale of interest, Harthill and Rusco, (another subject in this book), still seemed very good value at £52,000 and £42,000 respectively. But two others, Pitfichie and Fawside, together with an application from the architect David Leslie in respect of his own Castle Leslie, (Fig. 22, above right), which had also once been a prime candidate for guardianship, caused The Historic Buildings Council to take stock before making any further recommendations to The Secretary of State. Harthill and Rusco had suffered scarcely any masonry loss, but Pitfichie had partly collapsed in 1936, Fawside had lost the cap houses of its ancient tower and had crumbled at the wallheads, (Fig. 23), and Leslie had suffered a serious collapse and other lesser falls of masonry.

At Pitfichie an authentic restoration was possible as a good deal of the fallen masonry was still on site and the castle had been fully surveyed before the collapse. As it was one of the most interesting of the medium-sized Aberdeenshire towers, the Council eventually recommended grant-aid. Masonry retrieved from the debris on site was reinstated wherever possible and all the new dressed work was skilfully cut, but the missing rubble work was largely made good in blockwork. The final result was archaeologically convincing inside and out, and apart from a slight wobbliness in the wall plane at the junction of the ancient rubble and the new block-work, the result was visually little different from that of other restored towers which had suffered no masonry loss. Fawside, also

Fig. 23
Fawside Castle, viewed from S.E. (MacGibbon & Ross).

one of the subjects in this book, was rather more of a worry. It was a particularly interesting example of a big early tower extended for more comfortable occupation in the late sixteenth century but in the course of its rebuilding to designs by Ian Parsons the original internal planning was less completely reproduced than at Pitfichie and the brickwork patching of the wallheads showed through the harl in wet weather. Both had been expensive in terms of monetary values at that time, £62,000 over four years at Pitfichie and £77,000 over a similar period at Fawside.

The Council consequently instructed a review in 1981. It was found that expenditure on tower houses had only occasionally been a double figure percentage of its allocation of funds. It was concluded that the restoration of Castle Leslie should proceed. Built in 1661, it represented a critical stage in the transition from tower house to late Stuart country house and at David Leslie's own wish the rebuilding was carried out in solid rubble work, the first occasion on which an applicant accepted that new-built stonework could or should be harled over. Predictably Castle Leslie proved expensive and a further review was called for in 1985. That review showed that of the fifty-three grant-aided restorations of castles which had not been continuously occupied as country houses, thirty-five had been roofed, even if inadequately, at the time of application and thus fell within the normal parameters of building repair. Of the remaining eighteen, eight had lost hardly any masonry, a ninth not much and at the tenth, Niddrie, it was decided not to reinstate the fragmentary seventeenth century upper floors, the original form of which entailed an element of guesswork. Thus in only eight cases was there significant rebuilding of fallen masonry and at all but one of them there was reliable survey or early pictorial evidence, the single exception being Fawside where the deficiency of reliable information was resolved by omitting the main cap house.

Since 1985 the pace of tower house restoration has been slower, partly because the best preserved, best-located and most readily available subjects for restoration had already been undertaken, partly because the building repair grant scheme was again, for a time, as over-committed as it had been at the beginning of the decade and partly because the very high costs involved in restoring the larger towers had begun to be more widely known. The main projects of those years were the restoration of the Earl of Mar's Alloa Tower by a trust promoted by Clackmannan District Council; Tilquhilly which was still roofed but very neglected; Midhope, an ancient monuments grant-in-aid case where the roofs had largely fallen in (all three in this book); Oakwood, which was fairly complete, for Sir David and Lady Judy Steel; the much more ruinous Hatton (Angus) and Forter (also included), at both of which there was fairly clear evidence of what had fallen, MacGibbon & Ross's drawing and a couple of early photographs being particularly helpful in the case of the latter; The Landmark Trust's Ascog, relieved of an out-of-scale and somewhat shapeless mid-Victorian addition; and Plean, (Fig. 24, overleaf), where the additional floor built early in the present century was respected on the advice of The Ancient Monuments Inspectorate, as it had

An Historical Review – David Walker

destroyed the evidence of the original treatment of the parapet walk and the cap house. Except for Midhope, which was part of the Hopetoun estate, nearly all of these projects were either for new owners, or, as in the case of the Leslies at Castle Leslie and the Oliphants at Hatton, for families who had bought the houses back. The most notable feature of the more ambitious late 1980s and 1990s grant-aided projects has been the consistent adoption of traditional rubble work throughout and some fairly intrepid structural engineering where the internal faces of the walls had fallen at the wall chambers and mural staircases, particularly at Hatton where a great deal of nineteenth century consolidation work had to be unpicked to recover them.

Fig. 24
Plean (or Plane) Castle and its restored Edwardian top floor. The palace wing, has since been rebuilt. Photo: Robert McCallum.

Fig. 25
Spedlins Castle. (MacGibbon & Ross).

Not all of the tower house projects carried out since the Second World War have been grant-aided. Some, such as Castle Fraser, eventually repaired as a museum project rather than a house by Clive Pearson's daughter Lavinia Smiley, the much smaller but essentially similar repair of Fourmerkland as a heritage project by Sir John Keswick, and the unique double pile tower of Spedlins, (Fig. 25), restored for Stephen Yorke, were carried out to high standards without any request for grant-aid, but in a number of other cases, where the owners preferred not to seek grant, the absence of the guiding hand of Historic Scotland's architects and inspectors shows. The same is true of several important towers where application was made and grant-aid recommended in principle but agreement on standards could not be reached. In a few further cases, notably Blackhall at Paisley, Levan Castle and The Landmark Trust's Monreith, grant-aid could not be recommended, mainly because of financial constraints, but the projects were nevertheless seen through with creditable results, while at Mains of

David Walker – An Historical Review

Fintry The City of Dundee's long-delayed fulfilment of its legal obligation to keep the castle in repair was successfully carried out as a Manpower Services Scheme in the early 1980s. In all some twenty tower houses were undertaken without grant-aid, while a further tower, the diminutive Z-plan Benholm Lodging, was removed from Netherkirkgate in Aberdeen to Tillydrone Road in Old Aberdeen to make way for a Marks & Spencer store. Appropriately enough that great authority on castles, Dr W. Douglas Simpson, was its first tenant. A somewhat similar transfer to another site had in fact taken place once before. During the Second World War William R. Thomas had planned to rebuild Otterston, but before he could do so it had largely collapsed, giving him the option of rebuilding on another site. This he did between 1946 and 1955, with the professional assistance of the elderly arts-and-crafts architect William Williamson of Kirkcaldy, at Easterheughs on the cliffs near Aberdour. It differs from the Benholm Lodging in that it does not exactly reproduce what existed at the previous site, although it did incorporate much of its stonework, together with some fine interior work rescued from Rossend, then derelict. Much more recently, in the mid 1980s, the neighbouring tower to Otterston, Couston, was the subject of an equally exceptional rebuilding, on this occasion on the original site. Not much more than the gable of the jamb of this L-plan tower had survived but the fine site on the banks of Otterston Loch induced Mr Alistair Harper - who had already re-roofed the ruinous early eighteenth century Skellatur in Strathdon - to buy it. At first he proposed to rebuild only the jamb as part of a new house of his own design but after an archaeological investigation of the site was suggested to him, and the original plan established, he commissioned Ian Begg to rebuild it as nearly as possible to its original form, the design of the lost upper floors of the main jamb being worked out by reference to an old view showing it prior to its demolition in 1830 and to other more complete towers of similar plan. Only those previously familiar with the site are likely to appreciate that what is seen today is approximately seven-eighths new. No other rebuilding, past or present, has had so little of the original structure to incorporate.

Looking back over what has been achieved, particularly in the best restorations, two observations may be made. The first is that the seventy or so restorations which can be regarded as successful more than match in numbers what is held on The Ancient Monuments Estate. They have consolidated a significant proportion of the fifteenth, sixteenth and seventeenth century heritage. Most of them would, sooner or later, have been lost had there not been such an intervention and the country would have been much the poorer in interest. The second is that re-roofed or re-occupied cannot have the interest that comes with the chattels accumulated over the centuries. Nevertheless, the absence of later adaptation often tends to result in the tower house which has long been roofless better demonstrating how such towers were lived in when first built than continuously occupied ones: windows have not been enlarged, mural stairs have not been blocked up, and the planning has not been altered. It is also important to keep the issue of authenticity, often raised as an argument against

An Historical Review – David Walker

the restoration of such towers, in perspective, since so many of these continuously occupied towers do not have their original roofs. When it is argued that the odd turret window, for which precise evidence was lacking, may not be exactly proportioned or located as it was originally, in the continuously occupied house the evidence of the original windows may well be almost completely lost.

In considering grant applications in these days of ever-tightening priorities, Historic Scotland and The Historic Buildings Council have to look ever more closely at what the restoration will achieve in national heritage terms: whether it is a building of critical importance not matched on The Ancient Monuments Estate, or indeed elsewhere, which may result in a small degree of intelligent guess work having to be accepted, as at Melgund; whether it is complete enough for an authentic restoration to be feasible; whether the applicant's proposals respect the original plan and are of a sufficient specification to merit scheduled monument or listed building consent, as the case may be (it is now fairly unlikely in the light of past experience that extensive use of brickwork or block work, other than as corework, will again be accepted); what the likely cost of the proposed works will be and whether the applicant can meet them, with assistance if necessary. Even where these criteria can be met, which will often involve full archaeological investigation beforehand, there should be no presumption of consent from either The Secretary of State or the planning authority. The officials of at least one planning authority favour picturesque ruins in the landscape rather than restored castles. Particular caution should be exercised in respect of early or remote castles. It has long been recognised that these are not really appropriate subjects for re-occupation and that restorations in remote island locations present particular difficulties: after a promising start, the final result at Kisimul was a disappointment with some compromises of detail which will, hopefully, now be rectified. It must also be recognised that there is a limit to what everything is worth: and that cost rather than merit can be the deciding factor, in deciding applications for grant-aid, given the other priorities which have to be faced.

Fig. 26
Kisimull Castle, MacGibbon & Ross's drawing, viewed from NW.

The lesson from almost all the cases of really big towers which have required significant rebuilding of fallen or unstable masonry has been that the eventual costs are not easy to estimate accurately and may prove a greater strain on the resources of their owners than anticipated. Experience has shown time after time that the cost of restoring a roofless or badly decayed tower house is likely to be far in excess of the market value of the end result. Nevertheless, Dairsie Castle was rebuilt to designs by Ian Begg and Raymond Muszynski, with scheduled monument consent, following a very full archaeological investigation, the most ambitious rebuilding project tackled in Scotland since Maitland Wardrop reconstructed Barnbougle for the Earl of Rosebery one hundred and nineteen years ago. Sadly the project ended in disagreement with both the architects and Historic Scotland, and the detail of some of the upper-works is not as sensitive as the remainder. A happier episode has been Lachlan Stewart's restoration of the unique "Z"-plan tower house at Ballone, which was pulled back from the brink of final collapse and where the detail would be hard to fault. Also as good as it could be is Melgund, where the restoration of the tower-house section is now reaching completion under the supervision of Ben Tindall. At the time of writing restoration is under consideration at Baltersan and Barholm, but inevitably the era of tower-house restoration is drawing towards its close for the very simple reason that the number of towers capable of restoration and available for purchase is now so limited. Looking back, not everything has been perfectly done, but in only a few cases (some of them, the writer regrets to admit, grant-aided) is there much real cause for regret at what has been done. What can be said with certainty is that the Historic Buildings Council's programme of grant-aid will result in there being perhaps as much as twice as many tower-houses in the year 2100 than there would otherwise have been.

[The writer gratefully acknowledges the assistance of Mr Harry Gordon Slade, Mr Ingval Maxwell, Mr Richard Emerson, Dr Deborah Mays, Dr Aonghus McKechnie and Mr Ian Dewar in writing this paper.]

Fig. 1
Viewed from SE prior to commencement of the works.

Midhope Castle

by William Cadell, MA, RIBA, FRIAS.

I have been in private practice for more than thirty years and my firm specialised in restoration and allied architectural works. During the 1970s and 1980s the firm was closely involved in various restoration projects in Bo'ness. I am a member of a number of conservation societies and have been on the National Trust for Scotland's Executive Committee, its Curatorial Committee and its Buildings Committee. Formerly I was the RIAS Representative on its Council. I was also a member of the Architectural Heritage Society of Scotland's Council and have been involved for many years with the West Lothian History and Amenity Society, Linlithgow Civic Trust, Linlithgow Museum, Bo'ness Town Trust and the Bo'ness Heritage Trust, amongst other societies and similar bodies. I have recently completed two terms with the Royal Fine Art Commission for Scotland and am currently on the Council of Management of the Architectural Heritage Fund. Active involvement in these organisations is interspersed with a keen interest in trees, shrubs and gardens.

The Background to Restoration

Hopetoun Estates, proprietor of Midhope, initiated a Condition and Proposals Report and Costing, in October 1985. Midhope Castle had not been used since the 1950s and there was concern about its state of disrepair and the danger of partial collapse (Fig. 1). West Lothian District Council Planning Department, the Scottish Civic Trust, the West Lothian History and Amenity Society and the exemplar of Colin McWilliam's handbook on Lothian had all played a part in encouraging restoration.

The Estate had a particular problem of access to a new home farm, which had been constructed in the 1960s, immediately to the West of the castle, with access directly through the castle forecourt. Under the circumstances of traffic, smell and noise, it was perceived that re-use of the castle was an unattractive, if not impossible, proposition. With the encouragement and assistance of the Historic Buildings and Monuments Department, a programme of consolidation only was agreed and Scheduled Monument Consent obtained. The annual budget available for the work was limited and a programme was agreed, setting estimated costs against annual budget and producing a phased programme over seven years. Work started in 1988 and was still in progress when the Castles Conference was held.

History

In 1438 Henry Luigstone, laird of Manerston, and John Martyne, laird of Medhope, agreed to divide certain disputed lands lying between them, and to do this by lot. "Sortes", made of wood and marked by each proprietor, were

Fig. 2
Carved letterings. That on the right states 'Et petiit corpus Jesus', evidently with reference to Joseph of Arimathaea asking for the body of Christ. (MacGibbon & Ross).

entrusted to a neutral party, who, on the altar of the parish Church of Abercorn, gave his decision. In 1478 Henry Levingstone was "infefted" by the bailie of the place "by passing to the chief manor place of Manerston within the wall that went round the tower thereof" ... "then to the old toft or mansion of Medhope." This is the first mention of Midhope Castle which has been traced, and it would seem that the tower, of which the arched basement floor still remains, was built by John Martyne, who continued to be laird up to 1478.

It appears that this was the castle where Livingston and his immediate successors lived, until 1582, which is the date carved on a stone, now built out of place in the wall immediately to the North of the gateway. The letters upon the stone refer to the initials of Alexander Drummond and his wife, and commemorate the rebuilding of the tower with turrets (Fig. 2). When the present front door that has a shield, coronet and the letters "G.L." above was reconstructed, the older lintel was re-sited. The monogram gives the initials of George, third Earl of Linlithgow and keeper of Linlithgow Palace, who succeeded to the earldom in 1646. In 1676 we find him signing documents from the Castle of Medhope.

Sir Robert Sibbald, in his 1710 'History of the Sheriffdome of Linlithgow' notes "Meidhope" as a "fine tower house with excellent gardens, one of the seats of the Earl of Hopetoun". Thus, change of ownership to the Hopes seems to have occurred prior to Livingston's involvement in the 1715 Jacobite Rising and his subsequent dispossession.

Inhabited by "Pensioners of the Hopetoun Family" when recorded by McGibbon and Ross, it was then being used "as residences of estate workers or

William Cadell – Midhope Castle

pensioners," when surveyed in 1921 for the National Art Survey of Scotland. This story continues with wartime occupation by Polish servicemen, followed by occasional use by seasonal workers and ending with use by the Civil Defence, for training purposes, and the development of the home farm.

Neglect of the castle in favour of the home farm and pheasants appears unacceptable to today's conservationists but, in Estate management terms, re-investment in the land rather than buildings was seen as being more desirable in the 1960s.

Architectural Description

I have known and loved this place for many years, my first memory being the view from the Estate road to the South, with the castle in the dip to the North and the hunt chasing up the ridge in the background, with the estuary and Fife hills in the distance beyond.

The castle is located near the Midhope burn, half a mile to the West of Abercorn, in one of the most favoured sites in Central Scotland. It is approached from the East through a gateway, of which one pier is apparently original and the other has been rebuilt (Fig. 3). To the left on entry is a late 17c double lectern doo'cot, set in the wall and there are good Victorian cottages to the North and South of the enclosed ground. There is an additional derelict Victorian building to the rear of the castle. An inner gateway gives access to the former forecourt, with overgrown garden grounds to the South, the castle to the North and the cattle courts of the home farm to the West. (See Fig. 7, overleaf).

The tower is high, having a vaulted basement, three upper floors, an attic and a garret (Fig. 4). It is oblong in plan. The masonry is of coursed rubble. At three angles two-storeyed turrets are corbelled out. At the fourth angle, the Northwest, a smaller turret is corbelled out at a higher level to form a turret-stair serving the roof space. The main turnpike is immediately below and rises from the entrance level. The windows of the tower are rounded at jamb and lintel. Originally there were dormers with pediments to the North and South, but the pediments were removed in the 17th century. The high main roof now oversails the turrets, which have been reduced in height. The entrance to the tower is at first-floor level and enters from the courtyard by a short forestair. There is a good Renaissance door-piece. (Fig. 5, overleaf).

The first addition to the tower consisted of the two lower storeys of the East

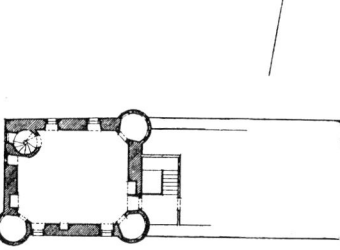
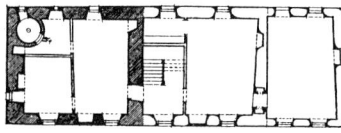
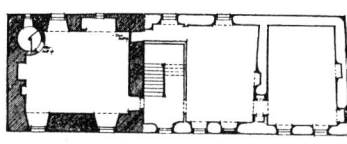
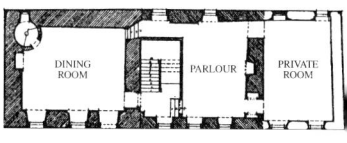
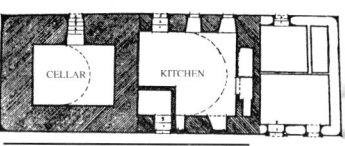

Fig. 4
Measured drawings by Hugh A. Dalrymple, 1902, published in The National Art Survey of Scotland.

Fig. 3
View from the SE at the entrance gateway. (MacGibbon & Ross).

Midhope Castle – William Cadell

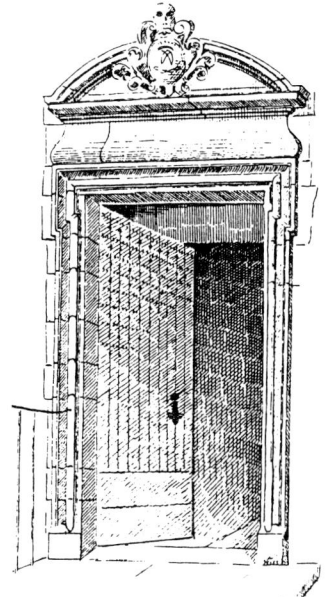

Fig. 5
*The Renaissance doorway.
(MacGibbon & Ross).*

wing (Fig. 6). The basement of the wing is vaulted and was the kitchen the large fireplace with segmental arch still remaining in the East wall. The kitchen is entered from the courtyard. In the next extension, probably dating from the late 17th century, the small wing was raised two storeys and carried Eastward. There was a fine old staircase and several rooms with 17th century panelling and cornices. Surviving features have been recorded and a good painted ceiling, found built up some years ago, was removed and restored. This latter now, and surprisingly, adorns the Abbey Strand Tea-room, outside the gates to Holyrood.

Reuse

The building has not changed hands since the late 17th/early 17th century, remaining the property of Hopetoun Estates. The consolidation works were half way through a seven year programme, at the time of the Castles Conference, and there was no intention to reuse the building on completion or to go beyond the maintenance, repair and renewal works of the then agreed programme. Being assisted by central government grant, access for viewing by arrangement was an imposed condition.

Thus, the castle will remain a shell on completion, with no floors, partitions, stairs, etc. Were the Estate to consider re-use in the future, access to the cattle courts would have to be re-routed and any user would either have to tolerate the rural smells and noise, or these would have to be accommodated elsewhere.

It would have been good if the restoration of the walled garden ground to the South (so complementary to the forecourt and castle), the gateway, doo'cot, walls and cottages to the East and North, plus the former walled garden to the N.E., could have been an extension of the present work (Fig. 7, opposite). Hopefully, if re-use of the castle is contemplated in the future, this necessary work will be undertaken, as all these buildings and associated grounds form the setting to the castle.

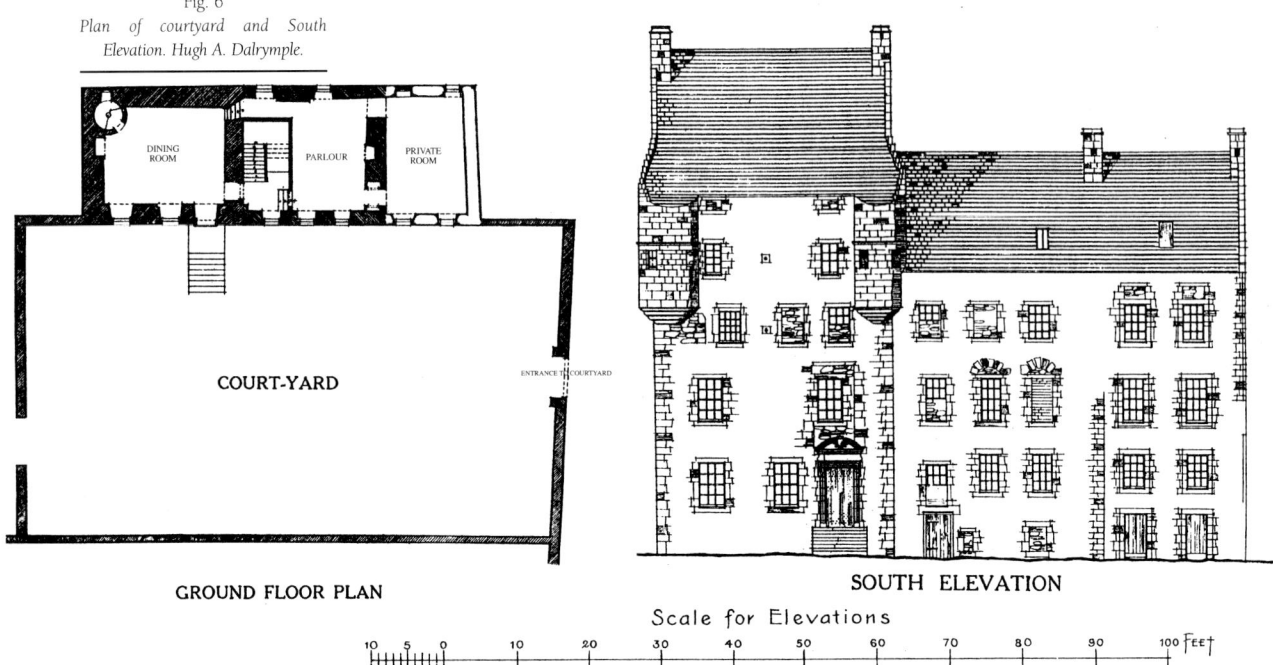

Fig. 6
Plan of courtyard and South Elevation. Hugh A. Dalrymple.

GROUND FLOOR PLAN SOUTH ELEVATION

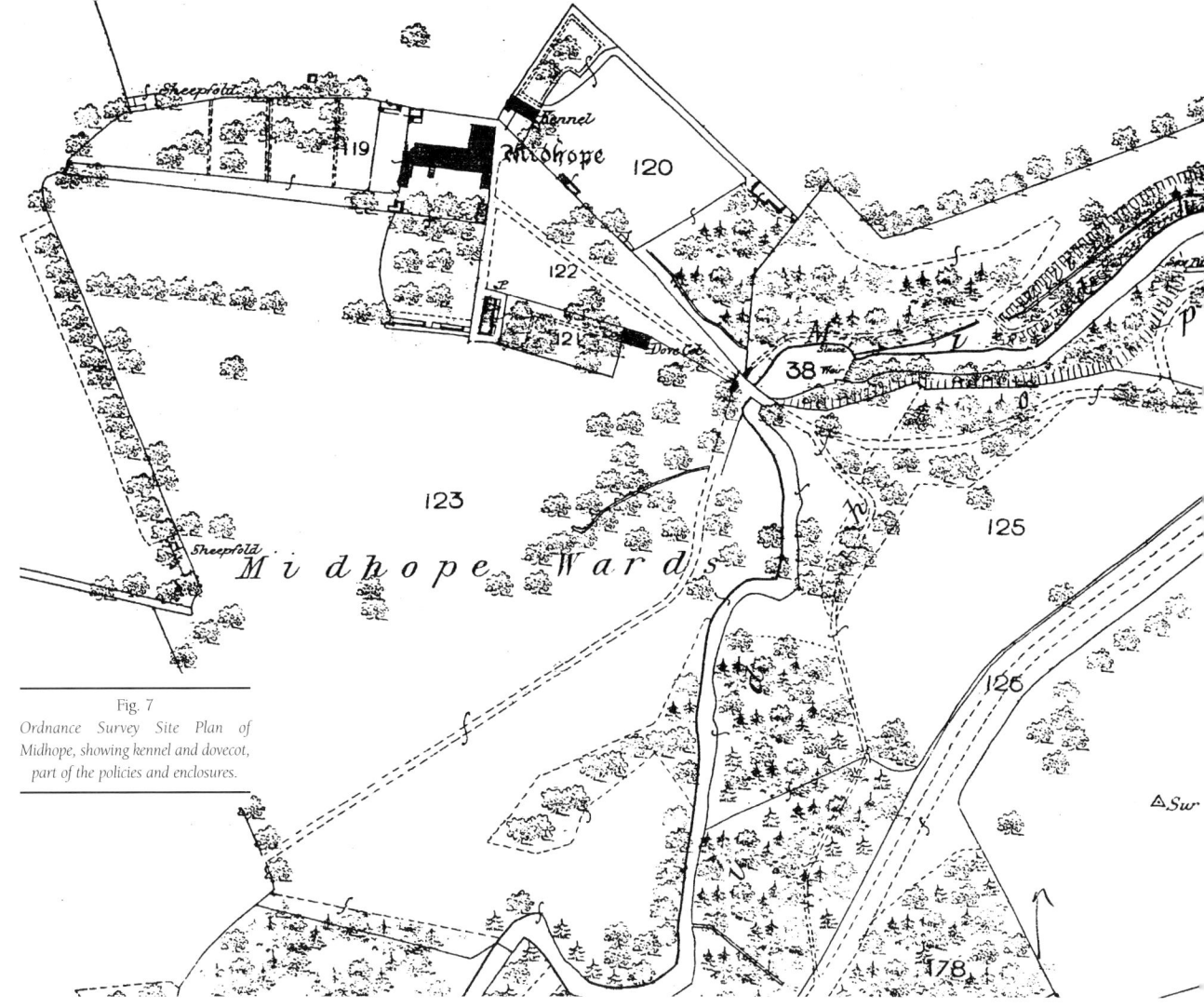

Fig. 7
Ordnance Survey Site Plan of Midhope, showing kennel and dovecot, part of the policies and enclosures.

Large land holdings, such as Hopetoun Estates, may quite reasonably find it very difficult in various management terms to consider sale or lease of a building, in a location such as this, buried within the private envelope. However, if it is considered that re-use is a desirable objective, it is undoubtedly going to become easier for the Estate to contemplate if the building only requires internal work. Even if only on the basis of keeping options open for the future and arresting deterioration, the present modest works may be considered a good investment for all parties involved. The location of Midhope, in terms of possible re-use, is to its advantage, as it has ready access to Edinburgh, Turnhouse and the electronics industries of West Lothian.

The Architect's Work

As you will know, to be effective as a conserving Architect, it is not just a question of doing the drawings and filling in the forms. This is the easy part: you have to see the problem form all points of view and consider the financial ways and means as well. My firm tried to fulfil this 'enabling' role since the mid 1970s recession, and had both welcome successes and irritating failures.

I was the job Architect, initially, and the firm continued to conduct the works in the person of my then partner, Thom Pollock who, with other colleagues, attended the Castles Conference. With the *modus operandi* of so many weeks a

Midhope Castle – William Cadell

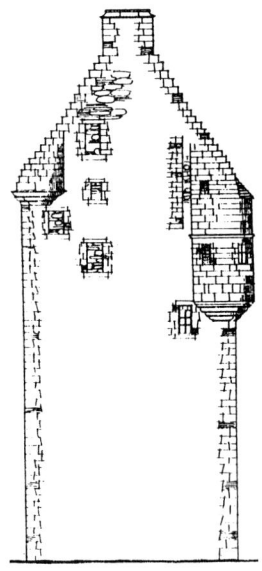

WEST ELEVATION

Fig. 6 (continued)
*West Elevation of Midhope tower.
Hugh A. Dalrymple.*

year, over a period of seven years, it was convenient that we were at Linlithgow, only a quarter of an hour's drive from the site. In this sort of situation, where budgets are tight, it is most helpful if the Architect's time, travel and expenses can be kept to the minimum.

The work was undertaken on the basis of separate trades. We knew who should do the job, their rates and the quality of their workmanship, as they had already done work for us in West Lothian, at various locations, including Little Mill at Linlithgowbridge and at Niddry Castle for Peter Wright. We had also enjoyed co-operation with a very effective Community Opportunities West Lothian team, who gave early help with site clearance and, indirectly, with demolitions. There was no difficulty in meeting the Historic Buildings and Monuments requirements, or those of the Local Authority. These factors may all be seen as advantages in employing local Architects.

However, a proprietor initiating such work also wishes to know that the Architect employed is both suitably experienced and has a record of competence in undertaking it. He or she may also wish to speak to former clients about performance on similar work, elsewhere, and it is helpful and reassuring to be able to provide the sort of information contained in the R.I.B.A. Practice Information forms, where previous experience, etc., is detailed.

Planning, Building Control, etc.

I first attended a meeting at Midhope about 25 years ago, with George McNeill, then the Director of Planning, John Gerrard of the Scottish Civic Trust and the then Estate factor, Jamie Douglas Menzies. The restoration of Midhope had been a Planning Department objective for many years. This objective was also shared by the Historic Buildings and Monuments Department, but it was not until 1985 that all parties met on site and it was decided to proceed with a report and costings. These were undertaken in early '86, approved with revisions by Historic Buildings and Monuments in early '87 and Scheduled Monument Consent and grant aid applied for in mid '87. The proposed work was judged to be that of repair, reinstatement and consolidation. Neither Listed Building Consent nor, as no re-use was proposed, were other Local Authority permissions required. Prior to work on site, access was provided for the Monuments Records to photograph, and surviving fragments of cornice, etc., were protected in situ.

It was Historic Buildings and Monuments (and currently is Historic Scotland's) normal practice to require working drawings, bills of quantities and competitive tenders, before offering grant. Due to the method, the scale and extent of the proposed programme, this was seen as inappropriate and it was agreed to proceed on the basis of the Feasibility Study and Costings, as revised and updated. An offer of grant was made in Spring '88 for the first year's work, to be expended in the financial year '88/89. Subsequent grants were made annually, with a percentage addition for index linking. The grant had to be reapplied for every year, but the principle of the programme had been accepted.

William Cadell – **Midhope Castle**

No other grants were received, but the C.O.W.L. work was carried out, free of labour costs and, in the event, virtually free of materials charges too.

Restoration Work, etc., and Costs

I have already mentioned that the estimated cost was divided by the annual budget to produce a phased programme over seven years. You may remember the old tale of 'The Black Bull of Norroway': "Seven long years I served for you"... etc. I do not think princesses are as patient these days, but this arrangement suited both the Historic Buildings and Monuments Department and the client. In addition there was no clamouring user. The work had, however, to be divided into a sensible sequence. In practice, and following the first two years, the programme had been reduced to six years, with the budget increased for the last four years to compensate.

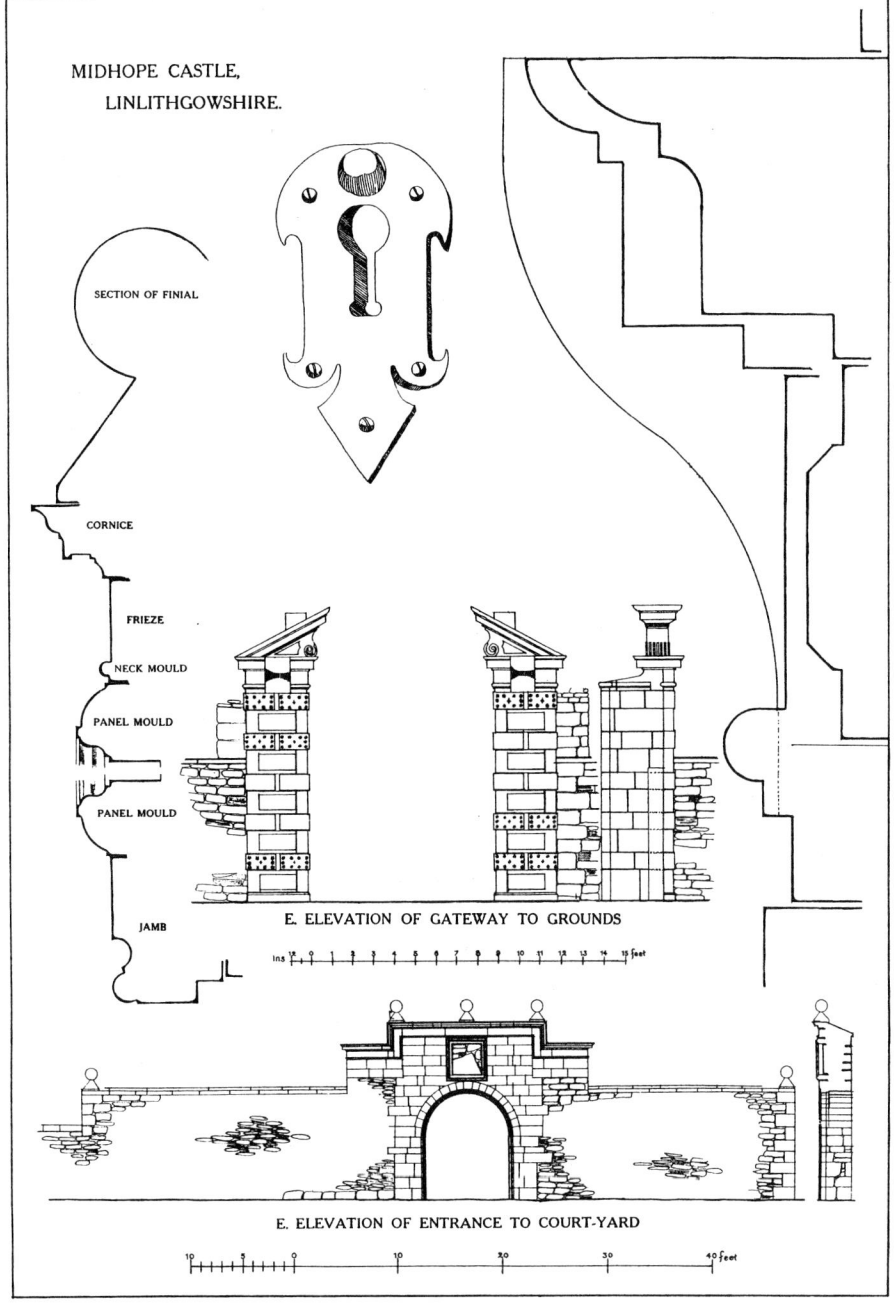

Fig. 8
Details of gateway to the castle grounds and entrance to the courtyard. (National Art Survey of Scotland). Hugh A. Dalrymple.

Midhope Castle – William Cadell

Year 1. 1988/89. Site Clearance

Demolition and clearance at East range.
4 weeks mason work at West Tower. £15,000

Year 2. 1989/90.

7 weeks mason work at East range.   Place tie beams. £15,000

Year 3 and 4. 1990/91 and 1991/92.

West tower complete.   East range complete internally. £40.000

Year 5 and 6. 1992/93 and 1993/94

East range complete. £40,000

Total for all works at August 1989 rates £110,000

Total including inflation £133,000

The reason for combining years 3/4 and 5/6 was to economise in scaffold charges by having only to scaffold once on each block, when all necessary external works and the roof reinstatement could be undertaken at the same time. The site was visited at least once a week during the course of the work and additional visits were made if required. We found it was very helpful for all parties to discuss progress and achieve better solutions through discussion and with mutual respect for everyone's contribution. In complicated work of this nature and scale it would have become even more complicated had communication been through the written medium and I am not certain that the best results would have been achieved.

Problems and Errors

There were few if any problems, but demolition of the East range roof and floors below undoubtedly presented a challenge or two! The state of these elements was so dangerous that working from below or from windows was impossible. The work had also to be undertaken carefully to avoid secondary damage and collapse, particularly at the wallhead, and at floor levels, windows, and chimney breasts. Niddry had enjoyed the assistance of a group of die-hards, some of whom had in their school days been responsible for the slogans, in impossible positions, so depressingly seen from the Glasgow/Edinburgh railway line: 'Wild Young Chungy' or 'English Go Home', etc. Spare a thought for the enterprise, skill and daring of such vandals! At least one had perished in attempting such literary achievements. The leader of our group, John Reid, was a competent man, with some experience in demolitions and, more importantly, a great love of old buildings.

William Cadell – Midhope Castle

A programme was devised and costed, including the hire of transport and plant, plus two jib cranes. Demolition was done from above, working off platforms suspended from the cranes - not an easy operation, as the worker had to hold on with one hand in order to work with the other, whilst at all times having to be very careful to avoid sudden movements! Instructions were passed from driver to platform by a third party standing on the wallhead. Once all was collapsed, the rubble and debris could, with greater safety, be shovelled out of windows for removal by tractors and lorries. The whole operation took approximately three days and cost £7,000, including hire of cranes at £3,450.

We had advice from the structural engineers, Messrs Wren and Bell, in the reconstruction of the West Tower roof. This previously incorporated accommodation at two levels, with access to the upper levels of the corner towers. The span was approximately 9m and the pitch 55%. In order not to apply too great a thrust at the wallhead, steel purlins were fitted half way up the rafters and the rafter ends anchored to the wallhead, which itself was restrained by steel beams a metre below. Made to measure roofs are likely to be the norm in work of this sort, but with this massive span, height and pitch it was particularly difficult and required all the skill and determination of the enterprising building team, consisting only of two masons, John Fraser and his father, one joiner and one labourer.

Following the demolition described above, the first phase of work was complete and the building shell left for action later. Neil Hynd made his inspection for the Historic Buildings and Monuments at this stage, pointing out the danger of leaving a building shell, following demolitions, without any tieing of the structure. As the structure was massive there was in fact no collapse, but it would have been better practice to have fitted the steel floor beams immediately, following demolition, rather than leaving them until the next year's work.

Fig. 9
View from SE, 1991: West Tower roof renewed, demolitions complete at East range.

Midhope Castle – William Cadell

Conclusions

The lack of a planned re-use for this building was unfortunate, although the possibility of eventual re-use has been greatly increased by undertaking the consolidation and re-roofing. Now completed, the building continues to be a drain on the Estate's resources, with the obligation to provide continuing maintenance and repair. Gradualism, where appropriate, is, I think, a good solution to conservation. Work planned in advance can be adjusted to the budget and what may appear to be daunting can be more readily and less painfully achieved, within a longer term project. There is time, also, for making improvements to the process and trust and faith are established over a period, on the basis of performance.

All parties, client, Historic Buildings and Monuments, Local Authority, architect, and builders showed flexibility in dealing with the problems of the building and the phasing of work over a fairly long time. The extended programme and budgeting, the use of separate trades of proven competence and the architect's time being used to best advantage, all contributed to what, at the end of the day, I believe, were very good value for money, given the building's size. The consolidation of this important historic structure and the provision of new roofs was achieved at a cost of only £135,000. *(1994 prices)*.

Fig. 1
Muckrach Castle in its dramatic setting, with views to the Cairngorms beyond the Spey Valley, prior to restoration. Photo: Ian Begg.

Muckrach Castle

by Ian Begg, da (edin), fRIAS, FSA (scot).

I joined Robert Hurd (Neil & Hurd) in 1951. Robert died in 1963 so I was sole partner until I joined firms with L.A. Rolland, Leven in 1965. I remained Senior Partner of Robert Hurd and Partners until 1983 but by that time I found that the firm had grown too large, so I retired and formed a new firm. My partner in the new firm of Ian Begg Architect was Raymond Muszynski and we had a good small office - five all told. Respect for our traditions in all aspects, particularly in buildings of quality, was the backbone of the practice. The erection of very good buildings, able to carry the tradition forward, was our goal.

For a long time I have been worried about the continuity of our architectural awareness and enthusiasm for design, and while I enjoy immensely our rich past of tower houses, bridges and other building forms, I see them as lessons for the future.

During my professional life, I have been involved in much restoration, conservation and new building, both in the centre of cities like Edinburgh and Glasgow and in country villages, country houses and castles, such as Aboyne, Blair and Paxton House. Paxton House, having been gifted to the Nation, is now open to the public.

I designed the Scandic Crown Hotel (now the Crowne Plaza) in Edinburgh and the Visitors' Centre on Cathedral Square, Glasgow – currently the St. Mungo's Museum – and have had a rewarding range of work: from an unsatisfactory job, trying to restore an Islamic castle in the north-west mountains of Saudi Arabia, where I was overwhelmed by bureaucracy and a demand that work had to be done by 'scientific methods' (the job was not finished under my care!), to the other extreme, and infinitely more satisfactory, the stabilising of the tiny ruin of Castle Maoil, Kyleakin, working with Alistair Urquhart as the stonemason. Muckrach Castle was a most enjoyable job, *en route*.

Various other responsibilities have come my way during my working life. I was Interim Director of the Edinburgh New Town Conservation Committee when it was set up in 1971; Interim Director of the more recent Edinburgh Old Town Committee for Conservation and Renewal (1984-5); and was Adviser on Architecture for the Edinburgh Old Town Charitable Trust. I have undertaken architectural teaching in design and was, for twelve years, a member of the Historic Buildings Council for Scotland. I have been an Architectural Adviser to the National Trust for Scotland and a Vice President of the Architectural Heritage Society for Scotland.

The Building and its Restoration

Muckrach is a very small tower house, near Dulnain Bridge, Grantown on Spey. In 1975 it still stood, on rising ground, ruinous and frail, but with enormous presence, overlooking the Cairngorms. The Inverness County

Muckrach Castle – Ian Begg

Planning Officer drew the attention of the owners to their obligation, under the Planning Acts, to look after their listed building.

The tower was originally built in 1598 by a cadet of the Grant family of Rothiemurchus, It seems slightly late, considering its style, possibly because it was a fashionable introduction, but it has shown fascinating complex construction, where timber has been introduced into the stone walls - perhaps because stone was an alien building element in the great forest of Rothiemurchus, and masonry construction was not understood, or trusted.

The building form dictated the restoration process and the planning of the house that has subsequently been rebuilt within the old shell. Muckrach was given every sympathetic treatment by the architect, who depended greatly on the stonemason and joiner. Even the Professor of Structural Engineering at Edinburgh University was brought in, not for a design, but to offer an opinion on the structure of the turning stair which was recreated. There is no other like it!

Nearly four hundred years ago, Muckrach was built economically by people with an exceptional awareness of three dimensional form. MacGibbon & Ross in "Castellated and Domestic Architecture of Scotland" sensed the unusual in this building. I had the rewarding and pleasant task of carrying out the restoration and formation of a modern house, within the shell, working with splendid tradesmen. These men were finely in tune with the work of the original builders.

The Background

Muckrach was a ruin when first I saw it, but it was a real little gem to work on. It is one of the rewards in life to work with colleagues in order to create something good and fine. It was one of the high points in my life, as an architect, to work on Muckrach with the mason, Alistair Urquhart, and Ronnie MacPherson, the joiner. We were a team depending on one another and I feel sure that we made a good job of it. I am very pleased to say that Alistair and Ronnie are still good friends of mine, twenty years on!

I remember this as a cold job, which wasn't warmed by the relationship between us and the son of the original client. In the wintertime, when days were very short, he couldn't bear go to the local hotel for food because we would waste daylight and time. We had very cold lunch breaks. My assistant, who was a vegetarian, once had a sandwich supplied – the contents of which consisted of one cold brussels sprout – from the previous night's dinner table, no doubt! In fact, it is during the breaks that we often learn most about a client and his (or her) aspirations. It is also, of course, where the builder and joiner also get close to the architect. Sadly, this close link is rarely pursued. I don't know why but it is most unfortunate and does the building process no good at all. It is not only on a relatively small job, like the one at Muckrach, where this should happen. It should happen almost as a matter of course, because building up a sense of respect and responsibility, which comes from contact, invariably pays off in the quality of work. But back to Muckrach.

Fig. 2
The conditions of Muckrach when drawn by MacGibbon & Ross.

Ian Begg – Muckrach Castle

It was, I think, in 1976 that we were first called in to look at the tower house. Just at the end of the days of Inverness County Council, Richard Cameron, who was Chief Planning Officer, had called the owners of Muckrach's attention to the fact that it was a Listed Building. The deterioration was hardly new but the place was indeed in poor shape. It was obviously a fine example of the small Scottish tower house and they had a responsibility to do something about it. In fact, it was much more important than anyone suspected at the time. It stands on a superb site, about 800 feet elevation, secluded but close to the A938 road running through the Dulnain valley. Built in 1598 by the second son of John Grant of Freuchie, now the Rothiemurchus family, it was unroofed in 1739 and seems to have been fairly ruinous by 1767.

Even as a ruin it had a wonderful quality - a marvellous presence on the hillside that impressed me on the first visit. It is truly wonderful how these early builders could create superb architectural effect out of comparatively simple but ingenious planning and building techniques. Here there are no six foot thick walls, no applied decoration at all; the hall was only twenty feet by twenty-one feet to the stonework, so that the whole building is smaller than many a bungalow - yet look at the quality and its striking posture on the side of the hill. (Fig 1) There was substantial dereliction, even from its condition as drawn by MacGibbon at the end of the 19th century (Fig. 2). The surrounding trees, too, had become derelict.

When, as architects, we took possession of Muckrach, it could only be regarded as structurally unsound. The South gable of the main tower had fallen in, taking with it the vault which supported the main floor and part of the wall which linked the castle to the little round tower to the South. This gable had obviously been the weakest one, containing all the fireplaces and flues, and most windows too, so it is hardly surprising that it failed. But why, precisely, is the interesting point. We have much to learn from such work.

Many features that were there to see were not recognised on our earlier visits. It is upon these that I will try to concentrate, as I describe the work and endeavour to offer some explanation for what we found. The only dating that could be given to the collapse of the South was that it was "recent", in that underneath all the stonework of the collapse was a bicycle crank! There were no other finds of any archaeological significance.

Muckrach is strange and 1598 seems rather late for this building. My guess is that the laird, John Grant, brought the idea of a tower to the area. He perhaps visited someone else's tower house and liked what he had seen. We have to remember that Rothiemurchus was a huge part of the Caledonian forest at that time and timber building would be the norm. Probably the stonemasons were also imported. I hope to show you why I believe this to be the case and that the timber builders of the forest were the dominant people in the building of this tower house. But I am not denying that the masons were very clever, too. I believe that they were the designers, with a three dimensional sense that is extraordinarily rare today.

Fig. 3
Plan of Muckrach MacGibbon & Ross.

FIRST FLOOR PLAN

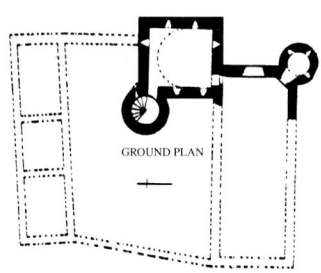

GROUND PLAN

Muckrach Castle – Ian Begg

The Job

As has been said, it is a small building and it was in very poor condition. The very first stages meant working only for short summer seasons to repair the structure. No firm end to the project was in view. The parents (the original clients), who were alive at this time, had no end use in mind for the little castle. They simply wanted to carry out their statutory obligations. I wish there were many more like them, in this respect, as I also wish there were more Planning Officers who would try hard to get owners of listed buildings, in a bad state of repair, to undertake necessary repair work, before building costs get out of hand.

The first essential was to repair the South gable by filling in the gaping hole (Fig 4) and also to rebuild the vault. This was obviously skilled work and potentially dangerous. No one in the Grantown on Spey area that we approached would look at this as a job. Everyone said the building had to be demolished. However, this was contrary to what might be regarded good conservation practice. Nothing original should be removed if it can be safely retained, at reasonable cost!

I had recently completed difficult work at Aboyne Castle with Alistair Urquhart, so naturally I invited him to come and see the new problem. "Nae bother! We'll put up a scaffold in the hole, put a bit of corrugated iron across the top...... and if it starts to move ye'll hear the chucky stanes fall on the corrugated sheet and A'll jump into the saund."

So we started. We used concrete blocks because they are quick to build and of course they are cheaper than rebuilding in stone. A decision to harl the

Fig. 4
South gable in a dangerous state.

Ian Begg – Muckrach Castle

finished work had been taken and I knew that Alistair was astonishingly adept at handling these most intractable heavy blocks. It takes real skill to build with them and present a soft undulating surface to the exterior for ultimate harling. The normal process of building fair-faced blockwork would present a surface much too flat and alien to the effect of harling on stone. One can argue that stonework should be used where stone has been. Of course, but cost is one factor; and also the extent of our repairs will be obvious to later generations, should they be interested.

Rebuilding the vault followed the completion of the South gable. We had a clear indication of the vault line on the North wall and we could also see evidence of a small cross vault over the entrance way. We built formwork from plywood, but I know neither Alistair nor I would ever use plywood again. We would use boards in the traditional way, we have since discovered, and we would plaster on top of these and set the vault stones in the plaster - thereby sealing the whole job and giving the easiest possible plaster surface when the formwork is stripped. It is a terrible job to try to plaster a vault from below, as was done at Muckrach. Imagine the difference - putting the stuff down at your feet on boards, rather than plastering a curve over your head, while standing on planks. As far as we knew, all the old vaults were plastered, and would show boardmarks.

The parents, our original clients, had now died and their son took over.

It was probably our third summer working there, when we got to the upper level of the main spiral stair. At the break, where the corbels carry the circle tower out to the square, for the rooms above, we found an extraordinary state of affairs which had remained unnoticed at earlier stages, even on photographs. Alistair found that immediately above the corbels there were great voids, about 9 inches by 10 inches, running about 12 feet from side to side of the tower and faced on the outside with tiny pinning stones (Fig 5). Hefty timbers of Scots pine had been placed, no doubt by the timber builders who, in my view, as already mentioned, dominated the works. How could a timber builder trust these stone corbels, built by masons? (I sometimes wonder how I do!). So they laid these great timbers to lace the structure together (Fig. 6 overleaf). However, these having rotted away, enabled us to see how the fine stonework, only 3 or 4 inches thick, continued to support the upper walls from the very outer edge of the corbels. Fine work indeed!

Fig. 5
Voids within the stair tower structure, running from side to side. See also detail of timber lacing the structure together. (Fig. 6 overleaf)

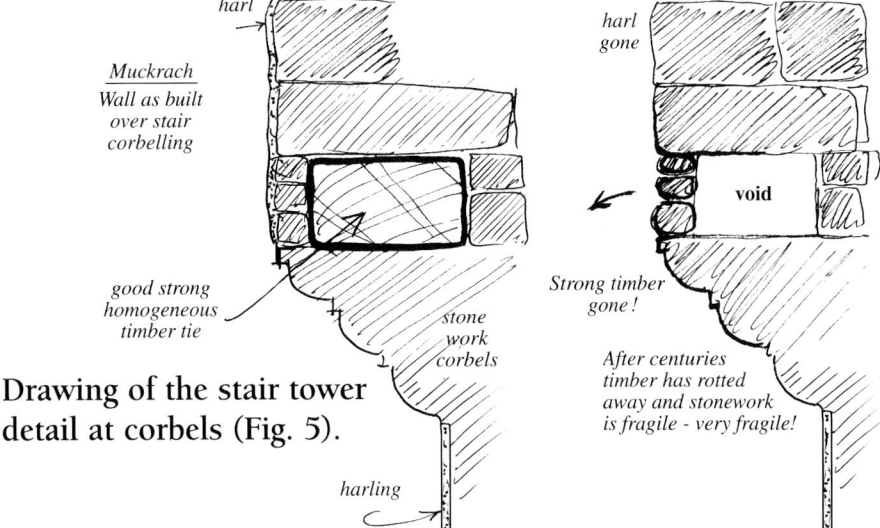

Muckrach Castle – Ian Begg

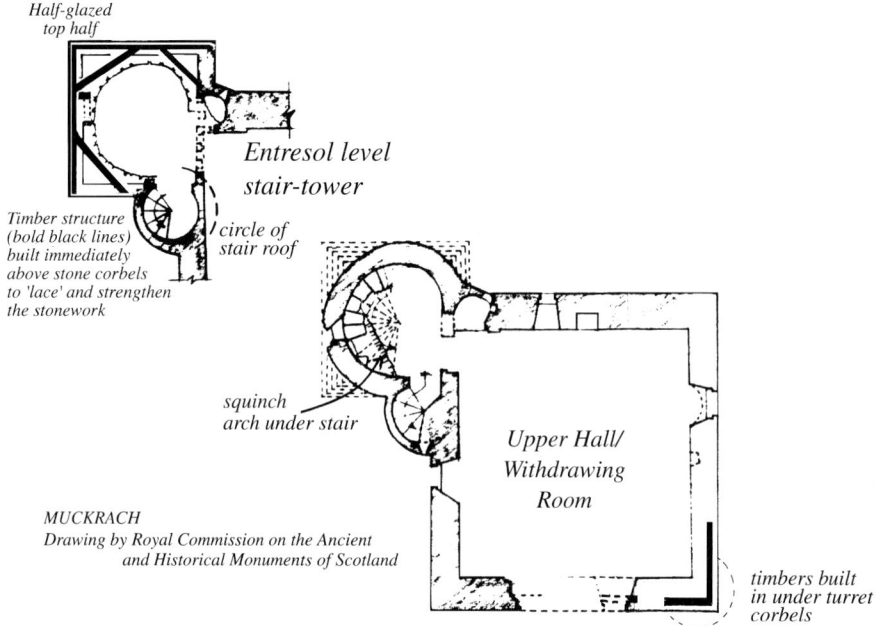

Fig. 6
Timbers lacing the structure together.

There were other examples of this lack of faith in masonry: under the corbelled corner turret where, again, the corbelling was not trusted; also at the wide recess in the South wall, where the failure of a timber beam may have triggered the major collapse of the gable and vault. A timber beam had been placed above a stone arch - something a mason would never do because an arch has to be in compression to work (Fig. 7). Here the weather over the years,

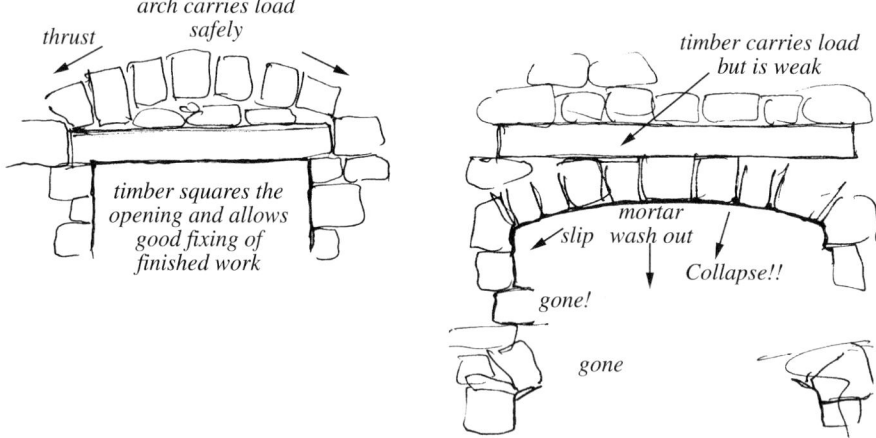

Fig. 7
Left: Traditional 'safe' lintel with relieving stone arch over. Right: Aberration found at Muckrach – timber over the arch creates an inherent weakness and caused unnecessary collapse.

wasting the timber beam, would also wash out the mortar between the scarcely loaded arch stones, so that they became unstable and failed with the timber. The timber builders, although they were the bosses, didn't appear to understand stonework. Muckrach is exciting because it is a misplaced little stone tower house. On the face of it, little different from dozens of others, but misplaced because it was built in the great forest, the one place in Scotland where timber was the plentiful building material.

There was another feature of the construction, unique as far as I know.

Ian Begg – **Muckrach Castle**

MacGibbon & Ross noted the fact that the main stair is different in its construction. "The mode in which these steps are supported is peculiar, a rough arch being thrown across a segment of the circular staircase under each." They saw the unusual but of course they did not have to rebuild it, so offered no insight into how it really worked.

Fig. 8
The staircase, showing squinch arch in stairwell,(below, left) and short stones corbelled out, forming the basic structure to carry the stairs, which have gone.

You are looking down the stairwell in Figure 8 and will see that there is a peculiar arrangement of stones, far too short for a stair, following round the circle. If you look back at the Royal Commission drawing (Fig. 6) you will see the plan. The segments, referred to above, are in fact squinch arches under the stone 'steps' that add support to these. Initially I imagined that these short 'steps' were broken remains of the original steps, but this was not the case - they were built like that. Precisely why, apart from providing supports for the stairs, we never discovered. We made assumptions in discussion with Professor Arnold Hendry, Professor of Structural Engineering at Edinburgh University and he visited the site to examine the detail carefully. We built a model to replicate what was there and added a stair, showing how it might have been formed. We came to the conclusion that this was a compound structure, employing both timber and stone.

Our solution, not necessarily the precise style of the original of course, was to construct a timber inner stringer made up of short lengths, forming a faceted helix. The balustrade was an integral part of this construction and was locked at top and bottom to the main structure. To analyse this a little further: having constructed this stringer, there was only one way it could fail, i.e., by bursting outwards in the direction of the 'steps'. So we filled in the space between the stringer and the short original 'steps' with flat stones, attempting to arch from the stringer to the wall, in order to keep the stringer loaded and therefore tight. So, in this manner, the new stair was formed. We have wire mesh embedded in

Muckrach Castle – Ian Begg

mortar, under the new work, to mak siccar but there is no doubt that it is a sound construction. and could easily be as it was originally built.

The probable reason for this form of construction was to overcome the shortage of long stones, as are necessary for the usual form of stone stair. The stairwell is about 9 feet in diameter and the staircase is barely 3 feet wide, finished. The Royal Commission drawing indicates exceptionally long steps. Nothing was found on site that might have been part of such a wide generous stair. So the original solution at Muckrach was most ingenious.

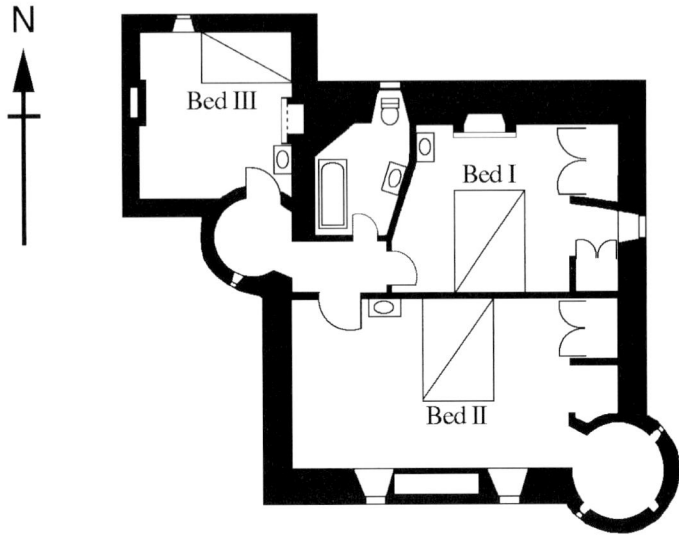

Fig. 9
Plan of domestic arrangements.

Fig. 10
Angle turret on SE corner.

The ground floor vault formed the kitchen. The first floor, reached by the stair just described, formed the Hall and from this level one climbed by means of a small secondary stair, crudely built but of normal stone stair-construction, to the bedrooms, bathrooms, etc., all very tightly and economically planned (Fig. 9). Remember the building is only 20 feet by 21 feet between the stone walls of the main block.

In the reconstruction there were many clues as to the original form. One just had to keep an eye open and have a sympathy with the original builders. Alistair Urquhart was an ideal 'medium' and I learned much through him. The little projecting angle turret had virtually disappeared, but there was enough evidence to give us a clear picture of the original, including its roof form (Fig. 10). Here you see it as built by Alistair. It is now a beautiful shape, slightly barrel curved and set on precast concrete corbels.

Slowly the building got up to the roof, the walls having been pointed and tightened all the way up. We had still not fathomed how the roof of the secondary stair would be built. Figure 11 shows the top of the tight, steep, secondary stair, with part of the wall missing - a gaping tooth. The picture is from my position, as I ponder. I am sitting right on top of the main roof, very cold indeed, one leg down each slope of the roof. Look at the drawing again (Fig. 9), entresol level, - you will see how, if we continue the circle of the outer form of the stair to the inside, in order to build a conical roof, there is nothing to

Ian Begg – Muckrach Castle

support either wall or roof. So we have to step back - figuratively - and consider carefully. Ronnie MacPherson the joiner - another extremely clever builder, if slightly impetuous in his younger days (here) - had just erected the basic roof. He was frustrated by stones at this staircase which projected above the roof line (Fig. 11) that otherwise seemed to be correct. "Knock the buggers off!" was his suggested solution, but Alistair wouldn't as he felt there had to be a reason for them being there. Let me explain this as simply as I can. Figure 12 (overleaf) indicates what we found. We had to build a regular cone but, in fact, it was truncated and we had stones sticking up through the roof (the ones that had to be 'knocked off'). Now imagine the cone. If you tightened the curve as the stair tightened over the inside of the building, then you'd find that the cone rose but one could build it perfectly normally on that rising line. On the bottom right hand side you see that as we did it, it worked perfectly. The strong line in fact was a natural drainage line to bring water from in behind the turret out to the front. It was extremely clever, and the original masons, of course, knew that this was what they were going to do, long before they got there in the construction.

Tradition has it that the original plaque, which had been in situ over the main door, was at Rothiemurchus, so a cast copy was made by Alistair. He had gone to another friend, the late Albert Cramb, a plasterer in Edinburgh, to learn the old technique for taking a cast from stone. The copy was built into the wall of Muckrach to complete the work. So Muckrach was more or less restored as it was originally built but, to some degree, adapted internally for modern day living. It is a lovely little building, which has settled down, with lichens growing, given the clear Grampian air (Fig. 13 overleaf). The glass roof, however, was not my work, but I can well appreciate its value!

Fig. 11

Muckrach Castle – Ian Begg

Fig. 12

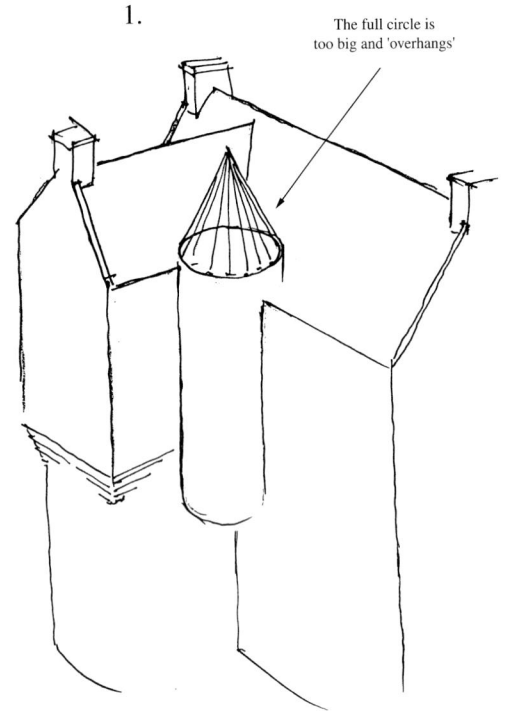

1. The full circle is too big and 'overhangs'

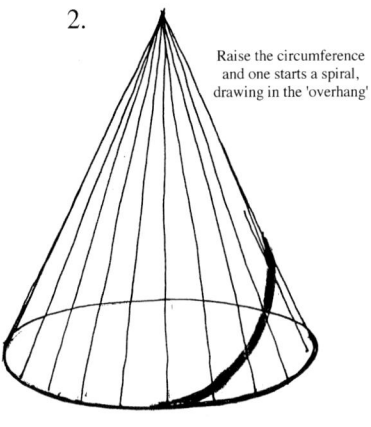

2. Raise the circumference and one starts a spiral, drawing in the 'overhang'

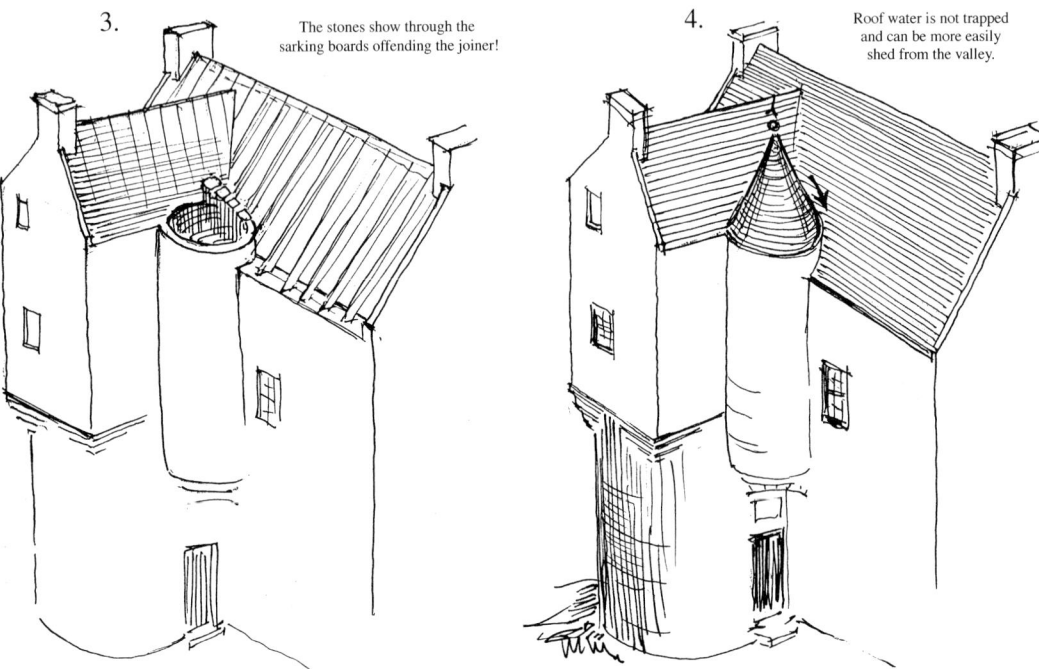

3. The stones show through the sarking boards offending the joiner!

4. Roof water is not trapped and can be more easily shed from the valley.

Ian Begg – **Muckrach Castle**

Fig. 13
Muckrach at the turn of the century.

Fig. 1
Tilquhillie in 1999. Photo: Robert McCallum

Tilquhillie Castle

BY FRANCE SMOOR, MSC, MRIBA, ARIAS, DIP ARCH AND TP (DELFT).

In 1985 Tilquhillie Castle was purchased by Dr John Coyne, a former diplomat, originally from Virginia, and his wife, Kay Hamlander, whose parents were from Norway. They have lived in Europe for many years, first in Switzerland and then moving to Scotland, where they purchased the charming 'miniature' castle of Murroes, near Dundee. Their great enthusiasm for Scottish castles is matched equally by that for their team of Siberian huskies, and dog sledging, so they sought somewhere rather more in the wilds, where these two interests could better be combined. I was involved in their search for a perfect mediaeval castle and Tilquhillie suited them well. Its late 16c architecture still retained a passive, defensive character and its remote setting on an exposed hillside, away from other settlements, complemented their desire for isolation and security.

I myself graduated from Delft as an architect and town planner. I came to Scotland in 1968 and started a private practice five years later, mainly occupied with restoring listed houses, sometimes castles or country houses, sometimes little houses in towns and villages in Fife and Tayside. I now live at Gagie House, a 1614 fortalice near Dundee, which has been altered or extended in each century, including the 20th, by myself. Gagie therefore contains a variety of periods and styles, expressing the changes in its history, which are still to be seen under the surface of modern life. My philosophy coincides with that of Historic Scotland, in that one should aim in restorations to consolidate the entire heritage and history of the building. I differ from them, however, in my belief that one should conserve or repair only what is worth preserving. Decay is also an aspect of history that one should accept and is a valid reason to remove what has no merit. This, of course, introduces subjective evaluation! Our forebears never had any inhibitions about adding that 'something contemporary', which was sometimes eclectic, sometimes historicising and sometimes radically new, depending on the builder's taste, but is almost always recognisable to the practised eye as being a product of its own period, without the need to date everything.

The Building's History

Tilquhillie was built in 1576 by John Douglas, a descendant of the Douglas of Dalkeith, whose grandfather had brought the estate into his family by the marriage to an Ogstoun heiress from Fettercairn. The coat of arms above the door displays both Douglas and Ogstoun quarters. His son, also John, was in his minority, under the curatorship of Morton, Regent for King James VI, who in adversity had to go into hiding in Tilquhillie, in 1591, under the name of James de Grieve. John married Mary Young.

Robert, one of their ten offspring, was knighted by Charles I but fought on the wrong side, lost a fortune and fled abroad in 1647. Covenanters were garrisoned

Tilquhillie Castle – France Smoor

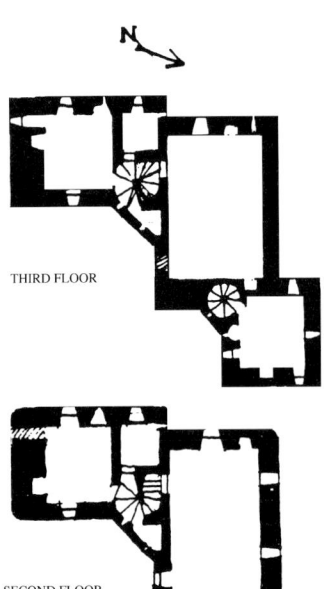

Fig. 2
Plans of Tilquhillie. Scale 1:250.

in his castle, which was not returned to the family until 1687, when another John succeeded. In the 18th century the family moved the main residence to Inverey, a country house in the fashion of the time, along the River Feugh, in the more temperate climate of the valley.

Tilquhillie consequently became a minor residence and latterly a farmhouse. The travel writer, Norman Douglas, spent part of his youth there and his brother, John, was married to Edith de Reuter of press agency fame. The last members of the Douglas family to own the castle were John Sholto, born in 1904, and his son, Hugh, who emigrated to Australia and sold the property to the present owners. By this time, the social degradation of the building was complete, as it had not been inhabited since well before the Second World War, and it was being used to house turkeys!

Description

As the castle was too large to build in one year, the original building project must have spanned a year or two, although I do not agree with MacGibbon and Ross that it was built in two stages, signifying a change in style. The almost excessive perforation of the external walls from cellar to loft, by recesses and openings, large and small, enables easy observation of the surrounding countryside and the building's walls, thereby eliminating any blind corners. To my mind this demonstrates a great concern for a passive defence system.

It was built on a Z-plan, (Fig. 2), with the corner towers very closely integrated with the central block, as if the transformation to a more convenient plan, with the rooms interlinked horizontally, had already taken place. Inside, however, each tower remains virtually a vertical unit on its own. This applies especially to the north-east tower, the laird's tower, which has a private spiral staircase up from the first floor. The main tower and that of the south-west share a more spacious staircase, so that the floors are all staggered and separated by short flights, taking in smaller rooms, as it winds upwards.

The corner tower rooms above the vaulted basement are all identical in layout, with a fireplace in the outside gable and a window recess beside. There is always a window in each side wall, however small and, in addition, a recess with a shot-hole to control the entrance or any re-entrant angle. These perforations provided all the rooms with a remarkable amount of daylight, but no doubt at the same time made the castle uncomfortably draughty.

In the 19th century, presumably to counter these draughts, the main rooms were all lined with an inner skin of lath and plaster. All recesses and smaller windows were turned into cupboards, or blocked up, and major windows were squared, losing some height internally, as their openings were originally vaulted. This made the rooms rather dark. Conversion to more classical interiors did not, however, extend to the introduction of larger or additional windows, placed in a symmetrical elevation design; at the same time the original shutter windows must have been replaced by sashes, fixed to the smaller windows, and sash and case for the larger. The detailing of the profiles was simply domestic. The modesty of these alterations presumably reflected the fact that the family had by this time moved their principal residence to a more gracious house, in keeping with the Age of Elegance, and Tillquhillie was refurbished in a small way for a lesser member of the family. The lack of ventilation must have contributed to the early decay of these alterations and by the time I became involved most of this refurbishment had already disappeared.

Due to the poverty of the soil on the estate, consisting mainly of dry sand and gravel - and therefore the relative poverty of the estate - the castle had remained virtually unchanged (Fig. 3) since it was first built and it presented a case where an almost complete return to its original state was an obvious decision; one, I should add, that was not entirely supported by Historic Scotland.

Fig. 3
Tilquhillie, largely unchanged, MacGibbon & Ross's drawing at the end of the 19th century of the SE elevation.

The Masonry

Structurally, Tilquhillie was very well preserved. The three towers, tightly fused together were only pierced by the many small windows and shot holes; a compact mass of masonry, bypassed by later fashions for larger openings. Alterations to the masonry were limited to a rear door on the ground floor and an interconnecting door, horizontally linking the north east tower with the main tower on the second floor, via the private stair.

When the Great Hall was converted in the 19th century from a sort of thoroughfare into a drawing room and was squared up and boxed in with dry lining, it was thought necessary to remove the squinches in the opposite corners where the doors into the north and south towers were located. These were built, arching the corners over the access doors, and were hacked out to form a square corner. In another corner was a cubicle in masonry that housed the steps rising from the provisions cellar, below. A similar stair is in Inverquharity Castle, Angus. This had also been removed to produce a square corner and the steps filled in. These were minor additions. No windows had been enlarged or added.

Internal Finishings to Walls

Refurbishment had taken place only in the three rooms on the first floor in the 19th century, and in a further two rooms on the second and third floors of the south tower, i.e., five out of eleven rooms above the cellars. This work consisted only of drylining, enclosing some windows and all shot-hole recesses to form cupboards, and inserting grates in the original fire openings.

The timber finishings were of a simple domestic detailing, as is still frequently found in farmhouses of the period. The remaining windows sat in lined and squared recesses to conceal the vaulted soffits which, as already mentioned, reduced the daylight further and, with their sash and case windows, resulted in the interiors looking decidedly claustrophobic and dark.

It was difficult to imagine how the dry lining could be removed and yet retain the cupboards and fire grates that were encased in its framing. Historic Scotland opposed its removal but, since most was already gone before we became involved, it was almost inevitable that we should return to the original interiors, which were present behind these later additions. This enabled us to re-open the smaller windows and shot-holes. Trying to re-create the 19th century refurbishment would have required more guesswork than exposing the hidden earlier detailing and it had certainly no architectural or historical merit on a par with the original interiors.

The romantic pre-occupation with one or other period of an historic building often leads the restorer astray, trying to peel away subsequent or even previous layers of architecture to achieve an ideal image. This is not a method of restoration to which I subscribe and certainly not if this idealised image is just a harled pastiche. In Tillquhillie, any wall repairs were carried out with the rubble that was to hand and the new rear door received a proper granite arch, salvaged from a nearby demolition, rather than retaining the decaying timber lintel.

The internal walls were plastered directly on to any sound old lime plaster or prepared render, leaving prominent stones exposed, as was found before, and then painted with an oil-based 'breathing' white paint.

Windows

We were anxious to return to the original shutter-type windows. This was strongly opposed by Historic Scotland. In the end, we were given permission to re-introduce them but only to discover that no grant would be given for this repair and so, for financial reasons, the idea had to be abandoned. I think that

Fig. 4
1. Tilquhillie NE elevation.
2. NW elevation.
3. SW elevation.
4. SE elevation.
Drawing – France Smoor.

this was regrettable, especially since I understand that Historic Scotland is no longer insistent on sash and case windows in tower houses. I welcome this development because often the installation of a sash and case window, with its quaint appearance of small panes, has been abused as a panacea to obliterate other forms of window tracery, for the sake of misplaced uniformity. Until the late 18th century, glazed windows were an expensive item in Scotland. When James V, on a royal progress, visited Powrie Castle north of Dundee, he sent his own glazier ahead to improve the illumination during his stay but no doubt the glazing would have departed with the King, once the food ran out! Glazing should therefore be regarded as a desirable but optional extra to the secure provision of shutters but it was not the only means of providing illumination, as often parchment or lambskin was stretched over the top opening, to combine the admission of an element of light with draught-proofing.

Shutter windows are well enough documented even though not many have survived. Since the principle is very simple, there is not a lot of scope to err when replacing them. It is certain that the leaded glass tops were inserted into the still extant grooves in the lintel soffit and upper stone surrounds. There it was held in position by an extension of the transom of the shutter frame. Below this, the shutters had to keep out wind and water. Very often there were also shutters above the transom and behind the glass but these shutters could easily be lifted off their hinges. There is a Flemish painting of an only slightly earlier date that shows the bottom shutters open, with a temporary grille against insects, placed in front. I would not object to having an extra glazed pane, that was openable, placed in front of the bottom half of the window opening, as an optional extra, in the same way that to-day one would regard, say, a blind, a lace curtain, or a pelmet.

Tilquhillie Castle – France Smoor

The sash and case windows that we installed had to fit inside very shallow recesses, sufficient only for the shutter type of window. To avoid revealing wide timber margins on the outside elevations, the windows could not be provided with enough space to use weights to balance the sashes; opening these windows would therefore be heavy work and will remain a lasting irritation for those who use the castle.

Internally, as previously mentioned, the window openings were vaulted over, with the arch springing set back from the wall top of the reveal, to allow space for the formwork to rest on. This produced a rather odd and crude mushroom-shaped outline.

I believe that in restoring an historic building, one restores not only stone, mortar and wood but something that is more important - the historical concept of an architectural space and form which, at Tilquhillie, was not only designed for comfort in front of the fireplace, under the dry roof and within the warm walls, but also for the reassuring relationship to the dangers outside. These could be controlled through the innumerable spy-holes and windows which, in turn, all contributed to producing a remarkable inflow of light. It gave us an almost addictive satisfaction to re-open these quaint perforations and to discover the magic of the light and the views in all directions, over the surrounding countryside. Historic Scotland, however, stopped us in our tracks in this agreeable pursuit of opening all these peep-holes – but only at the last window. In the end even they relented, for at the final inspection it was suggested that it be opened after all!

Floor Construction

The top two floors (the second and third) consisted of tongue and groove pine boards, resting on oak beams. Few of the oak beams were missing, although some had been cut in front of fireplaces when new protruding fire grates were installed during the 19th century refurbishments. Many of the beams, however, had some rot in their ends where they were resting in the walls. We were able to repair some floors in a way that had been done before in the castle. New longitudinal joists were placed below the beams and carried on stone corbels which protruded from along the parallel walls, thereby reducing the beams' span. This form of repair may not exactly be 'reinstatement' but it is a sensible way of minimising disturbance of the masonry and, in many castles, it is an accepted way of carrying the floor joists, thereby reducing the risk of rot from the outstart. In the case at Tilquhillie, the owners, moreover, had great satisfaction in introducing the 'art nouveau' corbel stones.

One floor had under-dimensioned joists and was sagging badly. We used acro-props to reduce the sag and then nailed twin joists alongside, their top halves higher up, creating little box girders in combination with the floor on top. Plasterboard was then nailed against the soffit of these additional joists, with insulation in between.

Most of the original, very wide floorboards were gone but the owners managed to save enough to repair one floor, which was a source of great satisfaction to them. They went to considerable trouble to find the extra wood that was still required, having to resort to splitting old 10" x 4" pine joists in half, a request that was not greeted with great enthusiasm by the sawmillers, who did not relish the prospect of using their circular saws to cut through old nails in the process!

The cellar floors were either of earth or cobbled with small, local granite stones but as these did not make an even floor they were later screeded or concreted over.

There was no evidence of the earlier use of stone slabs in the 'piano nobile' or Great Hall. As they were hard to come by locally, one assumes that this floor must have been of timber construction. It was likely that this was replaced several times in its history, because of rising damp from the vaults. The owners decided to cover both ground and first floors with Caithness slabs over underfloor heating pipes. Historic Scotland grant-aided only the ground floor, doubting that the first floor had ever been slabbed, but they generously contributed to the underfloor heating.

Fireplaces

There were two small cast iron fireplaces, intended for coal fires, which were insufficient for log burning. These were removed. The laird's room, off the Great Hall, still had the only original stone-carved, moulded fire surround.

The Roof

The original roof construction, in oak with rafters, double tie beams and an ashlar post and sole piece on the wallhead, was all still there and required only minor repairs. The sarking and slating had been renewed previously. The original roof covering could have been thatch or stone slates, hung from straps with pegs but there was no evidence of use of either material; however, the underslating course at the eaves consisted of large stone slabs to maximise the overhang.

Historic Scotland quite rightly insisted that the roof be renewed, although it was not visibly leaking. In my experience, I feel that it is wrong to remove the old sarking, for I believe that if at all possible one should treat it and leave it where it is. New sarking could be nailed over the old, separated by $1\frac{1}{2}$ x 2 ins straps placed vertically over each rafter, in order to create a ventilated space. It is then possible to place insulation in between the rafters, right up against the old sarking and to line it without obscuring the original roof structure. (Fig. 4.1 and 4.2). This is what we did. In the beginning I had some difficulty in persuading the slater and the dubious owners to conserve the old sarking. It was very fragile but lessons were learnt with the first roof and in the subsequent work on the two remaining towers, the old sarking was kept. In fact, during these operations, the old sarking kept the structure stable and saved a lot of shoring. Keeping the old

Tilquhillie Castle – France Smoor

Fig. 4.1
Roof repaired, showing old sarking retained, treated and repaired.

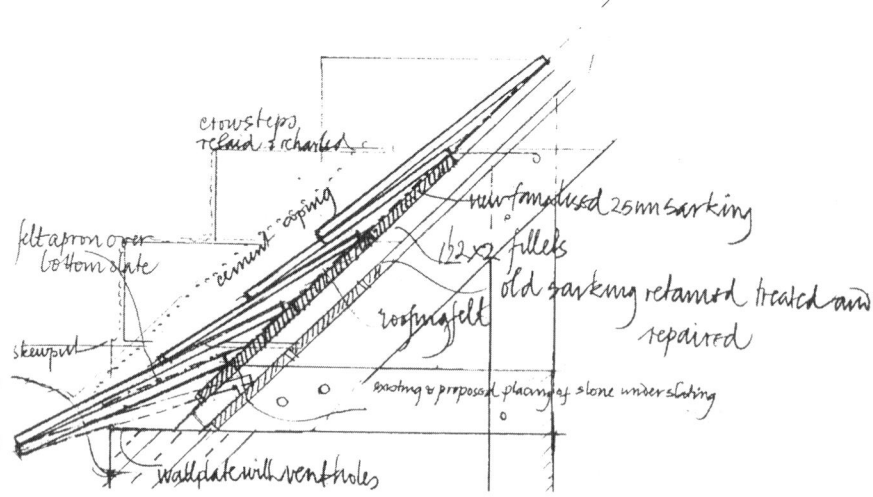

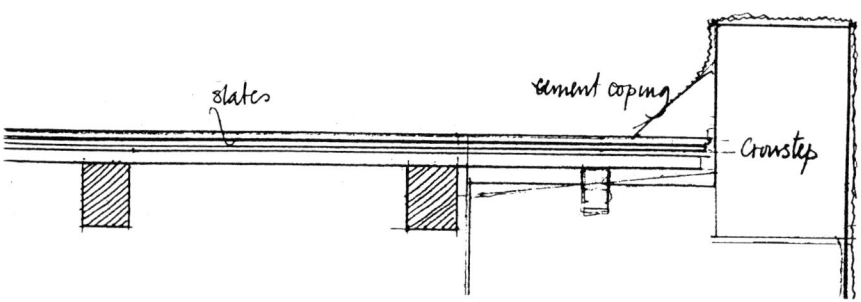

Fig. 4.2
1. *Gable section throught roof showing original construction.*
2. *Deteriorated construction, as existing, before work began.*
3. *Proposed correction, leaving ventilated gap between old and new sarking.*

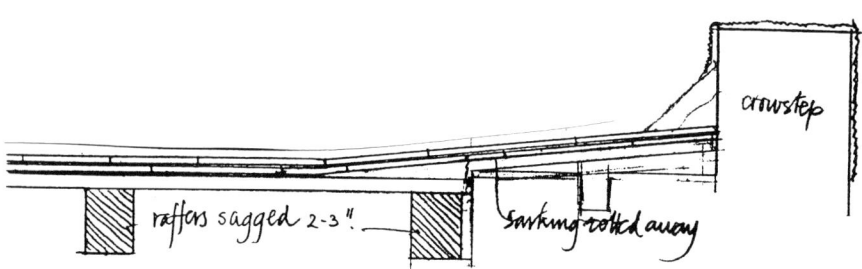

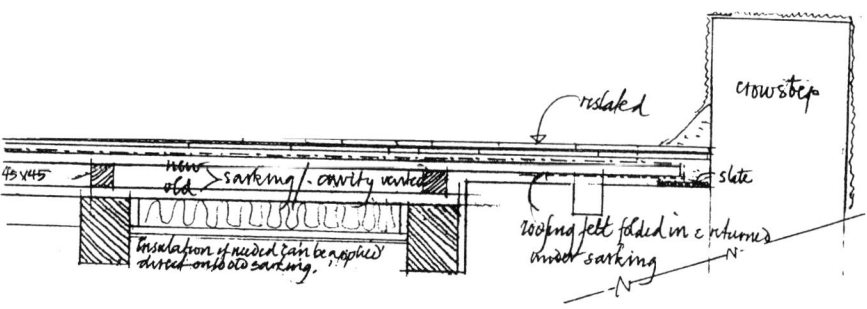

sarking also meant that the new roof was raised by approximately two inches. This is just the amount of sagging that the roof had suffered during its history, except of course at the gables. Here, double sarking with ventilation in between was essential, otherwise, as can be seen in almost every repair job, the sarking rots quickly, trapped between the wet wallhead and the slating and coping. (Fig. 5).

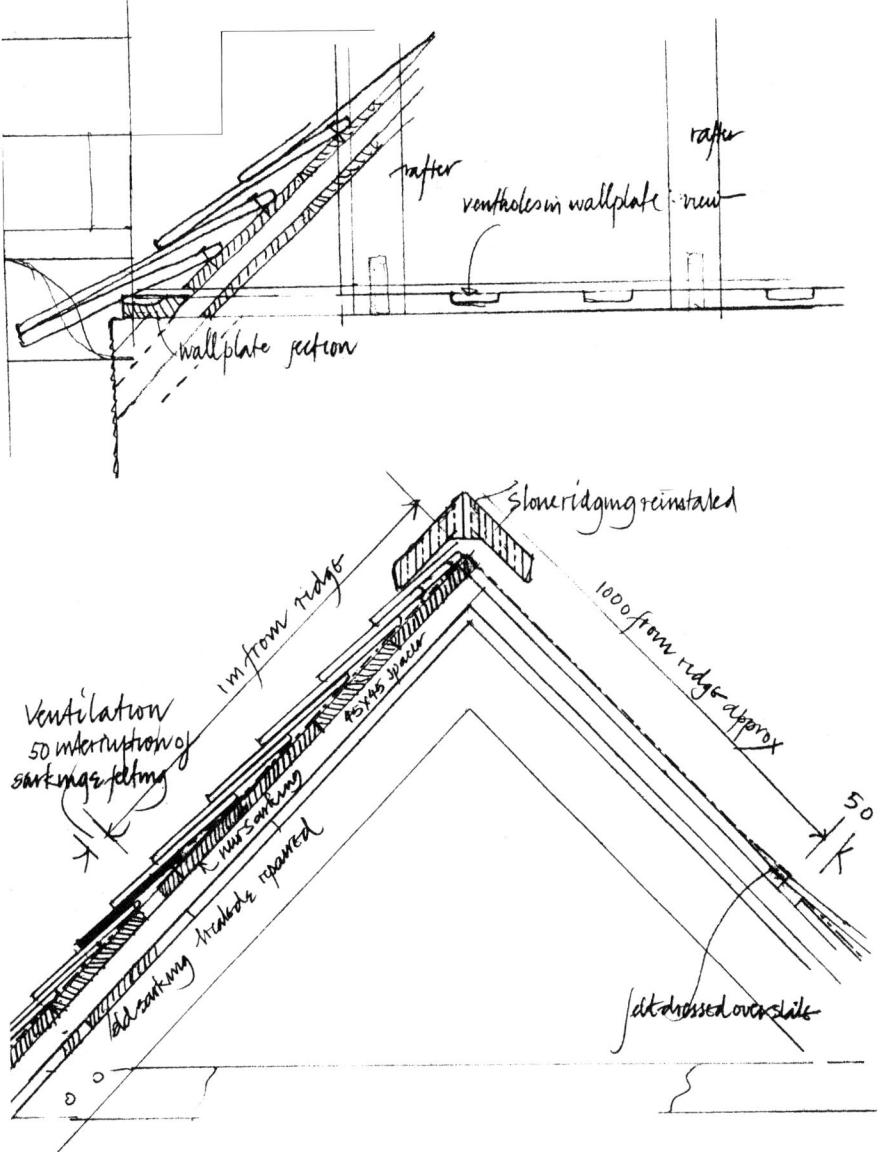

Fig. 5
Section through roof ridge and wallhead, showing roof ventilation.

The new slating, using second hand slates was laid on top of roofing felt. This requirement did more harm than good as it blocks ventilation whenever lofts are made draught proof, as was here the case. I applied a very simple solution, telling the slater not to nail the felt strips together at their overlap so that as the laying of slates progressed, a row could be inserted between the overlapping sheets of felt, so creating vent gaps over the entire roof.

Tilquhillie Castle – France Smoor

Doors

Only two of the original doors were left in the building, both hung and hinged on crooks and bands. Their construction was simply horizontal and vertical lining, nailed together. One door led into the provisions cellar. Its vertical outside lining consisted of three oak boards, tongued and grooved in a shiplap fashion; the inside horizontal lining was in pine, consisting of five boards, butt-jointed together. The oak on the outside may well have been used to try to keep out rats. There was a similarly constructed door on the second floor of the main tower but it was made only of pine and used twice as many boards for both the horizontal and vertical lining, also butt-jointed both ways, with the boards all tapering in width, as if it had been constructed at the end of the job, from left-over pieces of timber.

The later doors were braced, lined and framed and were left as they were. Those missing were constructed to match the others.

Harling

Generally speaking, the harling was in good condition but required a certain amount of patching. We decided against removing all of it in order to reharl so that the building would have a uniform appearance, as this was against the principle of removing something, for purely cosmetic reasons, that was still functioning well. The result was, of course, not to everybody's perception of a highland castle. It is strange that some individuals will accept a patchwork repair for stone walls but not for harling. In practical terms it was very difficult to find a matching colour for the harl, since old and new harling differ in texture and the colour varies considerably from wall to wall, according to the aspect of sun, weathering and wind exposure. I was against mixing pigments, so patience is required until weathering eventually blends all together through the passage of time.

Project Management

The project was executed by the owners, as main contractors or clerks of works. Dr Coyne and his wife were meticulous in their efforts to return to the original, especially over certain joinery details. Unfortunately, in establishing the grant eligible cost at the time, no allowance was made for this considerable imput. I believe that this is a method of carrying our a restoration project far more economically than by the full procedure of tender and main contractor, which public bodies are usually obliged to use.

Notwithstanding the differences of approach, however, we were very grateful to Historic Scotland for its grant aid.

France Smoor – **Tilquhillie Castle**

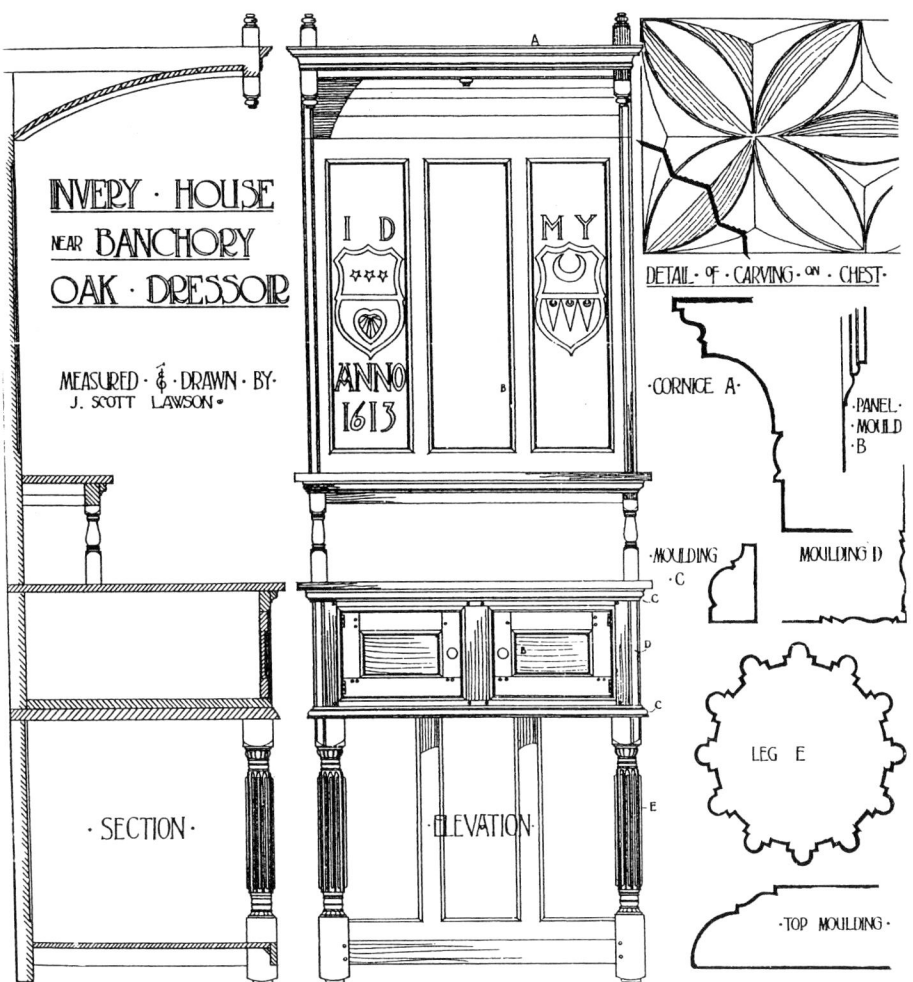

Footnote; Mention should be made of the only known, original piece of furniture belonging to Tilquhillie. (Fig. 6). It is the dresser bearing the initials of John Douglas and his wife, Mary Young, dated 1613. After three and a half centuries' connection with Tilquhillie, it was believed to be still there shortly before the castle was purchased in 1985 from the last Douglas. It now appears to be in safe-keeping at Towie Barclay Castle.

Fig. 1
SE elevation. MacGibbon & Ross suggest that the rounded angles of the building are brought to the square with corbels, near the eves, in such a manner as to preserve the idea (in the Scottish mind) of a projection where the turrets used to be.

The Restoration of Tilquhillie Castle

BY JOHN COYNE, BSCE, MA, PhD (Cantab), THE OWNER.

Introduction

Castle restoration is a highly idiosyncratic endeavour, requiring extreme levels of optimism, patience and, above all, tenacity. The obstacles facing the prospective restorer are of heroic proportions. Most of the castle restorers I have met have one thing in common, a near messianic dedication to the saving of Scotland's architectural heritage. It is a passion which controls their lives. For some it begins as a general love of castles, for others it is a particular building they come across, just by chance. A person may be smitten at any age. Many were trapped by the romance of castles as children. They went on foot or on bicycle, exploring all the castles and ruins near them. The childhood enthusiasm was carried into adulthood. Others discovered castles at a time in life when most of their contemporaries were looking forward to a lengthy period of tranquil retirement.

In my own case, I fell in love with Scotland's fortified architecture twenty-five years ago. What appealed to me the most was its austere functionalism, tempered with a rustic elegance. I am, by nature, a restorer of things. I had the good fortune or good sense to marry a person of a compatible disposition. Our first restoration was a rambling 18th century Colonial country house, which had seen better days. The woman estate agent hesitated to show a dilapidated structure like that to "such a nice young couple". She looked at it and saw what it had become. We looked at it and saw what it had been and could be again. It was the first of six restorations my wife, Kay, and I have undertaken.

I spent much of my professional life in Europe, but every holiday was spent in Scotland, exploring with our 'friends' Messrs MacGibbon, Ross and Tranter. We were depressed by much that we saw. It was difficult to understand how so many unique structures were allowed to fall into a state of decay. We began to photograph and catalogue them. We contacted people who had restored, or were in the process of restoring, castles. What impressed us was their dedication and willingness to provide us with information and further contacts. We started corresponding with the owners of ruins which we considered to be in urgent need of restoration. Our pile of correspondence is now two feet thick. Almost to a person, the owners were well-intentioned people, willing to discuss the buildings. Most agreed that the buildings should be saved, but they viewed the problems as insurmountable and were unable to undertake the task themselves. For various reasons, they were also unwilling to let anyone else do it. Over the years, many of these same people have relented and sold their buildings to restoring purchasers.

Tilquhillie Castle – John Coyne

Acquisition

The owner of Tilquhillie, a Z-plan tower house completed in 1576 (Fig 1), and I had been in correspondence for a number of years regarding the future of the building. He was genuinely concerned about the castle but, understandably, reluctant to sell this part of his family heritage. We discussed a rental agreement, but the financial commitment that was required made this impractical.

We continued to watch over Tilquhillie, keeping windows boarded up and the door secured with a padlock. Eventually, the owner contacted me and said that he had come to accept what I had said about the need to ensure the castle's continued existence. He had decided to sell it and flattered me greatly by saying that he could think of no one better to undertake the restoration than me. It is a pity that there are still some owners who lack the courage and responsibility he displayed in making such a difficult decision.

Just prior to our buying the building, the surrounding farm was sold and split into three separate parcels. We were effectively surrounded by three different parties, with their own intentions for the area. The first and most immediate threat to the castle's site was presented by the purchasers of the farmhouse and steadings. They planned to start a commercial kennel in the steadings, just fifty feet from the castle. We were reminded of so many other castle restorers who found themselves in similar situations, in conflict with unsympathetic neighbours. We adopted a direct approach. I met with the people and explained our intentions and determination to fight any developments which would have a negative impact on the castle's setting. It was apparent that there was no possibility of compromise. One of us would have to go.

After protracted discussions, they finally decided to sell the house and steadings to us. Unfortunately, they did not own the large modern byre which had been built, without planning consent, at the entrance to the castle. This was sold with the adjacent farm. Through further negotiations, we managed to buy from the farmer the 40 x 60 ft. plot of land on which the byre stood, for the princely sum of £50. Of course we had to rebuild the byre at another location on the farm. The byre eventually became ours when we were given the opportunity, at a later stage, of buying the farm. A final purchase gave us sole ownership of the access to the castle. All of this expanded our project enormously. We started out to restore a castle, but we ended up with the task of restoring part of the original estate. The advantage was that we were able to ensure the amenity of the castle.

From the earliest days, we were conscious of the need to plant trees and shrubs; nearly 10,000 have been planted to date. Each year, as we worked on the castle, we had the pleasure of watching the trees grow. Some are now thirty feet tall. It has given a sense of maturity to the grounds, as opposed to the usual barren construction sites which have surrounded many restorations. We are now actually in the position of having to consider thinning the trees.

John Coyne – **Tilquhillie Castle**

The Work

The castle was an ancient monument, thus necessitating scheduled monument consent before restoration could begin. Minded of many of the problems other restorers had encountered in meeting the conditions for grant aid, we were reluctant to apply for the relatively small amount of assistance which was available at the time. In the end, we realised that the conditions that would have to be met for scheduled monument consent were much the same as those for grant aid. As satisfying the conditions would entail substantial additional expense, we applied for the grant as a welcome means of helping to offset the increased cost. I drew up a schedule of works for the restoration, which I revised slightly after the inspector's visit. I was very much reassured after my meeting with him, as he was knowledgeable and helpful, and I found that we were in very close agreement as to what needed to be done.

At the outset, it is essential that a clear plan is formulated for the restoration. Although the advice of experts is invaluable, one should never give up direct control. The restoration of a castle is much too important to leave to the professionals, no matter how well-intentioned. This is not a viewpoint guaranteed of a welcome reception by such august bodies as Historic Buildings and Monuments, as it was then known. After much discussion and correspondence, it was decided that I would handle the actual restoration, as long as an independent architect verified that the works had been completed, as detailed in the final schedule of works. I hired a friend, a highly creative and talented architect, France Smoor, to fill this role. I am certain that I owe him a debt of gratitude for keeping me from developing an ulcer by assuming that risk himself. During a protracted period of time, volumes of correspondence were exchanged, a quantity survey was conducted by an independent firm, and all supporting drawings and documentation were submitted. Approval was granted, and the actual restoration work began.

In fact, we had not been inactive during the period. A previous owner of the farm once told me that, in his opinion, the castle should be pulled down, as it was dangerous and nothing but a nuisance, in that it attracted people up his road. He had given physical evidence of his disdain for the castle. He had access to heavy earth moving equipment. In addition to removing dykes and the remains of a stone circle, he had also cleared the fields of large boulders. Most of this material ended up piled against the back wall of the castle. We set about clearing the site, rebuilding the drystone dykes, and began our planting programme. We also converted the farmhouse for our use. Although the enforced delays were difficult to accept, they did have the benefit of providing time to acquire the materials we would need; stone slabs from Caithness, granite from demolished Aberdeenshire steadings and churches, reclaimed pavement stones from Aberdeen, timber from Speyside distilleries, Glasgow churches and the forests of France. I bought three different eight foot lintels to replace the one missing from the Great Hall's fireplace, trying to get just the right colour and surface. We were determined that everything we put into the building had to match what was

Tilquhillie Castle – John Coyne

still there. Even when work was to be plastered over, we used stone instead of block.

The first task in the restoration was to clean out the building. Tilquhillie was fortunate in that the family's increased wealth in the 18th century was not used to remodel the castle extensively, or to add a Georgian addition. Instead, they decided to build a new house on the banks of the Feugh and relegate Tilquhillie to the status of farmhouse, to be used by the farm tenant. As such, it did not escape change completely. Some alterations were made. Two vaults were converted to house cattle. A rough opening was made into the building by enlarging an arrowslit in one of the vaults under the Great Hall. The connecting passage between the vault and the rest of the castle was walled up and the area was cobbled. In later years, and over some time, the vaults became filled with debris, to a depth of almost two feet. It took days to clear them out. Another crude opening was made from the second floor of the main tower into the stair, which rose from the Great Hall to the north-east tower. To achieve this, it was necessary to remove one tread and a section of another, making it extremely difficult to use the turnpike stair from the floor below. The kitchen was moved from the south-west tower vault to the floor above, and the fireplace was enlarged to meet the increased demands of cooking. This required the original kitchen fireplace to be closed. A rough system of corbelling with bricks was used to accomplish this, creating an enlarged hearth. At some later date, piped water was brought into the kitchen, via a hole under a window.

The Great Hall suffered the most alteration (Fig. 2 & 3). The fireplace lintel was removed, the opening was restricted in size, and a cast iron insert was installed. The Great Hall was squared off by the removal of the wine cellar stair projection and the squinches at opposite ends of the room. The door into it and the door from the hall to the laird's room, at the opposite end, were both enlarged, the original stone being replaced by timber framing. The turnpike stair to the north-east tower was blocked up, eliminating any direct access to the floors above. They could then be entered only by the new door in the room above.

The corbels which originally supported the beams were removed. The room was then strapped and plastered. An historically minded plasterer left his name and the date of the work, 1906, on the ceiling. A similar treatment was given to

Fig. 2
Commencing the downtakings of the squared-off Great Hall. Turkey cages still in evidence.

Fig. 3
The Great Hall; windows, doors, squinch and fireplace restored.

the room above the Great Hall, but one of the corbels was left in place because it did not protrude far enough into the room to present a problem. The two bedrooms in the southwest tower were also strapped and plastered.

The windows in the mural chambers were both filled in with stone, creating space for closets. The laird's room had the only fine piece of stonework in the castle. The fireplace had a bolection style mantel in granite (Fig. 4). It had been painted several times, on the last occasion with a wood effect to match the woodwork in the room. An arrowslit and a small window had been blocked up, the latter to provide space for a cupboard. It appeared from the fireplace that the room had been panelled at some point in time. In fact, in MacGibbon & Ross, Volume II, 1887, it states that "some fragments of good old wood-work lying in one of the upper rooms are well worthy of being preserved". Unfortunately, their advice was not heeded.

Stone was removed from the wall heads in both the main and the north-east tower. It appeared that it had been used to block up the windows in the two flanking towers. Evidently, someone realised that it would be easier to carry stone down, rather than upstairs.

The next transformation took place in the 1940's. A tenant farmer "modernised" the new kitchen by lining it with tongue and groove boarding, installing a new cast iron stove and a Belfast sink. The building was abandoned as a habitation only a few years after this work was carried out, as it was simply too unpleasant a place in which to live. The last denizens were turkeys, participants in an unsuccessful estate enterprise. Several of the cages remained when we arrived on the scene, as did a flue which was run from the Great Hall, through the floor and into the chimney in the room above. After this, the castle remained unused for about twenty years. It was fortunate that slates were replaced from time to time. Almost all of the structural timbers, which are of oak, were in excellent condition. Woodworm had all but destroyed most of the sarking, in addition to most of the flooring in all the rooms, except that above the Great Hall. In fact, standing on the first floor of the north-east tower, one had a virtually uninterrupted view of the roof overhead.

Nature, with a little help from man, had also taken its toll on the outside of the building. The chimneys were in need of rebuilding. A large crack in the chimney wall of the main tower was the most spectacular structural fault. This extended from the chimney head almost to the ground and had been caused by rain washing the mortar from the joints, once the harl had been lost. From

Fig. 4
Fireplace in the laird's room, with carved rolled moulding.

Tilquhillie Castle – John Coyne

photographs of the castle taken in the 1880's we could see the reason for much of the damage to the harl. The front elevation of the building was virtually covered in some form of climbing vine, and the metal eyes used to support the plant were still in place. It is likely that water penetration behind the harl, and the subsequent frost, eventually broke away patches. Similar action took place behind a faulty downpipe at the re-entrant. Although there were other areas on the building where the harl had suffered localised damage, it was nevertheless still in an impressive state of repair, forming a thin protective surface over the random rubble of the structure.

Most of the windows were gone. Of those which remained we were able to save three early ones. In an upstairs room in the south-west tower there was a window that had four panes, with the upper right one hinged, providing the only means of opening the window. Sadly, there was only one of the castle's original doors remaining. It was constructed of vertical and horizontal oak boards, fitted together on the front, using a joining method frequently seen in early American Colonial Clapboard houses, called shiplap, after the resemblance to planking on the hulls of wooden boats. Although it only led to the wine cellar, the door had been eaten at the bottom by rodents, and several of the horizontal boards had been removed, making the door rather flimsy. Fortunately it had retained an early handle and Suffolk style latch, minus the thumb lever. The handle was surprising, in that it was relatively ornate (Fig. 5), considering the simplicity of the building.

Fig. 5
Handle on the only remaining original internal door.

Once the final approvals had been granted, work started on the exterior of the building. We stripped all of the slates from the roofs and set them aside for re-slating in the same locations. Broken slates were replaced with matching reclaimed ones. Lichen was not removed from the slates as I was determined to avoid the possibility of having the replaced roof looking somewhat new. The sarking on the main tower roof was the worst affected by woodworm. It crumbled to the touch. After much searching, I found a sawmill which agreed to cut boards to the non-standard dimensions needed to match the sarking which had been removed. I might have also removed the old sarking on the other two towers, if it had not been for the convincing argument of France Smoor, who had the ingenious idea of double roofing the towers. Battens were nailed up the roof, and the new sarking was nailed to them, leaving approximately two inches of air space between the new and the old sarking. Ventilation spaces were left between several boards at the top. At these locations, the felt was overlapped but not nailed at the bottom, thus allowing air to pass through. In effect there was a good circulation of air from the eaves, where I placed short sections of one inch polythene water pipe through the void and out through the stone ridge gaps. This system has had the added advantage of allowing alternative living quarters for the bat colony, which was well established in the roof space.

Re-slating had always been one of my major concerns about the building. I photographed the entire roof before we began, paying special attention to the slated valley joining the main block and the south-west tower roofs. I kept a

Fig. 6
An early slated valley, providing an effective and aesthetic joining of the main and SW tower roofs.

constant check on the slaters and their work. I went over the slates on the ground and on the roof after they were put in place. Any slate that did not look right was pulled out and replaced. The end result was a roof that did not look as if it had just been reslated, but it was still not as appealing as the original. As I expected, the valley was a real problem. I had it lined with lead, but was determined to reinstate the slate valley as it was originally. At this point the photographs came in very handy (Fig. 6). In the end the valley had to be re-slated three times. I must admit that I am still not pleased with it, as the slaters were never able to replicate the excellent work of the original slater.

The other major job to be undertaken was the repair of the large cracks in the walls. These were stitched with large granite blocks instead of concrete. The joints were raked out and slots were made for the granite bonders. Once these were in place, we refilled the remainder of the rents with stone and mortar. When finished, only the long narrow blocks gave evidence of our work, but this was soon to be harled over. We went over the building from top to bottom, looking for boss bits of harl. I took samples of the harl and analysed them. I went to every sand quarry in the area and took samples, looking for a sand which would most closely match the gradations of the aggregate in the existing harl. For lime I chose Hargreaves. It was not available in the area, so I contacted Mr Hargreaves, directly, and arranged to have a shipment sent to us via one of his customers in Montrose. I chose Hargreaves lime because of its dirty-white-to-

Tilquhillie Castle – John Coyne

beige colour. We harled all the patches. The end result was a near perfect match, as far as texture was concerned, but we could not hope to match exactly the colour of the old, weathered, existing harl. When finished the building had a rather piebald appearance, but every year the old and new harl blends in more satisfactorily. (Fig. 7). Kay and I resisted the temptation to lime wash the building, preferring to let nature take its course. In fact, in wet weather the patches are hardly noticeable. It is interesting how the colour of the building changes with the weather, from a deep rich tan when it is raining, to almost white in bright sunshine.

The windows presented us with one of our major problems. Initially, we wanted to use a leaded glass and shutter configuration. This was because the glazing grooves were clearly in evidence. The Historic Buildings architect, who did the original inspection, agreed with this choice for the same reasons. At some point there was an administrative volte-face and Historic Buildings came out strongly in favour of fenestration based on the existing early 19th century windows. We argued our case most strongly and won. The delay in winning approval gave me time to think about the windows in more detail. What continued to plague me about the shutter-board windows, was the shutter itself. We had no model for it. It is unfortunate that so few shutters have survived. All the examples we had seen or read about were much too ornate for a building as plain as Tilquhillie. In the end I opted to go for what we knew. We used the earliest remaining windows as our models and hired a local joinery firm to make them for us, as I had seen previous work undertaken by them which was of a very good quality. I made regular visits to the workshop to monitor the progress.

Fig. 7
The finished harling on the SW elevation, showing the old and new harl. The kitchen block and large chimney is on the right; central tower, left. Photo: Claire Smoor.

John Coyne – Tilquhillie Castle

We worked out the placement of astrigals and other details on the spot. I had the joiner re-do any work that was not of an acceptable standard. I have to credit him with his control, as he kept smiling all the time, but the owner of the firm did tell me that I had almost cost him the services of his master joiner. It was worth the trials and tribulations, as every window now fits perfectly. We then had to decide how to finish them. The thought of painting them white did not fill us with excitement. Fortunately, Kay has an artist's eye for colour. She chose a grey Butinox stain, which had the effect of drawing one's attention away from the windows. In the end we were quite happy with them, but if we ever come across a sketch, painting or description of the original windows, the probable result is not difficult to imagine.

Many of the window openings and most of the gunloops had been blocked up with stone. There were some interesting discoveries. One was an obvious window, high up on the main tower's east elevation. What made it rather unique was that there was no opening on the inside and the stonework gave no evidence of a window having been there. I spent many hours staring at the wall, trying to puzzle out what had happened. I thought that the answer would be found when we erected the scaffolding and could take a closer look. As soon as it was in place, I scrambled to the top and peered in through the opening, only to be confronted by several hundred years of birds' nests. I spent hours with a small hoe, pulling out the twigs and bits of dried plant matter. There was no immediate answer. The window opened into a small cavity in the wall. I resumed my frequent vigils in front of the interior wall. The room below had two fireplaces. In fact, there was evidence on the walls and floor of a previous partition. The fireplaces were of exactly the same construction. The assumption had always been that they were both contemporary. We tend to forget how frequently changes are made in houses today, during a ten year period. When we are looking at buildings which are hundreds of years old, we somehow do not expect that changes were made within a similar time span. It eventually dawned on me that it was most probable that the fireplace on the east wall was added very early in the castle's history. They took out a fairly large portion of the wall, but in the room above, they made use of a garderobe. The flue was built inside and run into the main chimney which formed the inside wall of the chamber. Afterwards they walled up the opening to the garderobe, but left the window on the outside.

Kay and I discovered additional windows, mainly by examining the interior stonework. For the most part, they were crudely filled and had not been harled over. There were, however, other window outlines that could be clearly seen under the harl in wet weather. One small window in a vault was completely unexpected. Kay found it when she removed some loose stones in the vault wall. She pulled them out only to find that there was more loose stone behind. Then part of a metal bar appeared. We photographed what she had found and continued to remove stone. She also came across part of an old cauldron and broken bits of glass. It seems that anything that was to hand was thrown into

Tilquhillie Castle – John Coyne

the void to fill it. A little more effort was rewarded by the sight of a perfect small window opening, with an iron bar fixed horizontally across it. Too small for anyone to crawl through, it appeared that it was intended to keep anyone inside from passing things to someone outside.

One window remained unopened. The stonework used in filling it was of such a high quality that I hesitated to open it. I thought that there must have been a good reason for closing it up but now we regret that decision, particularly, as even the Historic Scotland inspector who last visited the castle advised that we go ahead and open it.

The glazing of the gunloops was one of the worst jobs in the castle, therefore it fell to me. I cut a cardboard template for each one. It sounds much more simple than it really was. Many times I had to wedge myself into the opening, arms outstretched - not a job for anyone who is claustrophobic. I then cut a piece of glass and crawled back in to fix it in place, using a weak lime and sand mix. I had learned from past experience that anything stronger would eventually crack the glass.

Most of the windows originally had iron bars or grilles, but the demands of modern living had resulted in most of them being removed at some point in the castle's history. Fortunately, this was not the case with the yett. (Fig. 8). They had cut the top off to allow it to be removed, but it was still there and in remarkably good condition, complete with a sliding draw bolt, which had a huge hasp for a padlock. There was also a draw bar, still in position, in a recess in the wall. The bar was two inches square, but to keep the weight down, the ends were solid, while the interior was drawn out thinner. To keep it the same dimension along its length, the bar had been quartered, and the four sections were spread apart, leaving voids between them. We resisted the pressure to paint the yett and bar. Instead we cleaned them with fine steel wool and oiled them. This produced a much more natural look.

Fig. 8
Yett with draw bar and draw bolt.

One last exterior item had to be taken care of. I have already mentioned the slated valley. It channelled rainwater onto the roof of the re-entrant and across the main entrance. We had a lead gargoyle and rhone made to take care of the rainwater. It took a year to complete and weighed about an hundredweight, but it still had to be put in place. Our local blacksmith gave me the loan of his pneumatic drill to use in mounting the brackets, and I hired a hydraulic platform for the day. The blacksmith arrived with the drill - it was then that I noticed the bees. When we first saw Tilquhillie, a room in the south-west tower had one of its walls and part of the floor coated in wax. During the first summer I realised where the wax came from. The tower roof was home to most of Deeside's bee population. Despite all the disruptions during the restoration, the bees never left. The main hive area was, and still is, under the slates of the re-entrant roof. The morning I picked to install the rhone the bees had decided to swarm. It was obvious that it would be a two man job. The blacksmith informed me that he was afraid of only two things in life, heights and bees. Nevertheless, he volunteered. I managed to borrow a beekeeper's smoker to calm the bees. Up we went. For two hours we swayed back and forth in the little bucket of the lift, in a cloud of bees and smoke. Finally, it was done. We leaned back to admire our work. The blacksmith asked if the gargoyle had a name. I wonder how many blacksmiths have gargoyle namesakes.

Our first task in the interior was to clean out the building. Worm infestation was so great that just about everything we had hoped to save had to be removed. We are still using parts of the interior for kindling. In the Great Hall we found that the strapping had been used as structural timbers, providing support for the beams overhead. Woodworm had reduced these timbers to powder, necessitating immediate remedial work. I decided that the only course of action was to replace the corbels and the supporting timber that once rested upon them. It was easy to locate the positions where the corbels had been removed, as the plaster was gone and patching was obvious. We used the remaining corbel in the upstairs room as the model for the replacements. It is possible that the original Great Hall corbels were ornate, but the replacements were purely functional in nature. It was interesting that there were corbels only on the south wall. The beams ran from the south to the north wall so we used the corbels to support a trimmer beam, upon which the floor beams rested.

Upon examining the beam-ends, I discovered that the north ends were all in very good condition. By contrast, many of the opposite ends had suffered from damp. This actually corresponds to the prevailing weather pattern as wet weather mainly comes across the Grampians, from the south-west. Corbels had therefore been used on the south walls only. There were slots for the floor beams which gave an indication of the original beams' lengths and the size of the trimmer beam. We didn't have to replace any beams, only the trimmer. I found suitable old timber balks at the Aberdeen docks. I talked the director of the company which owned them into selling me two. The next problem was to cut them, so I persuaded an Aberdeen timber merchant to quarter them, with the

Tilquhillie Castle – John Coyne

understanding that if they hit any metal I would be charged £500 for a new saw blade. I spent quite a bit of time going over the balks with a metal detector and removing every nail. It was amazing how much metal there was. I nevertheless still kept my fingers crossed as they headed for the saw. The quartered timber resulted in two freshly sawn surfaces and two which retained their patina. This was ideal, as only two sides would show when they were in their final position.

Each beam was about fourteen feet long and weighed about three hundred weight. It was obvious that they had to be brought into the building through a window in the Great Hall. I erected staging outside the window and created a ramp. With two men on the ground, one on the staging and one inside the Hall, we managed to pull each beam up and through the window. To be sure that the trimmer beams had a bearing contact with both the floor beams above and the corbels below, we used a rather backward procedure for securing them in position. We shored up the trimmer beams, tight against the floor beams, then jacked the corbels into position, underneath them, and mortared in the corbels. The beams and corbels were left supported for several days, in order to let the mortar set.

The missing Great Hall fireplace lintel had to be replaced. The alternative to a new piece of granite was a reclaimed lintel from one of the many steadings which have been demolished in our area to make way for modern farm buildings. One had been spotted by a friend while walking in a forest near the castle. I spent hours locating it, but even longer loading it into a trailer, single handed. I had acquired three other lintels but this one had the best colour match. It took less time to install than to find and recover it; the installation was one of the few things that went smoothly and according to plan. We put two supports through the front of the fireplace and removed the stone where the missing lintel had been. I erected a short scaffold at the exact height of the opening and extended it to the window adjacent to the fireplace. A hired rough terrain forklift was used to raise the lintel up to the level of the window. We then slid it onto rollers, through the window along the scaffold, and into position in front of the fireplace. Levering it into position and mortaring it in place was the easiest part of the job. It took days to rebuild the inside of the fireplace and to repoint it. I felt like one of Dickens' chimney sweeps, wedged up the lum, working in soot and darkness.

Mention has already been made of the projecting stair from the Great Hall to the wine cellar. To avoid thinning the outside wall excessively by constructing a stair within it, the stair was erected along the inside of the wall. The inner wall of the passage projected into the room about three feet. Once the wooden floor was lifted and the stone infill removed from the stair, a clearer picture emerged of the original stair. The left side of the door jamb was found hidden under the plaster. From the jamb, I was able to determine the height of the original door and its angle of projection into the room. The sill had been removed, but a close examination of the floor showed distinct indications of where it had been located and where the other jamb joined it. One question remained unanswered. "Was the roof of the projection horizontal, or sloped?" The wall had been patched to such a degree that it seemed impossible to see what had been done. Days were spent staring at the opening, trying to determine what the original builders would have done. One day, I found the answer. A bit of original plaster was still there, running in a horizontal line. It even projected slightly outward into the room, showing that it had continued, at least for a distance, over the roof. The roof of the stair projection had, indeed, been level, rather than sloped. The finished product may not be exact, but it is very close.

As previously indicated, the door from the Great Hall to the Laird's room and the main door into the Hall had been enlarged and the original stone lintels replaced by wooden ones. In the case of the former, the door was also shifted to the right, so that the room could be squared. The window ingo was made symmetrical with the opposite side by being built up with stone, probably the stone from the projecting stair enclosure. One set of jambs for the main door remained, indicating its original height. As with the wine cellar door, it was possible to determine the width of the door from the floor markings. The case was not so plain for the door to the Laird's room. The width was no problem, but the height was another question. In the end I decided to make the door just high enough for me to walk through, without ducking, to ensure that the door would not make my head a phrenologist's playground. Unfortunately, when the time came to lay the Caithness slabs on the underfloor heating system, I found that there was not quite enough space. The door ended up being one of the most lethal in the castle - one which is just high enough to deceive the unwary. It looks fine. A slight tilt of the head, and one passes through without incident. A moment's inattention and the top of the head is concussed. I have thought of inventing a hat with a built-in air bag, but the market would obviously be limited.

We were able to save seven early doors. The original door to the wine cellar was minimally repaired with pieces of contemporary wood, reclaimed from the castle. The others were more recent, but not being of oak they had suffered severe worm infestation. They should probably have been replaced, but we were determined to retain anything we possibly could. One door we kept had late 19th century graffiti on it. Farm workers and maids left notes about their loves. We could not keep the door where it was, so we used it to replace one in a mural chamber. The replacement doors were made to the same design as the remaining original door. I used kiln dried oak, which we allowed to air dry further for several months. Hand-made iron studs were ordered and a local blacksmith made copies of the original handle.

The finished doors were excellent, but as the months wore on, we watched them warp, much the same as the original ones must have done. The problem was that the vertical boards shrank more, along their lengths, than the horizontal ones along their widths. At first, they only compressed the horizontal boards. When this was no longer possible, the vertical boards continued to shrink, pulling the horizontal boards over them. The result was the formation of a warp. This is very much the same way a thermocouple works in a thermostat, where two different metals are joined, back to back. As the temperature drops, one shrinks more than the other, bending the metal strip over to a point where it makes an electrical contact. From the very start I knew that warping was possible, but wrongly assumed that the kiln dried boards would not suffer this extent of shrinkage. I did not repeat the mistake on the main door. Several of the horizontal boards were removed and a sufficient amount of wood was planed off to allow them to fit back in place, with ease. After a few weeks the door straightened. On the positive side, gaps in the doors did help to keep the building ventilated. In winter they are not quite so welcome.

Not all of the surprises were unpleasant like the warping of the doors. Several interesting discoveries were made in the first floor room of the south-west tower. This had become the kitchen some time in the 19th century. In 1947 it was 'modernised' for the new tenant farmer. We knew the year because the son of the farmer paid us a visit. His memory of the date was confirmed by newspapers we found behind the tongue and groove boarding which was used to line the room. When we removed the panelling, we found that it hid several important features. To the left of the fireplace we found an old salt box built into the wall (Fig. 9). It was unusual, in that it looked like a large bird box, with pitched roof and circular opening. The wood was well worn, giving evidence of the number of hands which had reached into the hole to take out salt. An even greater discovery awaited us on the other side of the room. Here we found that the cladding covered a mural chamber. We eagerly sifted through the dirt on the floor of the chamber and found one of the few artefacts to come out of the building. It was the remains of an early percussion pistol, so small that it almost seemed to be a child's toy. We also found bits and pieces of early wallpaper throughout the kitchen, suggesting that the room had once been put to more genteel use.

Fig. 9
The salt box.

The heating system presented one of the major challenges of the restoration; how to provide a comfortable temperature for modern living standards, without detracting from the building's early character. I had seen underfloor hot water systems in a number of European countries, but they had not been widely used in Britain. Here, due in part to a good bit of salesmanship on the part of the electricity boards, most of the underfloor systems in use are electric and costly to run. I decided that a hot water underfloor system was the only answer. It has the long term benefit of not being tied directly to any one energy source. I hope, eventually, to be able to heat the building from material grown on the farm. At the present time, oilseed rape is the most promising, providing the government creates the right fiscal climate for its development as an alternative fuel source.

I contacted all the major manufacturers of underfloor systems and talked to a few people who had installed them. Months were spent going over charts and diagrams. Finally I opted for a Swedish manufacturer, with good representation in the U.K. Once this decision had been made, the real work began. On a floor plan it was relatively easy to draw the runs for the plastic pipe. It was another matter determining how to get to them and to know if there was sufficient depth

John Coyne – **Tilquhillie Castle**

to install the system. We needed a minimum of five inches to accommodate the insulation, the screed and the pipe work. Almost as much again was required for the stone slabs and bedding. This was no problem in the vaults. It simply meant digging almost a foot through the hardest hard pan imaginable.

On the first floor it was much more complicated. Whatever the original floors had been, they were removed and replaced by wood, now badly worm-eaten, nailed on roughly sawn timber sections. As the whole of the ground floor is vaulted, the voids at the sides of the vaults had originally been filled with dirt and loose rubble, to create a level surface. Much of this had been removed to accommodate the floor joists. It was obvious that I would not be able to put heating coils under every part of the floor. It was even difficult to get them to cross the tops of the vaults. In the end we managed to get all the floor levels the same as the original ones, but there was no room to spare.

The effect of the underfloor heating was quite pleasant. Because the heat was so evenly distributed, there was no sensation of heat at the surface. Instead, the stone floors simply lost their characteristic cool feel and became more like a wooden floor to touch. It took, and does take, a while to bring the building up to temperature - from 36 to 48 hours, but once heated the building acts as a giant night storage heater, keeping warm for approximately the same amount of time.

My determination to get the floor levels correct led to an interesting discovery in the wine cellar. The night before we were to pour the foundation screed, I went into the cellar for a final check. Deciding that the underfloor electrical conduit might be just a little high at one point, I got a spade and started digging. As usual, it was difficult cutting through the hard pan. Suddenly I hit some loose soil, just to the side of the conduit. I continued digging with renewed enthusiasm and found a ring of stone. It was the top of a well. Long past midnight, I stood back and looked at the three foot hole I had dug. The well was in excellent condition. Over the following days I continued the excavation, taking photos and recording what was found. No treasure, just broken wine bottles and bits of broken crockery. It was obvious that when the well was no longer needed, it became a glorified waste basket. The well tapered as it went down. To dig, I was forced to sit back on my heels, using a garden trowel. I could just squeeze my hand and the towel past my legs, take up a bit of soil and put it into a pail on my lap. The work was agonisingly slow. I managed to excavate ten feet in this manner; however, at that point I could no longer fit in the well. The water table had obviously lowered over the centuries, as there is still no water in the well, but as there are two other wells outside the castle, we will get a better idea of the original water table when they are eventually excavated.

While problems were encountered in laying the heating coils, it was even more difficult locating the main runs for the services. This is not a problem if reconstructing a building. One simply builds service shafts. I ended up by bringing the water feed, waste pipe, telephone and electricity cables through the same channel, under the stone threshold of the exterior door and under the floor

Tilquhillie Castle – John Coyne

of the main vault. From there, I was able to run under the vault wall into the adjacent vault. As the end wall in this vault was slightly skewed, it was possible to hide the vertical pipe run with a wall cupboard fitted straight across the wall. The pipes came out under the threshold of a small mural chamber off the Great Hall. From there, I was able to direct one set under the floor of the chamber and through a relatively thin wall into another chamber off the kitchen. This took care of water, waste and electricity to that room. The other set crossed the Great Hall at the wall, but there was still the problem of how to reach the upper floors. The main door into the Great Hall had been enlarged. Since I had decided to reduce the opening to its original size, the solution to the pipe problem was solved by building a channel into the reconstructed section of wall. Fortunately, the opening emerged tight in the corner of an upstairs chamber, destined to become a bathroom. We ran the pipes up tight against the corner in this room and brought the wall forward, slightly further into the room, in order to conceal them. By careful framing and the use of metal lath, it was possible to make the wall look as solid as the rest of the bathroom walls. I padded all the waste pipes with heavy rockwool insulation to deaden any sound.

The situation was not so easily dealt with in the upper bathroom. Since we had opened all the upper floors to the roof, there was no loft space for the hot water cylinder or the concealed cisterns for the boxed toilets. As a less than satisfactory solution, I framed the cylinder in a very irregular manner to imitate the look of a chimney rising through the room and out the roof. This will remain until the day we become clever enough to devise another method of dealing with this modern 'inconvenience'.

Some of the original wooden flooring still remained in the upper rooms. The room directly above the Great Hall had whole sections of floor still in situ, but there were also gaping holes. Several old boards rested on the beams overhead and, while there were no floors in the north-east tower, many of the original boards were still lying loose in the rooms. The worm infestation was extensive. We managed to save and treat enough to repair the room over the Great Hall and we had enough bits and pieces left over to lay another floor over the laird's room. However, these were not sound enough to be walked on, so I laid a new floor on top. Most of the flooring was cut from old battens, one and a half inches thick, matching the sizes of the original floor boards. In one room we were able to lay some very old boards which came out of a distillery. They were so strong that we could have done without the beams. We even found that in nailing them down, we tended to lift one of the beams which was loose in its slot at the wall.

Most of the beams throughout the building were in excellent condition. We simply cleaned each one. 'Simply' is perhaps not the best description of what had to be done. Each beam required over two hours of hard physical brushing and rubbing to clean. The beams in the second floor room of the main tower, however, were not as deep as those on other floors and were severely bowed. It was almost as if they had run out of the best timber by that point. We were faced with trying to lay the floor above on beams which bowed by as much as eight inches. Much of this was natural, but several beams were actually split and in danger of cracking further. Also, many beams had very little timber resting in the wall. One of the corbels was still in place, so we copied it and replaced the two missing ones. I was still concerned about the opposite side of the room, where there had never been corbels. I decided to bolt a plate to this wall and to run a series of six by two inch joists alongside the beams. Before doing this, I thought it would be worthwhile to try to take some of the bow out of the beams. I set up a system of acroprops and shoring, under the floor below. This was bearing on the top of the vaults. Then I aligned another system of props directly over them to lift the beams up at the centre.

Slowly I extended the props, watching and listening for any sign that a beam was about to crack. When I had raised them as far as it was thought safe, we nailed the six by twos to the side of each beam and fastened the ends to the wall plate. While the beams were jacked up, I repaired several which were severely cracked. I drilled them and inserted large brass screws, then filled the holes with oak pegs, made from reclaimed bits of original oak from the castle. When the supports were removed, I was elated to see that I had corrected more than half the sagging. The floor still has a dip in the centre, but it is no worse than any other floor in the castle.

Many of the walls had early plaster still on them. We brushed them all down to remove any loose material and filled in all the gaps with British Gypsum's renovating plaster. Everything was then covered with a finish coat. In a number of places, the new plaster became boss, lifting away from the wall. I took samples and had British Gypsum's laboratory analyse them to see if we could identify the problem. They agreed that we had done all the right things in preparing the surfaces and could offer no explanation. We cleaned the damaged areas, resorted to a bonding agent, and re-plastered. For the most part it worked, but in several places we had to plaster three times. In the end, it would have been much cheaper to have lined the walls, but this was never an option as far as we were concerned, as it would have hidden the character and strength of the walls.

It was difficult to decide how to finish the plaster. What remained had lost most of its surface with age and abuse. In places it was possible to see that the surface had been worked to a degree, making a hard but not especially smooth finish. It looked as if it had been brushed down. They may have used bound handfuls of straw or crude brushes. I decided to try something similar, so the plaster was finished using a wet wall-paper brush, avoiding the temptation to create any sort of pattern, and following the contours of the wall. In some places it is hardly noticeable. In others, the striations are quite pronounced and definite dust collectors.

The plaster was left to cure for over a year before we even considered painting. We found samples of a shocking yellow paint in the kitchen, but everywhere else in the building the colour was white. A similar shade of yellow had been used in a previous 16th century restoration we had undertaken. We opted for the simplicity of white. I had seen a paint called Classidur being used in restoration

Tilquhillie Castle – John Coyne

work in Switzerland. Fortunately for us, it had just begun to be stocked in this country. It allows the surface to breath, requires no primer, no undercoat and covers anything. I did not believe the claims. To put it to the test, Kay tried it on a chimney breast which was badly stained, due to the absorption of tars and soot from the chimney. Anyone who has dealt with this sort of problem will know how difficult it is to get a permanent solution. The Classidur covered it in one coat. We felt like we had participated in a washing powder commercial as we stared in wonder and exclaimed, "It really works! The stains are gone and the wall has never looked whiter!" Two coats were applied, but in many applications one would probably be sufficient. It was the one product we had found that we would recommend without reservation. Yes, there was a catch. It was extremely expensive, about three times the cost of an ordinary emulsion.

Throughout the restoration, we took great care in employing tradesmen. For the most part we made good choices. We were especially fortunate in our choice of a master mason, Slesser Troup. If he had been born 400 years ago, there is an excellent chance that he would have been the one who built Tilquhillie. He had the craftsman's feel for stone. I frequently found, when doing some masonry work, that I would ask myself, "Would Slesser approve of this?" Many of the other craftsmen developed a real feel for the castle. It is interesting how often one or other of them would express amazement at the quality of work done by their 16th century counterparts, with nothing but the most rudimentary tools. In a paper* presented to the Aberdeen granite workers in 1898 by the noted Aberdeen architect, William Kelly (whose floor plans of Tilquhillie have been reproduced on page 66) wrote, *"Architecture cannot exist without sound craftsmanship."* He went on to observe, "These old Aberdeenshire castles, although rude, perhaps even rough, are neither coarse nor vulgar. They have each and all that salt of *character,* that expression of a strong individuality about them." His observations, made over a hundred years before we undertook our restoration, provided us with a wonderful insight and guiding spirit. Restorations must be accomplished with craftsmanship worthy of the original workmen, with results which are never coarse or vulgar, but which preserve the unique character of the building. How well Kay and I have succeeded is for others to determine, but we can say with few reservations that we are indeed happy living with our restoration.

*Kelly, William, 'On Work in Granite' in **William Kelly, A Tribute offered by The University of Aberdeen,** *1949, The University Press, Aberdeen.*

Fig. 1
The north facing elevation at the time of acquisition. The wall to the left really did lean out several feet and the tree on the sky line was successfully replanted.

Aiket Castle

by Robert Clow

Buildings have always fascinated me. I am uncertain why this should be so, but having read the Forsyte Saga, at a tender age, I do recall thinking that had I lived in an earlier epoch I would have liked to have been the builder, Old Jolyon. Perhaps Nash's Regent Park terraces also had a formative influence, for I used to cycle twice daily, past their changing elevations and perspectives, on the way to work in Gower Street, in one of the most dreary of the (then) very dreary London bookshops.

I was born in China, where I lived until nearly eleven. Thereafter, boarding school in London, National Service in the Air Force, plus an apprenticeship in London and Geneva all served to sharpen my interest and appreciation of things Scottish. Returning to my parents' native city of Glasgow, at the age of twenty six, this early interest in architecture developed into an enthusiasm for Scottish vernacular buildings, tower houses and the extraordinary quality of the architecture of Glasgow. It wasn't a fashionable interest, for at that time both politicians and planners had the intention to sweep away as much as possible of the City's 19th century buildings.

I have been fortunate in the career into which I fell, quite by chance, for whilst working as a bookseller one has access to most books currently in print, or to new publications, in addition to the standard works of the past. Work, and a close involvement in The New Glasgow Society in its early days, brought me into contact with architects, town planners and people of a like mind, who became good friends. In a more practical manner, by moving into St Vincent Crescent when we were married, more than 30 years ago, my wife and I became closely involved in urban regeneration through our St Vincent Crescent Area Association. Alexander Kirkland's spectacular development, nearly four fifths of a mile in length, was deemed in those days by the planners to have a mere five years of life left. Zoned officially for 'industrial' purposes, along with the whole of the south side of Argyle Street from Finnieston to Old Dumbarton Road, it was due to be demolished in 1973. It currently is still standing. It was the recipient of most of the urban renewal grants that were on offer over fifteen years. It is now "A" listed and forms an Outstanding Conservation Area, all thanks to the work of the Association and the residents. It was a hard slog, as most of the initial opposition, we eventually understood, came from the Planning Department, strangely enough. My wife and I also cut our teeth, in a quite different experience, by restoring an abandoned mediaeval house in the small village of Mouthier, near Ornans (of Courbet fame), in the French Jura.

In 1976 we acquired Aiket Castle (Fig. 1), or rather:- two intact vaults and traces of a fifteenth century stairway on the ground floor; a generous stair to the first floor; three walls on the first and (what had been) the second floors; the open sky above; a short stretch of the River Glazert; three acres of undulating cattle-grazed land, plus five very large, old sycamore trees.

Four years after completing the rebuilding of Aiket, we acquired, renovated and extended the adjacent Millhouse of Aiket (see Michael Davis, *Castles and Mansions of Ayrshire, 1991*) and sold it on, under a conservation agreement. A decade later, we were fortunate enough to be able to buy a further half mile of the Glazert, adjacent to the Millhouse fields.

Most of my working life has also been involved with amenity societies. Some twenty five years ago Katrina was asked to start the Strathclyde Group of the Architectural Heritage Society of Scotland, on whose Cases Panel we worked for more than twenty years. I have served on both the Council and Executive of The National Trust for Scotland, each for two terms, and concurrently was a member of the Historic Buildings Council for one. Unbelievably, these two Edinburgh-based organisations managed, for at least three years whilst I was a member of both bodies, to arrange that their Councils or Executives almost always met on the same days in the year! Currently I am a member of the Executive of the Strathclyde Building Preservation Trust and am Chairman of the St. Vincent Crescent Building Preservation Trust. I also serve on the Council of Management of the Architectural Heritage Fund, in London.

The search for a building to restore

Starting before we were married, and over a period of fifteen years, my wife and I must have visited nearly every tower house in the central belt of Scotland. I think that after two years of marriage it had finally dawned on her that I wished to restore and live in a tower. In our looking, we were guided by Nigel Tranter's small volumes on "The Fortified House in Scotland" and the larger, more comprehensive five-volumed "Castellated and Domestic Architecture of Scotland", MacGibbon and Ross's excellent work. As James Thin had kept it in print for more that a decade it was (and currently still is) available from all good bookshops.

We started to look in earnest for a tower to restore, within the Glasgow and Stirlingshire area, aware that work required us to be within easy distance of the City. We made unsuccessful offers for Auchinvoil on the banks of the River Kelvin, then owned by the late Willie Whitelaw, M.P., (now inevitably demolished) and for Old Sauchie (still standing with the wallheads neatly slated). However, the owners of the latter didn't wish to sell "unless the price was right". Obviously our offer wasn't. Subsequently, as touched on by John Coyne, the owners put Old Sauchie on the market, more than 20 years later.

Each tower was duly circled on the appropriate Ordnance Survey map and dated. Sometimes two or even three were seen on a Saturday or Sunday. Katrina had fortunately acquired a heavy, prickly, Harris tweed trouser-suit, of a soft sandstone colour, which still hangs in one of the wall cupboards at Aiket. This doubled for a castle-climbing outfit, perhaps a bit stylish, but at least it was warm.

However, I am digressing. Slowly, the maps extended to include towers in Fife and Perthshire and the southern extremities of deepest Ayrshire - even to Dumfries. Most ruined towers, as all enthusiasts soon discover, are either on estates, where an intrusive new owner is unlikely to be welcomed, or near a farm where, should an interest in acquisition be expressed, the farmer immediately assumes there is an inflated value to his ruin!

We looked at Aiket Castle in the late 'Sixties. It sat in a cowfield, bereft of roof, beams, its eastern wall and all internal divisions. Cattle used it for shelter - a situation not dissimilar to that prior to its being burnt down in 1957. Then, according to neighbours, the cattle lived in the ground floor, two tenant families on the first and the chickens in the attic. The two families were related, managing to live in the four very small rooms on the first floor, three of which were formed by the 17th century division of the Great Hall. There was no running water or electricity. We dismissed the building as being 'too small and rather uninteresting'. The Secretary of State's Inventory listed it as late 17th century, but there were traces of a 15th century spiral staircase on the ground floor, directly underneath a later 16th century spiral stair that at one time had risen from first floor level. In the kitchen the cross vaulting of an older and larger chimney was also to be seen. Within its space a smaller (but still large) 17th century fireplace had been built, but unfortunately, at the time of this alteration half of the original bake-oven was destroyed.

Offers were subsequently made for other towers, including Duntarvie, near Winchburgh, where near-impossible terms had been suggested by the Hopetoun Estate. Enjoyable though we found this period of perpetual search, we eventually realised that we were unlikely to find something that met our rather vague criteria. We returned to Nigel Tranter's volume on Ayrshire and started again at Aiket. The owner, a farmer, liked us, or so we thought. His cows splashed manure on our city clothes, as we talked in his byre. This we believed to be a good omen. He was obviously interested in our proposal and willing to sell, so we agreed a price of £2,000, our total savings, but infinitely higher than the previous going price of £50, suggested by Nigel Tranter in one of his lectures we had attended in Falkirk.

Sadly for us, the farmer's canny Kilmarnock lawyer thought there must be other idiots out there and advised him to put it on the open market. So, with three very oddly shaped acres and a stretch of the River Glazert flowing a few feet away from the west gable, it went for over £6,000 to another buyer. We were desolate.

Some three or four years later we were about to conclude the purchase of Duntarvie, as the Estate had come up with much more reasonable terms, when out of the blue came a phone call from Bill Jack, the senior partner in the St Andrews architectural practice of Cunningham, Jack, Fisher and Purdom. Having advised us, the first time round, that he thought Aiket was restorable, he reported that the tower might be coming on the market again. We went to see the new owner and found this to be true. He had been unable to start work on its

Aiket Castle – Robert Clow

restoration, so we negotiated its purchase and settled for the price he originally paid, plus £1,000 for fees and planning permissions. Fortunately for us our personal financial position had altered over the intervening period, and by then we had just £10,000 in the bank.

History and architectural changes at Aiket

The earliest history of Aiket is, to-day, not known. In 1479 Alexander Cunninghame received a charter, the lands of Aiket having fallen to the Crown by recognition, in consequence of Elizabeth Cunninghame of Bedlands having disposed of them to Lord Hay of Yester, without having first obtained consent from the Crown, as feudal superior.

The Cunninghames appeared to be a fairly fractious family, particularly the third generation at Aiket, during the later part of the 16th century and their nefarious activities have inevitably left their mark on the structure of the building. Feuds with neighbours culminated in several deaths - the murder of Sir John Mure of Caldwell, five miles to the north-east; a man being hanged from his own rafters; and allegations of uxorial poisonings at the hand of Cunninghame's wife, Helen Colquhoun of Luss, whom he sent to the Court of Session in Edinburgh, but never arrived to face her accuser. Presumably she met an unfortunate end *en route* at his indirect hand! Then, in 1568, Cunninghame of Aiket "was shot near his ain hoose at Aiket" for his part in the murder of Hugh, fourth Earl of Eglington, a Montgomerie, who lived five miles to the south-west. The family were made rebels and the house largely destroyed, so it was interesting to discover the structural and architectural alterations that were the direct result of this murder.

The 15th century tower faces south, overlooking the Glazert Burn at a point where the river turns through 90°. There the river is pinched by the rock outcrop on which the tower stands. To the south-west, Barr Hill overlooks the bend in the river and the castle – originally built to a fairly standard pattern. The entry door to the south led into a small vaulted chamber (Fig. 2), from which a turnpike stair rose on the left hand side, up to the parapet walk, serving the upper three floors. In front and to the right were two stone-vaulted storage chambers. The Hall on the first floor was fairly standard for a 15th century tower, approximately 24 ft x 17 ft in size. The divisions of the rooms upstairs remain unknown.

Towards the end of the 16th century the tower was enlarged to the west, when the widow of the last-mentioned Cunninghame regained her destroyed home. She rebuilt the tower in the late 16th century manner and either she or her son added a lower kitchen wing to the west, with two floors upstairs, using the narrow outcrop of rock on which to build, that runs down to the Glazert Burn. The house was therefore rectangular in plan, rather than being built on the more normal L-plan. At some stage the entrance was switched from south to north and a barmkin wall was constructed. Later, a larger, grander staircase was inserted, leading from the ground to the first floor, just inside on the right of the new entrance. There is a suggestion that in the 17th century the west gable was largely rebuilt. The evidence is found in the considerable reduction in size of

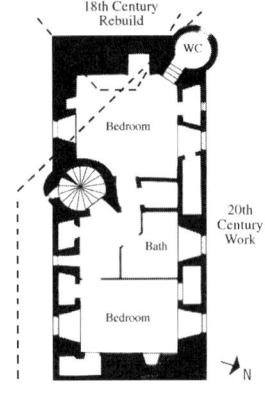

SECOND FLOOR PLAN

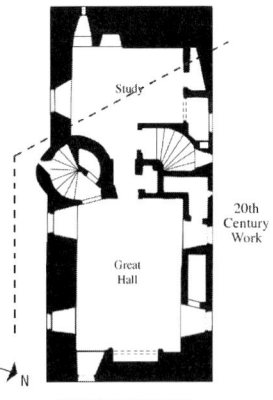

FIRST FLOOR PLAN

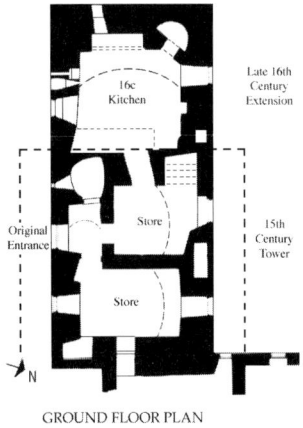

GROUND FLOOR PLAN

Fig. 2
Measured drawings by C. Plaickner and J. Rose.

the original kitchen chimney. (Fig. 3). In addition, there was the remains of a large 17th century fireplace in the west wall of the small first floor chamber and, externally, there was a distinct fall-off in the quality of building and stone size on the west gable, from about 9 ft upwards. In the late 17th century this branch of Cunninghames passed into obscurity, as the then head of the household had "dispensed all by cavorting with harlots in Paisley!"

Fig. 3
Four centuries of fireplaces. The broken vault and the cross-vaulting for the original 16c fireplace can be seen above the bake oven. The 17c fireplace had been infilled in the 19th century. The 20th century's contribution is an Aga. Photo: Copyright: RCAHMS.

In the 18th century, ownership passed to one of the branches of the Dunlop family and subsequently the house changed hands many times. Further alterations were made during this period when, in 1743, a long byre/cottage/cart shed was built, attached to the castle, within the barmkin. About the same time the tower was reduced in height, all traces of fortifications were removed and a gable was built on the north elevation. (Fig. 4). The west gable was partially rebuilt, again, during these alterations and period stone fireplaces were inserted on the first and second floors in the process. The spiral stair to the south (which was corbelled out from the first floor, as a result of the rebuilding in the late 16th century) was replaced internally with a stone and timber stair to the upper floors and, for some reason, the bottom three of the spiral stair's corbels were left protruding from the south facing wall. Windows were enlarged, in an not very successful attempt to make the building appear more fashionable. The result only succeeded in giving the mansion a tall and ungainly appearance, whilst internally it remained late mediaeval in layout.

By the 1950s it had fallen on sad times, having been a well-kept farm until the Second World War. Thereafter it was tenanted by two related families until it was totally gutted by two fires on the same day, and left a roofless and beamless ruin on the 28th May, 1957.

In 1976 my wife and I bought the ruin and three acres, by which time much of the mortar had been washed out, the sandstone had become friable – due to the intense heat of the fire and subsequent weathering over twenty years. Trees

Fig. 4
View from NW (MacGibbon & Ross). The remains of the barmkin below the thorn trees and the ash can be seen on the lower right.

Aiket Castle – Robert Clow

grew from the higher cornices. To add to the structural problems, the east gable had collapsed earlier, in a storm. This caused further damage to the adjacent cottage and also brought down the two central vaults. Had the building been left much longer it would no doubt have had to been bulldozed into history, as the front and rear walls were in a more dangerous condition than was immediately apparent. By the time we discovered this we realised that we had something more than a simple restoration on our hands and for two good reasons our original intentions to renovate within the shell, as drawn by MacGibbon and Ross, became quite impossible.

Preparation and professional advice

Our initial intention had been to rebuild the fallen east gable and the central vault that had collapsed, knit the shell together, re-roof it and move in. With our acquisition of the ruin came listed building consent for the Geoff Lodge plans and the plans themselves. These we didn't wish to follow, as we had our own ideas of using the old kitchen as a kitchen, once again, and there was a number of other ideas that had been formulating in our minds over the previous fifteen years, whilst looking at other tower houses.

We were deeply indebted to Roy Spence, an architect in Bill Jack's practice, who, with his wife Betty, had restored Pitcullo Castle, near St Andrews. Putting up with a stream of simple and repetitious questions, all of which were patiently and fully answered, he and his wife kindly took me through their experience at Pitcullo and encouraged me in what we planned to do. The information gained was invaluable and we shall ever remain more than grateful to them both. In the meanwhile, a Scottish friend from earlier castle-viewing days had become an Inspector of Monuments in Eire. He came over to revisit Aiket when he heard we had acquired the ruin and declared that its tower must be restored, along with the parapet walk and open rounds on each corner, as internally the building was

Fig. 5
South elevation of Aiket showing the three remaining corbels of the turret stair in the centre of the photograph and the infilled, original entrance to the south.
Photo: Copyright: RCAHMS.

still late mediaeval – a fact belied by the awkward appearance of the 18th century alterations. His opinion had strong appeal in that the three corbels that remained on the south elevation (Fig. 5) could again serve their original function, instead of remaining protruding, somewhat forlornly, out of the wall. His recommendation to reinstate the parapet walk was left in abeyance, partly on account of cost and at the back of my mind was the nagging thought that virtually all parapet walks leak! In addition, we had come across Timothy Pont's *Topographical Account of the District of Cunninghame, 1604 - 1608*. In this, Aiket tower and its late 16th century extension were described as a "pretty duelling belonging to Alexander Cunninghame, laird therofe. This name is properly from the Saxon, Aikhead - or wood of oaks". From this description it was obvious that by that time Aiket had lost its defensive appearance, its four corner rounds and water spouts, one of which we subsequently found when clearing rubble. Pont's description corroborated our belief that the rebuilding of Aiket - some thirteen years after the murder of Lord Eglington in 1586 and the revenge shooting of Alexander Cunninghame - must have been in the contemporary manner. The roof had obviously been carried over the wallhead, for if the parapet walk and corner turrets had been reinstated, the building could in no way have been described as a "pretty dwelling". We decided therefore to rebuild to Timothy Pont's description, as that was the last occasion when the interior related, with integrity, to its exterior.

In working to clear the shell, it had become more apparent that we had acquired a building which was at least as old as the 15th century. Originally, the entrance had been to the south. The floor plan on ground and first floor levels was almost identical to that of Badenheath, near Stepps. As Badenheath had been owned by the Boyds of Kilmarnock, and given the similarity of floor plans, it was more than likely that the band of masons working at Badenheath and Dean Castle had also worked at Aiket. When we found the reveals of the south-facing door were the same dimensions as those at Badenheath and that there were traces of moulded door jambs, we decided to recut the door's stone mouldings to the same dramatic pattern, as illustrated in MacGibbon and Ross (Fig. 6), when they drew what remained of Badenheath castle.

The original spiral stair to the left of the entrance had been cut off by the

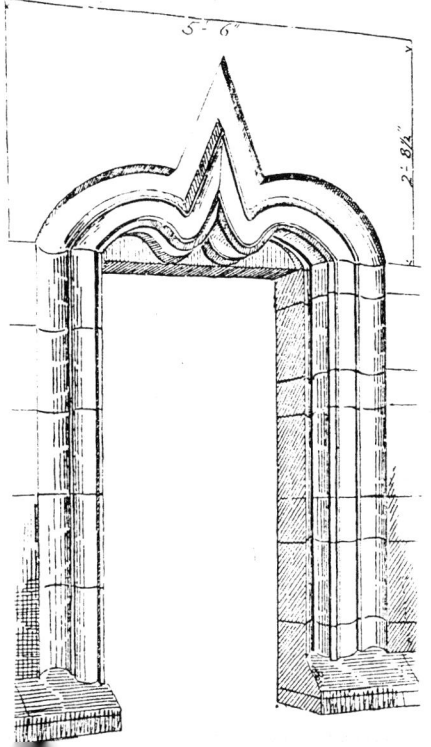

Fig. 6
Left: Badenheath as drawn by MacGibbon & Ross. Entrance doorway as re-cut,

building of a later stair, directly above. We therefore initially thought that in the late 16th century there had been no connection between ground and first floors. However, in the book *Dunlop Parish,* the Lady of Aiket, having been restored to the place and lands thirteen years after the murder of Lord Eglington, complained bitterly of "the destruction of the policie of the place of Aiket, housis, yairdis, orcheardis and growand trees, swa that the samyn has been rivinous and laid waist, but door, windo, lok ruf or but ony repair, and the dewties prescrevit, rigourouslie exacted, to the great wrack of the poor tenantis, quha ar not addetit in so mekle mail as is extortionat be thame." The castle must have been badly destroyed and it was she who had the new turnpike stair built on the (then) south west corner, corbelled out at the first floor level. On examining the north front more closely, a small stair light that had been infilled was found and reopened. This turned out to be at floor level, on the first floor, in what originally had been the north west corner of the old tower, suggesting that at one time a small interconnecting stair descended to the store chambers below, thereby giving access between floors. Had there been a stair at this point, it would have facilitated the opening up and insertion of the new, broader stair, up to the first floor. There is little doubt that this broad stair was a later insertion, as the back of the steps have broken into the vault of the kitchen, below, and the remains of its heavy D-nosings suggested a 17th century detail.

As to the reason for switching entrances from south to north, the answer remains open to conjecture. Perhaps the alluvial soil to the south and river was inappropriate to carry a barmkin wall, when these became necessary, whereas to the west and north of the tower the rock is exposed or close to the surface. However, the old entrance was blocked up (only to be re-opened in a narrower form in the 18th century) and the new opening was made, with entry from within the barmkin. A photograph of Aiket taken in 1916 shows three, eighteen foot high, thatched haystacks in the courtyard, encompassed by what remains of the barmkin wall. Where it was built on clay it had collapsed and had been removed, no doubt, in the 18th century. Where there was rock to provide a good foundation it still partially stood in 1976. We intended to rebuild it, in due course.

Before clearing started, the east gable was an apex of collapsed rubble that descended on one side of the gable's stub into the first floor hall and, on the other side, out to the byre, below. In collapsing during a storm, it had brought down the central vault in the building and the roof of the byre outside. It took two of us a year and a half's hard work to clear. Friends came and helped; for some one day's heavy labour was sufficient. Others returned time and time again. Removal of the rubble uncovered the 15th century jambs of a large fireplace in the Great Hall and a cross section of the lintel (Fig. 7). This caused great excitement and confirmed the earlier dating of the building. Unfortunately, this fireplace had been destroyed in the 17th century, when the room was divided into three apartments. The remains were therefore hidden behind the new plaster, so existence of the fireplace was unknown to MacGibbon and Ross. At

Fig. 7
Left, view of the remains of the Great Hall, first floor of interior, looking east, after fireplace had been cleared. Right, as rebuilt. Fig. 8.

least we knew the size and detail, so later the lintel was recut and we reset it on the original jambs (Fig. 8). Two garderobe chutes were also found, both within the north wall. An architect friend, Peter Clucas, developed unarchitectural skills in clearing them, suitably swathed in boiler suit, gloves and Wellington boots. The soil excavated at the bottom was rich, as might be expected. Bones, pottery shards and a discarded seven inch high costrel were recovered, the pot being modelled on a leather saddle-flagon. We took it to the Hunterian. Eventually it was decided it was a 15th century Scottish pot and it was written up in the Journal of the Scottish Pottery Society.

We proceeded to draw up our plans whilst we cleared out the rubble. Ideas changed and developed as we discovered more about the building. The late Rev. James Currie provided us with the names of three local and trusted builders. Two quoted to cover all eventualities. The third, Willie Burns, overlooked the castle from his home at Borland Hills. We went to discuss a quotation and explained how we wished to reknit the walls and reinstate the tower. "It will fall doon", was his response. "You'd better go and see a structural engineer, or you'll be wasting your money." His advice was taken and Gavin Walker duly met us on site, having requested we produce a really long ladder to take plumb lines. I was sent 45 ft up on this vibrating structure - presuming the intention was to teach me just how poor was the condition of the structure. I had no idea how flimsy long aluminium ladders actually are, when used. I had never been so nervously high in my life and every tremble appeared to make the ladder wobble to an even more alarming degree. However, I found out that the north elevation of the wall leant out two feet to the east and the central pediment swept elegantly, but not intentionally, inwards, by two feet, so there was a whip along the front of the building, due to the former supporting beams having been destroyed in the fire. We complimented Gavin on his subtle approach to ensuring his clients accepted his professional recommendations. He remarked that it wasn't cleverness on his part. He had to ask his clients to take their own plumb lines as he had a terrible head for heights. Anything higher than five feet caused him to feel giddy! However it did teach us a lesson.

He also advised that half the southern wall was cracked along its length, at first floor level, and had started to slip inwards. His advice was therefore to take the north wall and eastern half of the south wall down to first floor level, having photographed and measured them beforehand, thereby leaving the sound west gable and half the south wall (the western half) intact. A concrete raft would then be constructed on top of the first floor vaults to stabilise them and to provide a firm structure on which to rebuild the walls. At the same time the fallen central vault would be recast. Walls would be rebuilt in brick, a nine inch wall delineating the inside of the old stone wall and an eleven inch cavity wall forming the outer skin. Window surrounds would be recut in stone, as they had all been played out by fire, subsequent weathering, or movement of the walls. Having previously been harled, the reharling would cover both stone and new brickwork. We were not very happy with the idea of rebuilding in brick, but the intense heat of the fire had caused most of the sandstone to become friable and there was insufficient whin with which to rebuild. Besides which, the cost of rebuilding in whin would be phenomenal and we had not intended to apply for an HBC grant.

We refused to accept Gavin's proposals at first, and spoke to our Irish adviser. He suggested taking each stone down, numbering them and rebuilding them in their former position. He was currently supervising some such project on an 11th century monastery, in the heart of Ireland. We thought it might be a little expensive and inquired of his budget. It was over £200,000 (1976 prices!), so we decided *not* to do something similar at Aiket, besides which, the mixture of whin and sandstone made rebuilding in those materials almost impossible. Gavin gave us ten days to consider his proposal and come back to him with our decision. His parting offhand comments, "If you don't take my advice it will fall down." and "what's more, you will never get a mortgage," somewhat concentrated our minds, but only after the lapse of nine days. We accepted that the original builders had used the cheapest local material to hand, from the disused quarry behind and, in the twentieth century, our minds inevitably ran along similar lines, so we accepted his advice and selected the good local Kennet brick, which proved to be incredibly hard, once built.

We progressed our plans. However, in drawing the north elevation, the strange imbalance of the windows became more pronounced. They were weighted to the left, in relation to the building's façade - already noticeable from the ground. On the second floor, above an 18th century fireplace, three old turret stones had been reused to form a relieving arch for the lintel. One stone had interesting late 16th century moulded ropework ornamentation (Fig. 8). - a debased example of the type of carved detailing found at Blairquhan, perhaps? This suggested there had been at least one turret of a similar period which could only have been on the late 16th century extension to the west. When the turret

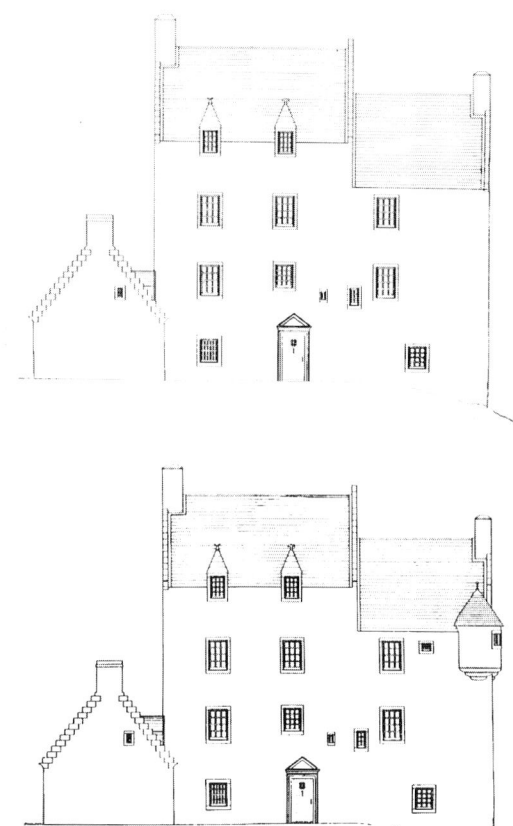

Fig. 8
Left, Ropework ornamentation on curved stone (top right of photograph) above 18c fireplace, reused as a relieving arch.

Fig. 9
Right, measured drawings of N. elevation with and without the turret by C. Plaickner and J. Rose.

was drawn (on paper) on the north-west corner of the north elevation (Fig 9), the whole façade fell into balance, bringing to mind Timothy Pont's description of a "pretty duelling." When rebuilt in this position (but sadly without the ropework moulding which we left exposed above the fireplace) the view from the turret looked dramatically down the River Glazert.

Given the controversial nature of the building, we thought it prudent to take the local Building Control Inspectors with us, so we sought their advice on a number of matters, as we drew up our plans. We were apprehensive of the problems that might arise in having to meet the building regulations of the time. The Inspectors were in fact extraordinarily helpful, as the local Inspector had been one of the part-time firemen who put out both fires. He could not have been more enthusiastic over seeing the castle rebuilt. Our warrant came through quickly, in addition to a Standard Grant for installing running hot and cold water, electricity and a damp course. However, the plans went off to the HBC in Edinburgh and for ten months we awaited a second listed building consent. Despite several reminders and yet more inquiries, nothing happened. With inflation rising above a rate of 27% p.a., and nearly a year's delay, we became distinctly nervous over the cost implications of yet more delay. Waiting became intolerable, so we commenced the downtakings. Two days later the HBC Inspector for the area arrived in my office in Glasgow and made it clear that our plans were not to his liking! He was concerned that we were planning to remove

Aiket Castle – Robert Clow

the gable in restoring the tower. As it was part of the building's historical development he wished it left. However the detail was well recorded in MacGibbon and Ross and we believed the 18th century alterations to be not only uncomfortable, but also inappropriate for a 15th century building. We saw little difference in unfortunate 18th century 'improvements' and the unsympathetic alterations inflicted on 18th century burgh architecture over the past forty years. If restoring an 18th century building to-day, one would no doubt remove all unsympathetic alterations, such as boxed dormers, flat roofs, uPVC windows and inappropriate additions. One would also reinstate landscape window-openings to the vertical, leaving the building as it originally appeared.

Who was to say whether his or our view was more appropriate for this particular building? We did not believe that there was only one policy solution to the restoration or rebuilding of *all* towers. Each has to be considered on its own and what is appropriate for one is not necessarily appropriate for all.

The delay in obtaining the second listed building consent had cost us an additional £20,000, which we could ill afford, and at that time no one could foresee the subsequent years' rates of inflation. We parted on speaking terms but agreed to disagree. Having completed the building, we heard through the grapevine that the tower had been delisted, but a not dissimilar construction to Gavin Walker's suggestions for rebuilding at Aiket is to be found at Lorimer's Formakin Mill, an early 20th century rebuilding, and it is "A" listed. Whether we would have taken the same decision to use the local and cheapest material to hand, some ten years later, remains an open question. This was the late 1970s and attitudes have altered considerably over the years. Good stone masons are no longer a rare and dying breed and Ian Cumming, no doubt, was too young in those days even to have started serving his apprenticeship!

We agreed the builder's price for the brickwork, based on his time, with our providing all materials and undertaking all the other work, except for the consolidation of the vaults, which was undertaken by another contractor. However, the quotation was conditional on a further agreement in that should the work cost the builder more, he would charge accordingly. This was agreed on a shake of hands, but not before he had accepted our condition, that should it cost him less he would charge less. That was the basis of our contract.

The rebuilding work

We were extremely fortunate in the men who worked on site, and in Mrs Burns who plied them regularly with tea, twice a day. The weather also was good. Complicated though the plans were, as windows were different in size and not exactly one above the other, the rebuilt walls shot up at the rate of one lift per thirteen working days, exactly as calculated. All the work was undertaken from inside the building, so there was no need for scaffolding until we came to slate and harl. A bonus was paid to the men if each floor's target was met. In doing our own contracting, there were problems in ensuring that nothing delayed the builders, or our contract would become more expensive. We were therefore closely involved in heavy crane hiring, ordering dressed stonework for delivery, as required, transporting it from St Andrews by Volvo estate, craning in the beams on each floor, shuttering, and pouring concrete. The beams had to be carefully craned onto the codding pads in which the heavy steel brackets had been embedded in the beam pockets on the old walls and on the new work. Then we had to coach-bolt them on each side of every beam to the protruding 2/3rds of the brackets, in order to provide strong cross ties at each floor level. There certainly were advantages in having no roof overhead at this point in time. Whilst this was going on the rebuilding activity continued all around. One of my great concerns was how to avoid the lime mortar in the old work swelling or moving when damp, and bursting or reacting to the builder's cement. I was fearful that some years later we would have done something that we would live to regret or would be unable to resolve. As a result, I obsessively installed a damp course whenever the new work touched the old and used steel ties to overcome any weakness. I still do not know if it was worth all the effort and time.

I visited the site each evening, in order to check on what might have to be altered next day. In addition, I arrived on site at 8am every morning, in order to effect any alterations that we perceived were necessary, after the previous evening's observations. I then went over the day's work with the builders, leaving the site at 8.30am for my regular work in Glasgow. Every morning the men were already hard at work when I arrived. The gables and crowsteps gave problems, in that they were much higher than apparent, but otherwise all the deadlines were met. At last we had the roof joists, the rafters, and their oxters in place, strong enough to carry the weight of the Forfar roofing stones, and the building was ready to reslate and reharl. The builderwork costs came to £300 more than that originally estimated.

Once work started, word got round on another (restorers') grapevine. Various individuals wrote or phoned, offering to exchange invaluable information on sources of materials, techniques, or simply to share experiences. So it was that we met Mike Rowan (he with the problems of the copper-bottomed bath tub, in preference to our more traditional, but avacado-coloured bathroom suite) who was restoring Mains Castle, and Graham and Buffy Carson of Rusco.

The latter put us in touch with Mr Hanton, the master slater at Glamis, who generously supplied the huge Forfar sandstone roofing slabs and offered advice on cleaning, sizing, pegging and mortaring them in, when laid. Having failed to persuade him to undertake the slating, owing to a weak heart, he did however prune Katrina's roses, but in the Forfar manner, right down to the soil. They eventually revived! Willie Burns's youngest son, James (then aged nine), Katrina and I spent two weeks chipping the old lime mortar off the slates, then sizing them. The largest, "Royals", were often up to two or two foot six inches wide, and very heavy to lift, as they could be one to two inches thick. Fortunately, repetitive strain injury was unheard of in those days, but wrists ached every evening. We had decided to use plaster board sarking, rather than timber, in order to avoid later problems of rot developing under the slabs. On Mr Hanton's advice they were to be mortared in and double nailed. A very weak mortar mix was to be used. Our local slater undertook the work but, charming though he was and armed with Mr Hanton's advice, we were not sure that he had fully appreciated what he was undertaking and his men refused to take advice or direction. Fairly quickly the mortar skews cracked when drying, as they were much too strong a mix and on the first night we moved in there was a severe storm. The wind drove the rain under the skews and through the cracks, into the attic. Down the wall it ran, into our bedroom below and onto our pillows, propped against the wall. When it was dry I had to go onto the roof myself and insert lead flashings, raggled into the walls, to cover the skews. I set up a ladder on the roof slabs, tied a rope around my waist, using the Scout's traditional bowline, and attached it to one of the rafters beyond the window which led onto the lower roof. Had I slipped the knot would have held, but our Glasgow builder, Jack Derrick, advised me that without a harness the rope would have broken my spine, so on his advice we let him and his brothers finish the job in a more professional manner.

Our principal aim had been to get the building water-tight and harled within the first summer, so that frosting wouldn't cause the brickwork to spaul at a later date. To this end we had to have the building harled before the end of September and on Roy Spence's recommendation chose James Murray and his son, from Anstruther. In selecting individuals to work on the castle, we endeavoured to use firms that had already worked on similar buildings. At least, we reasoned, experience would stand both parties in good stead. However, Mr Murray initially refused to be lured so far away from his native Fife. Fortunately his relatives in

Fig. 10
Harling the S. elevation (left) with the final coat, one section to be completed on the one day, and on completion, (right).

Ayrshire required a visit and we persuaded him and his family to stop, en route, for a picnic at Aiket. The weather was kind and over lunch Katrina's parents helped to charm the Murrays, as we consumed an extended meal on the banks of the Glazert that lasted till 5pm. By this time Mr Murray felt that Ayrshire wasn't really all that far from Fife. We doubted that they ever reached their relatives, but they did come and reharl Aiket.

Three coats were applied to the walls. The first was a fairly strong mortar mix, the second weaker and the third consisted of a mixture of white sand, white shells, lime, a little cement, sharp sand, a whitener and a waterproofer - goodness knows in what proportions. It was applied whilst the previous coat was still wet, but had to be thrown on over one whole area of wall, from top to bottom, in one day, in order to avoid knicker-line marks being left where one day's work ended and the next began (Fig.10). The final coat required eight hours to set, prior to raining, otherwise the mix would run. The weather held, off and on, after a period of fifteen wet days. By this time autumn was setting in; however, on completing the final (north-facing) elevation, it started to rain after the lapse of only six hours. Some twenty years later one scarcely notices the staining on the wall, as there are so many additional weathering scars on the building. In fine weather it still glistens brilliantly in the sunshine. When it's dull or wet the building looks dreich, not unlike an uncared-for, old French farmhouse. According to Mr Murray his harl has still another eighty years of life and should see both parties (him and us) out.

The dressed stone also came from Fife, from Bill Watson's yard in St Andrews, where he had a good source of second hand stone from the Nydie quarry. We didn't know the sources of the Aiket sandstone (those of the quoins and some of the rybats being different from the mix of varying sandstones used in the body of the tower) but they must have been quarried at some distance, as the local stone is whin and extremely difficult to use, given its multifaceted and obtuse angled shapes.

A cold winter gave us time to get back our breath and to slip into lethargy for several months, but Spring and the thought of the Inland Revenue's somewhat demanding requirement that the work should be completed within only two years, galvanised us into action once again. At the end of the rebuilding, when claiming the tax back on the bridging loan, the Inspector initially refused to grant us the tax relief. He claimed that he had advised us that double relief would only be given if the work was completed within two years of the date of *purchase*. I panicked, as I waded through my files whilst we spoke on the phone. Fortunately my mother had kindly filed all the documentation under subject order, when having little to do one day. To my intense relief I quickly found his original letter and it clearly stated "two years from the date of commencing work." When advising him of the contents of his own letter, he merely said, "Oh, did I say that?"

Other financial problems arose with HM Customs and Excise, over VAT. At that time Zero Rating could be obtained if the building costs were more than 50%

Aiket Castle – Robert Clow

of the cost of new build. This was before the 60/40 rule. In due course we received confirmation that the work would be Zero Rated. Unfortunately it was worthless, as we had made the mistake of undertaking the work as individuals and there was therefore no commercial vehicle for reclaiming VAT. Had we set up a company and registered for VAT it could all have been claimed back, but at that period Customs and Excise were less user-friendly than they are to-day and didn't offer the appropriate advice. By the time the problem came to light they said it was too late to do anything.

Having made the building relatively watertight during the first summer, the second year's work concentrated on the interiors. Our honeymoon had been spent in a small tent, touring the towers and castles of north east Scotland. At Barra Castle, the late Mrs Irvine had charmed us and extolled the virtues of an Aga in the kitchen, to keep the vaults warm. The advice had not been forgotten, as the kitchen is the first room to which people appear to gravitate in a tower house and an Aga would also provide copious quantities of hot water. (Fig. 12). However, the hot water output was insufficient to heat the house, so we had to look at an alternative heat source. A friend of ours, a refrigerating engineer, had installed a heating system in his Park Circus flat, based on the refrigeration process, in reverse. Black iron pipes had been bedded, in a weak screed, in his basement and connected up to a small gas boiler. Hot water was then pumped round whenever heat was required. As his basement was extremely comfortable and dry, this formed the basis of our approach to supplementing the Aga heat in the kitchen, as well as effectively heating the other stone-slabbed rooms on the ground and first floor. Geoffrey Jarvis, an architect, who had been our best man, when sorting out our problems with the varying ground floor levels and sketching the dormer details on the largest "back of an envelope" that I had ever seen, suggested a more sophisticated system of plastic pipes, thermostats and room-by-room control. Manufactured by Multibeton, the system had been operating in Germany for some twenty years and the new Scottish agents, Gibson Wight of Kilmarnock, were prepared to pay for the labour costs of installation, in return for publicity. As money was short and an unsecured overdraft somewhat large, we were very grateful for their offer. The plastic pipes were laid above polystyrene, so the heat could only rise, and were embedded in three inches of weak screed. Caithness slabs were laid on top, in the kitchen and entrance hall. These replaced the few original limestone slabs we had uncovered. In the other vaulted chamber, our dining room, and on the first floor, two-inch sawn York sandstone slabs were laid as the finished surface. We did find a problem in that grease, food, milk and red wine are particularly difficult to remove, without the use of biological detergents, therefore having the York sandstone in the kitchen would have been impracticable but, on the other hand, the Caithness slabs, although more practical, do make the room darker. On the second and third floors we installed second hand 19th century cast iron radiators, somehow more acceptable to the eye than modern heating panels, and more generous in the radiant heat emitted.

The local authority, in offering their Standard Grant for the installation of water and electricity, made the installation of a damp course in the walls one of the grant conditions. In the ground floor rooms a damp course had been installed underneath the heating system and up to the slabs' surface where these touched the walls. We therefore had to obtain three quotations for the wall installation. The first quote from Rentokil came in at £1,500. The second lad who quoted asked us what other quotations we had received and for how much. As it was a rather strange request, we advised him of that from Rentokil. His quotation came in at £1,495! The third man's name was found at random, after a quick look through Yellow Pages. He told me that although his system was based on a low voltage current, it wouldn't work, along with all other systems, as our walls were between five and eight foot thick. He drew down the castle's plan, accurately, and his quotation came in at £570. This we quickly accepted and he returned just to check that everything was in order, before his firm started on the job. When we met, he inquired if his price had been the lowest. All I could do was to look at him straight in the eye and tell him that we thought that, of all those who quoted, we felt he had the greatest integrity! Sadly, when paying his bill, we discovered that the inevitable had happened and his firm had been taken over. When claiming the grant, the Inspector confirmed to me that he also knew that none of the various systems could work, as the walls were too thick, but the conditions had been laid down by Parliament, in its wisdom, and all three aspects of the work were required or there would be no grant - a bit of a waste of public money!

Fig. 12
The Aga replaces the 19c infill within the 17c kitchen fireplace. The bake oven to the left finds a new use. One of the reused rolled moulded stones from the first fireplace is left exposed, above the cruize lamp. Caithness slabs were salvaged from St Vincent Crescent when the council tore them up. (cf., Fig. 3 on page 91).

Aiket Castle – Robert Clow

Ceilings and floors

We had acquired our second hand beams which were 42 feet long for a mere £25.00 each and as the internal width of the castle, from wall to wall, was only 17 feet, each length provided us with two beams, so they were excellent value. Although they had come from a Glasgow graving dock and had been in salt water they were not affected by marine "beetle". We wished to expose them, for although there were no corbels left we had found one when clearing the rubble. We had also seen several somewhat harsh 19th century restorations, where beams had been precisely measured apart and carefully levelled, so we decided to determine their level, width apart and position, by eye. This made the cutting of plasterboard and its insertion between the beams that bit more difficult, but we were anxious that the result should not look too precise.

We worked on the ceilings ourselves, cutting the plasterboard to fit between the 12 x 12 inch beams, with a two inch overlap of plasterboard onto each beam. One and a half inch wide timber battens, the same depth as the plasterboard, were laid along the edge of the two inch overlap and nailed down. This gave a good firebreak and prevented the plasterboard from being crushed by the joists, which were then nailed down onto the slim battens on the beams and the beams themselves. Plasterboard was then nailed up onto the joists. Marginally the plasterboard sagged between each joist, as it absorbed moisture from the atmosphere. This gave the ceiling a subtle softness. In between the joists the required insulation and deafening were installed and the flooring laid on top.

Needless to say, the uneven beams gave some problems when levelling the floor above, as the joists rose and fell, depending on how far out our eye-level had been. However, when working at a later stage, John Phillips, the works' joiner, was somewhat impressed by the whole undertaking and offered to lay the third floor, at his expense, as his contribution to the project. We were grateful for his generosity, as the beams in the guest room, below the third floor, were the most uneven of all. Some time beforehand, Katrina had spent hours and much effort on denailing all the second hand joists we had acquired, then applying creosote generously, out of doors - a hard and thankless task, but at least the joists were dry and odourless when we were ready to carry them up to the higher floors.

Our efforts to install the joists and plasterboard were not without mishap. Late one Sunday afternoon, in the winter gloaming, after a heavy day, I was jumping as usual from beam to beam, in order to get to the other end of the room of the top floor. Set at about four to five foot intervals and 12 inches wide, there was a fairly broad area on which to land. However, I missed my footing and my toes slipped backwards, off the edge of the beam. Fortunately my momentum caused me to tumble forward. By the Grace of God, I caught my shin a cracker on the beam. As I fell and regained my balance, I looked down on the concrete floor some 25 feet below. After that incident I never jumped, but put down planking on which to walk, until the flooring was laid.

On different occasions, my Secretary Eleanor Macfarlane, (who was kindly helping us one day) and I put our feet through the plasterboard, by mistake. It was infuriating to have to replace it, but at least it was not quite so dangerous as jumping from beam to beam. However, it was more than painful when one scraped one's thighs on the roughly sawn joists as one went down, until one was caught by the eighteen inch gap between two of them.

Plastering

The finished internal appearance of the building depended principally on the quality and style of plastering. Fiona Walker of Newark Castle, Ayr, had recently renovated the 15th century tower attached to her home. We were particularly impressed with the quality of the neatly recessed pointing of the barrel vaulted dining room. On inquiring who the plasterer had been, she gave us the name of Tam McBlain of Sorn, so we invited him to tender for the work at Aiket, with the intention of using him and no one else. We explained that we wished the plaster to be applied by eye, not by rule, and for it to sit 'fat' on the exposed stonework. It would therefore be smooth and curvaceous. We also wanted it to run down to meet the stone slabs. There would be no timber skirting, so it had to be strengthened for six inches above the slab level, to avoid damage by vacuum cleaners or brushes. As the Cunninghames had lived such awful lives in the 16th century we suggested that the pointing of exposed stonework on internal door surrounds, in the vaults and on ornamental mouldings should be fairly crude. (Fig. 13). He took this all to heart and, with his son and an

Fig. 13
Initial measurement takings of the S window in the 16c extension (left). An enlargement of the window is indicated by the protruding rybats on the right of the window. Right: crude pointing, as the Cunninghames were so awful, but perhaps a mistake as they had 'style'. The 'fat' plaster, on the right hand face of the window, behind the shutter, hides the protruding rybats.

apprentice or two, pulled the building together, internally, exactly as we required. After having lived in the house for a number of years, we felt we had been somewhat uncharitable in our views on the Cunninghames, in so much that they did have style and were interested in the appearance of their building. The rooms were pleasantly proportioned, the later 16th century windows were embellished with rolled mouldings and there was ropework ornamentation around all the pistol loops we found. When Tam McBlain asked us how we had heard of him, we explained that we had been most impressed by the barrel vault at Newark. "Ach," he said, "that was the only room the architect wuldnae let me touch." In all the other rooms the architect had required the walls to be straight!

Taking possession and moving in

We left St Vincent Crescent, undertaking the removal of all our furniture and possessions ourselves, a step I would dissuade anyone from taking. It took us a fortnight and the tenement stairs in Glasgow and the spiral stairs at Aiket nearly killed us. Thanks to the tax inspector, it was almost five hundred years to the date that Alexander Cunninghame received his charter, in 1497, but of course the building was older than that, as previously it had belonged to Elizabeth Cunninghame of Bedland. Lord Hay had married, secondly, in 1469, Elizabeth, daughter and eventual heiress of George Cunninghame, son and heir of Sir William Cunninghame of Belton, (Burke's Peerage). We have still to find out when Elizabeth Cunninghame of Bedland or her forebears received their charter, in order to establish when the older half of the tower may have been built. There is a legend about the faithful bride of Aiket that centres round the Crusades, so it is possible that the site had been fortified for a much longer period. No doubt the former marshlands and the close proximity of the river were ideal for defensive purposes.

By the time we moved in, the plasterwork had been completed, although it was still wet. The rooms were all without doors, as we had only brought back sufficient green oak from France to make those for the front and back of the castle. The joiner eventually made the internal doors and I installed them. They were constructed by clamping six inch pine flooring together, the vertical face of the door to the approach and the horizontals behind. They were then screwed together, but not glued. Glued joints would have been much stronger than the actual timber, so the latter would eventually split along the grain, as it dried out. The idea instead was that the gaps between the planking would open slightly, to give a repetitive ribbed effect and the pine would eventually turn a mahogany colour in sunlight. Doors were fixed on iron crooks and bands, hand-made by the blacksmith in St Andrews, which we copied from those found when clearing the rubble. With these installed, our winter heating bill dropped from £3,000 to half that figure, as up till then all the heat had been carried up the spiral stairs and into the attic by a well-felt rising draught. A French antique dealer sold us a job lot of fifteen hand-forged doorhandles and latches, in varying degrees of disrepair, for the sum of ten francs. These the blacksmith also repaired, at the same time as he made the hand-forged nails with which we studded the front and rear doors.

We sold our flat in St Vincent Crescent. This eased the unsecured loan from the Clydesdale Bank, which by this time had risen to over £80,000. Therefore our next step was to secure a mortgage, but Gavin Walker's earlier thoughts about the problems of mortgage raising almost became a reality. I had opened a savings account at the Nationwide, with a view to approaching them to take out a mortgage when we moved in. At that period, in common with most other building societies, they appeared to believe that offering a mortgage on a castle was too high a risk! We were looking for £25,000, which sounded a large sum in those days, but the Assistant Manager in the Glasgow Head Office was not impressed by the plans and inquired as to how large was the garden. Having been advised, he turned us down on the grounds that "they didn't lend on houses with such large gardens." I couldn't believe my ears and asked him how many houses in Bearsden had gardens of a similar size. I doubt he was used to irritation being expressed by prospective borrowers, as it was before the days of easy finance and the concept of 'putting people first'. I departed, advising him we would be closing our (modest) savings account. I am not sure that this threat was taken very seriously. Several other Societies in Glasgow were approached, without success. In the end we had to go to London to get a mortgage on the open market, a sad reflection on the timidity of Scottish building societies, at the time.

The next task was to complete the adjoining byre that ran at right angles to the tower and formed the east side to the courtyard. (Fig. 14). Built on clay, part of the walls had fallen outwards, so they had to be rebuilt, where required, on the lines of the old walls, but on new foundations, and to the same thickness.

Fig. 14
The triple dormers on the 1734 building can just be seen through the trees, lower left.

Aiket Castle – Robert Clow

Money ran out before we finished, but at this stage Strathclyde Regional Council, who had changed the criteria for awarding heritage grants, because no one could meet their politically correct but practically impossible conditions, kindly gave us a grant of £6,000 for re-roofing the byre with second hand scotch slates and for installing astragalled, sash and casement timber windows. It was most welcome.

Over the next several years we continued to work on the rebuilding of the barmkin wall. Formerly it had snaked round on a lower outcrop of rock, near the river, and up to meet the gable end of the byre, the walls of which no doubt were once part of the barmkin. There was plenty of whin stone from the tower and we rediscovered how relatively simple it was to lever really huge stones into position in the wall, particularly at the lower level, by using a long batten as a lever and a piece of whin as the fulcrum. It wasn't until the barmkin wall was some four feet high that we recalled that the west gable of the castle had been constructed up to a height of eight or nine feet with carefully dressed and rounded whinstone, all the same size. As already has been mentioned, above that level the wall had been partially rebuilt in the 17th century and again in the 18th, for when it was reharled we found that all the turret stones had been reused to rebuild below the chimney head, at the top of the gable (Fig. 15, overleaf). It was therefore fairly clear that whin could be dressed and indeed was, in the 16th century. This we tried to do, but it was slow, hard work and dangerous, as the stone had a tendency to shatter and splinter. Fine shafts of whin inevitably headed straight for the eyes. It was clear that sizing the stones before using them was much simpler. The youngest son of our neighbouring farmer, David Hamilton, having helped us with much of the stone building, developed an eye for the work and it was he who finished the barmkin wall. We left the part to the west unfinished, as its height started to block our view from the courtyard, down the river. It was also becoming somewhat high in relation to Katrina's water garden in front of the wall, as the land falls sharply away from the wall's outer foundations.

Almost twenty years have passed since the builders signed their names on the east chimney cap and during this time I have been slowly working at most of the "snaggings". There is little doubt in our minds that had we not undertaken the rebuilding, Aiket would, by now, have gone the same way as have several of the towers that we had visited. Subsequently we understood that the farmer had sold because he was fearful that someone might have been killed when climbing the ruins, and he might therefore be held liable. Alternatively, there was a possibility that a dangerous building notice would be served, requiring him to pay for demolition. The loss of three acres of grazing and the possible gain of our two thousand pounds may have been a small price to pay to get rid of any liability.

In its historical context, the building has been rebuilt or partially rebuilt at least four times, once in the 16th century, after its destruction at the time of the murders of Lord Eglington and Alexander Cunninghame; once in the 17th; once in the 18th to make it more fashionable, when there was insufficient money to

Robert Clow – **Aiket Castle**

extend or build anew, and once by us in the 20th century, two decades after the disasterous fires. We received an Europa Nostra Award of Merit for our efforts, which was much appreciated.

At the time of acquisition we planted shelter around the land we had bought, particularly to the north and west, for it had been Katrina's intention to re-create an informal garden on the undulating terrain, the river banks and former gardens. Work is still progressing and in the intervening period we have planted over 7,000 trees on the 100 or so acres we have been fortunate enough to acquire, over the years. For Katrina there is much satisfaction in creating an appropriate setting for the house. For me, perhaps, there is the satisfaction in hearing the words of Timothy Pont, recorded some four hundred years ago, repeated by those who come to the castle for the first time.

Fig. 15
The west gable, twice rebuilt. The harl unfortunately hides the finely dressed whin on the lowest ten courses. The stair tower narrows as it rises higher and part of the byre and the ash tree (as drawn by MacGibbon & Ross) are to be seen to the left.

Fig. 1
The tower and its mansion house, as planned in 1727.

Alloa Tower

BY ANDREW MILLAR, PROJECT OFFICER,
ALLOA TOWER BUILDING PRESERVATION TRUST.

I first became interested in architecture at school, electing to study the history of architecture (as opposed to art) for Higher Art. I followed this through for part of my MA degree and throughout this period of study I particularly enjoyed sketching buildings and townscapes. Good books on Scottish architecture were relatively rare at that time, but Colin McWilliam's Scottish Townscape was a particular milestone. After a stint in publishing, I qualified in planning and progressively engineered a move over to building conservation and environmental-based work, within the local authority field. I have therefore been the 'conservation officer' in all three planning authorities for whom I have worked. What particularly excited me about the Alloa Tower project was the chance to manage the whole development process and see a project all the way through, from concept to completion, by running a building preservation trust. I have now acted as client and organised the funding for five building conservation projects, whilst continuing my mainstream work within the planning office. I am glad to say that other projects are currently being programmed. Although only part of my work, this is a particularly rewarding aspect and it is a privilege to have the opportunity to contribute to something so worthwhile and long lasting.

The Trust

The Alloa Tower Building Preservation Trust was formed in August, 1988. It was primarily a partnership between Clackmannan District Council and the Earl of Mar and Kellie, but there was scope for widening participation as the project developed. The Trust was a company limited by guarantee and had charitable status. It was one of only ten other building preservation trusts in Scotland, as recognised by The Architectural Heritage Fund. This recognition was a specific legal and financial mechanism to enable it to obtain funds at low rates of interest, to save and restore buildings which the private sector felt were uneconomic to sustain. The Memorandum and Articles of the Trust were wider than the name implied and allowed intervention to protect and preserve old Alloa's landscape in addition to its historical and architectural heritage.

The Trust's first project, the Tower itself, was perhaps its most challenging. How did this come about? The mediaeval tower's raison d'être was effectively eroded when the adjoining mansion house was burnt down in 1800 (Fig. 1) and a new house subsequently built in 1834-38. Significant deterioration of the fabric of the tower, however, was largely confined to the last forty years, following vandalism to the lead walkway. In 1973 and 1987, local enthusiasm did result in clean ups to the lower floors, with temporary opening of the building and events to coincide with Princess Margaret's visit and the 400th anniversary of Mary Queen of Scots' death, respectively. Also in 1973, the newly formed Clackmannanshire Field Studies Society published an authorative booklet on Alloa Tower. (E. Roy, K. Mackay, L. Corbett). In 1987 Adam Swan made a notable contribution with "Clackmannan & the Ochils" in the RIAS/Landmark series of architectural guides. Margaret C.H. Stewart also gave a number of lectures on her research into the Earl of Mar's early 18th century plans for Alloa Tower, Alloa and his estate lands, with vistas planned that were as dramatic as (or even more dramatic than) those at Versailles. The development of Gartmorn Dam as a Country Park also highlighted the historical links between this structure and the Erskine family at Alloa Tower.

The moves actually to save the building were instigated in 1987 by Clackmannan District Council. This was part of a new desire to 'get their hands dirty' and address market failure. The revamped Policy Planning Department, through Alan Stewart, Garry Dallas and Mike Thomson, engineered a pro-active role and it entered into negotiations with Lord Mar who agreed to the principle of transferring ownership of Alloa Tower in favour of a Trust - a major consideration, given his family's six hundred year connection with the property. Following these negotiations, the Council promoted the "Alloa Tower Preservation Project and Old Town Enhancement", highlighting the need for positive action within the Old Alloa Conservation Area. This report, issued in November 1987, was quickly followed three months later by a decision of the District Council to award a major grant of £100,000 over three years. The decision to appoint, in principle, Bob Heath, architect, was to prove crucial, as will be demonstrated later. In September 1988, with all the legal paperwork concluded in-house by Bill Scott, a solicitor in the Policy Planning Department, the Trust held its inaugural meeting with Lord Mar and Ian Smith, Chief Executive, as co-founders. Mr Graham Watt, Convener of the District Council, was elected Chairman and Lord Erskine as Vice-Chairman. In January 1989, at the second meeting, I was appointed Project Officer, following my appointment as Principal Planner with the Council that same month. In September 1989, the Tower and five acres of land and buildings were formally disposed to the Trust and in January 1990, after a hectic year of raising finance and negotiation over the repair proposals, the scaffolding arrived and the process of repair began.

The Trust aimed to carry out an exemplary repair of the Tower and to turn it into a Visitor Centre to tell the story of Alloa and its people. The Alloa Tower BPT also was interested in assisting the wider aim of economic regeneration, by further restoration/conservation and, in an enabling role, to assist additional investment and job creation in Alloa. To this end the Trust had assembled, with the co-operation of the Council, a development site for a pioneering dementia care centre and ten amenity houses with, incidentally, the proceeds from the land sale going towards the repair programme. In addition, at the time of speaking, it embarked on a joint venture scheme with Ochilview Housing Association to convert the Tower Square (the old stable block) into low-cost housing for sale. It was also a participant in the 'Tomorrow's Alloa' partnership and established a 'Friends' organisation, to develop wider public participation.

Meeting three or four times a year to agree matters of policy, programming and finance, the Trust delegated operational and administrative control to me. Although I had access to clerical and graphic support, all day-to-day matters of finance, project management and publicity were handled by myself. I also served the Trust as Company Secretary for most of the time.

History of the Tower

Alloa Tower is more than matched for its architectural value by its historic value, as the Erskine family residence. The Erskines of Renfrewshire were granted land in the Alloa and Clackmannan areas by David II, in 1348. From the time of their arrival in Alloa, the Erskines played a major role in the history of Scotland. For loyalty to David II, Sir Robert Erskine was appointed Keeper of the Royal Castles of Stirling, Edinburgh and Dumbarton. The present Earl of Mar is still hereditary Keeper of Stirling Castle. The third Lord Erskine was made responsible for the safety of the young James V at Stirling Castle, after Flodden (1513). For six years, the young Mary Queen of Scots resided with the Erskine family, before being taken to France. It was at Alloa House (i.e., the Tower) that Queen Mary was reconciled with Darnley, when she granted the fifth Lord the long-sought title of Earl of Mar, one month before her wedding in 1565. James VI was also taken under the protection of the Earl of Mar and lived his early life in the prescints of Alloa and Stirling.

The Erskines were obviously the area's most prominent and affluent family and were instrumental in promoting its early agricultural and industrial development, most notably through the Sixth Earl, "Bobbing John" (1675-1732). His immediate influence came to an abrupt end after he was exiled for ineptly leading the Jacobite force at the ill-fated battle of Sheriffmuir, in 1715. He went into exile and died impoverished in France. However, he left a considerable legacy, resulting eventually in the development of Alloa at the forefront of the Industrial Revolution. The building of the harbour, Customs House, coal mines, and the Gartmorn Dam to provide water power to drain the mines, were all executed by Earl John. His talents, as Margaret C.H. Stewart's extensive researches have ably demonstrated, also extended to the development of early classicism in Scotland, through his abilities as an amateur architect and as a patron and designer of extensive landscaped gardens in 1710 and 1728 (Fig. 2, overleaf).

The forfeited estates were bought by his brother, who restored them to the family in 1739 and, over the rest of that century, in particular the estate's and Alloa's prosperity grew, thanks to industrial development. Following 1800, when the mansion house next to the Tower was destroyed by fire, the Tower effectively lost its raison d'être as a focus within Alloa. The role of the Erskine family still continues today, but is comparatively diminished in terms of power and influence.

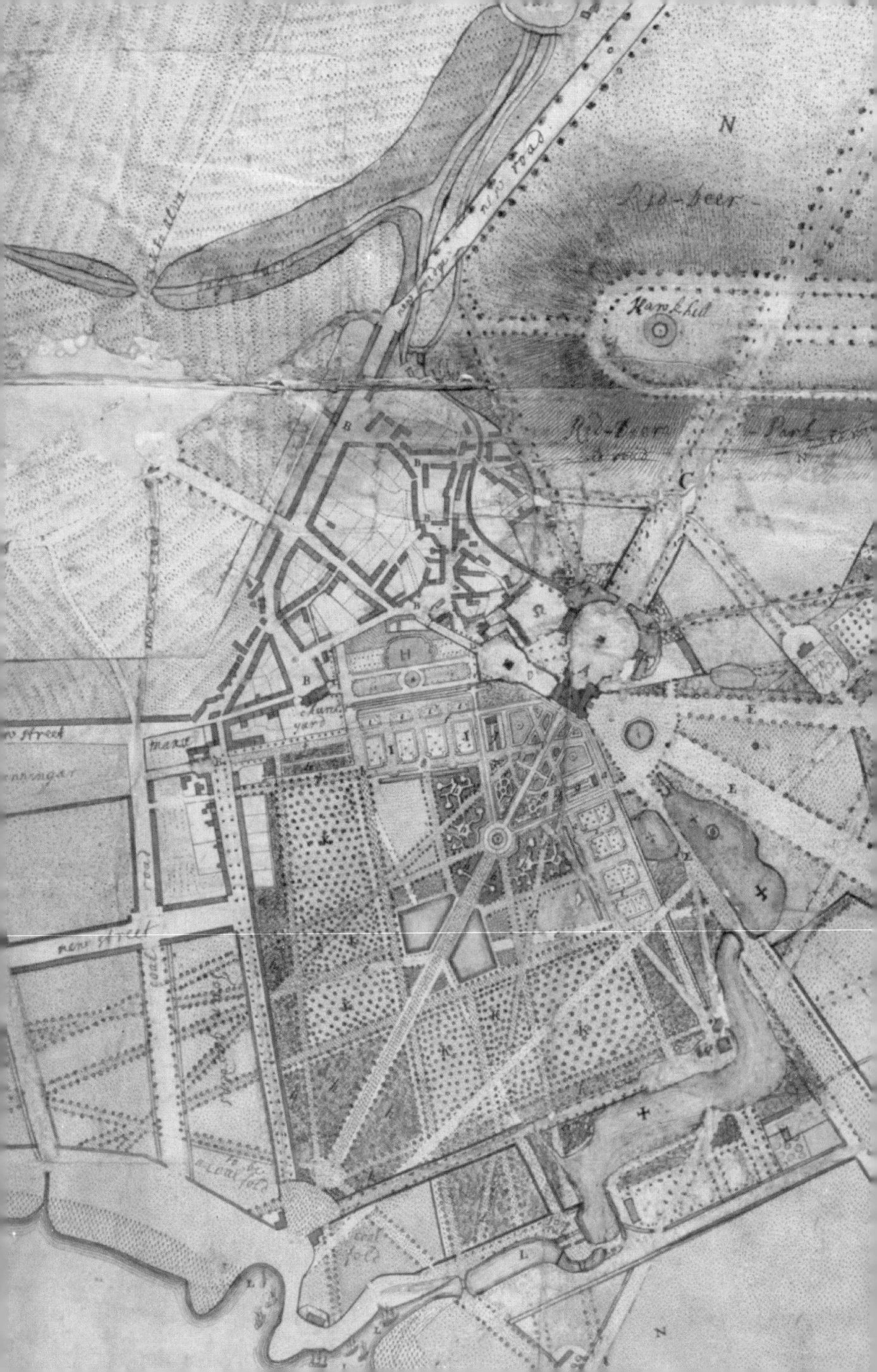

Andrew Millar – **Alloa Tower**

Architecture

The Tower is Alloa's most important building, both architecturally and historically. Not surprisingly it is both a Category 'A' listed building and, more crucially, a Scheduled Ancient Monument. As one of the largest rectangular-plan tower houses in Scotland, one commentator stated, "Alloa Tower certainly needs all its massive girth and height to retain its dignified appearance", for it is wedged in between a large factory and a housing estate, on the southern perimeter of the town. Its floor measures 62 ft x 40 ft and it stands 66 ft to the parapet walkway, or 88 ft to ball finials, (Fig 3). It is one of a series of fortified structures (Stirling, Manor, Alloa, Clackmannan, Tulliallan) along this ten mile stretch of carse-land and tidal river, the control of which played a vital part of the history of Scotland.

The Tower is reputed to be of 15th century origin, but a number of experts now feel that its characteristics indicate that it should be more correctly attributed to the 14th century. The first reference to a 'manor' or 'castle' at Alloa exists in a 1497 Charter and as the Erskines were granted Alloa as their principal seat in 1363, a tower and associated defences would naturally have quickly followed. Its appearance is, however, rather curious for a mediaeval tower with two elevations. In particular, they have the regular fenestration pattern of a classical mansion, as a result of the 11 ft thick walls having new windows punched out, old windows out of alignment being blocked up and a number of dummy windows being created. This is the external manifestation of the considerable remodelling which took place, internally, around 1700, undertaken by the Sixth Earl. The south-east elevation or rear, by contrast, is a hotchpotch of window openings, blockings, former corridor accesses to the main house and raggles, highlighting the varying ridge heights of the house extensions. Of major significance, however, is the double collared trussed roof, dating from mediaeval times. (Fig. 4, overleaf). Roofs of this size and calibre are few and far between on secular buildings in Scotland and it is amazing that this feature survived. Unfortunately, despite the 8 inch sections of oak, insufficient continuous tree rings survive to allow dendrochronological dating. The roof, with its 28 chunky trusses, formerly carried sandstone flags, but the Sixth Earl substituted Ballachulish slates and lead over the flags of the generous walkway, which runs right round the structure and, save for the bartizans, is formed utilising the depth of the walls. Equally impressive is the chamber below, which spans the full length and width of the structure and (with the removal by the Sixth Earl of the mid floor, which separated the apartments from the guardroom in the attic), now extends to a total of 34 ft in height, to the ridge of the open trusses.

The Sixth Earl reinforced the subdivision of the massive Great Hall, with its two groined vaults, into two levels and in contrast to the original form of turnpike stair in the south-west corner, still lit by mediaeval slits, inserted a new semi-circular classical staircase and dome to serve a new main door. This was enriched by Ionic pilasters, a pediment and the sculpted Erskine crest and motto "Je pense plus", designed after correspondence with James Gibb. The insertion of the stair resulted in the north-east walls being reduced to a mere 6 ft thick. The dome

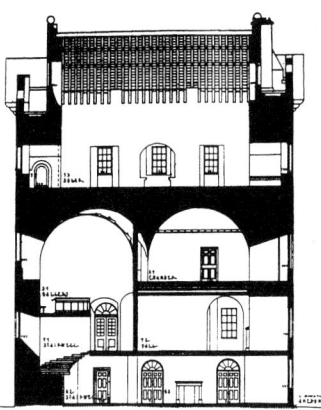

Fig. 3
Cross section of Alloa Tower.

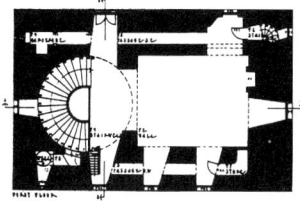

Alloa Tower – Andrew Millar

also featured a minstrel's gallery of uncertain but later date. Further investigations will hopefully shed light on the development of the interior but discoveries already made include:- a garderobe at the third floor level, an anteroom at ground floor and, most surprisingly, an exquisite mediaeval well at first floor level, 22 ft to bedrock and formed by blocks of circular ashlar. This was blocked up and hidden for three centuries by the works to the stair and only found when the removal of cement slurry pointing revealed half of a mediaeval slit window, the top half having been obliterated by a dummy window. The creation of a well at first floor level is extremely rare and can be regarded as a deluxe item, thereby highlighting the comparative power and wealth of the Erskine family.

Fig. 4
Looking up at the double collared trussed roof, unrestored.

Financing the restoration

The basic principle adopted by the Trust was incremental implementation, namely letting a phased series of contracts, as resources permit. Putting a £1 million package together for the Tower and letting a single contract was never a realistic option. The Trust had to 'jack-up' the credibility threshold and prove itself as a delivery mechanism, able to spend other peoples' money, wisely and effectively (Fig. 5). With most of the money essentially being a loss leader for posterity, the amounts involved being considerable, and with no sale at the end of the day to relieve the burden, phasing was the only option as far as the major core funders of Historic Scotland, Clackmannan District Council and The Architectural Heritage Fund were concerned. Historic Scotland, despite continuing major funding problems, were enthusiastic in their support, throughout the restoration. The District Council's up front money was to prove crucial, as it enabled the first contract to be let for scaffolding and a temporary roof, thereby saving the mediaeval roof from collapsing like a pack of cards (Fig. 6).

116

Fig. 5 (left)
Alloa Tower – derelict 1989.

Fig. 6 (below)
The tower's roof and parapet walkway scaffolded and under repair 1990.

Alloa Tower – Andrew Millar

This phased approach had other advantages, the most obvious being the ability to respond to new funding opportunities (European Commission - ERDF), or to take advantage of quick spend monies (S.D.A.). A programme over many years allowed relatively small financial increments (such as those from the Central Regional Council) to become a useful contribution.

At the time of my talk, the Trust had let four contracts on the Tower, ranging from £12,500 to £190,000. In all cases, the principle that the Trust followed was to ensure that each contract was worthwhile, in its own right. This would make certain that no expenditure would be wasteful, should the money ever dry up and the programme have to be mothballed. Cash flow was very important and this was assisted by preferential loans from The Architectural Heritage Fund in London, guaranteed by the District Council.

The Tower Project was, of course, much wider than the Tower itself and within a four year period the Trust had been involved in a total of twelve contracts on the whole site. These included an archaeological dig, landscaping by the Youth Training Scheme, approach landscaping from Alloa's Ring Road, a new access road (setted) and a visitor centre car park, re-creation of historic gardens (three contracts) and the conversion of Tower Square (imminent at the time of giving my talk). Values ranged from £25,000 to £600,000 and a number of different mechanisms was employed.

Suffice to say, the series of contacts, or their phasing, were not pre-planned but evolved to take advantage of specific opportunities to spend money. The basic philosophy was to work to a sketch Master Plan (Fig. 7), putting the puzzle together and hoping that at the end of the day the joins of the jigsaw would not be visible. Many other agencies were also involved in the wider picture, most notably Scottish Homes and Forth Valley Enterprise.

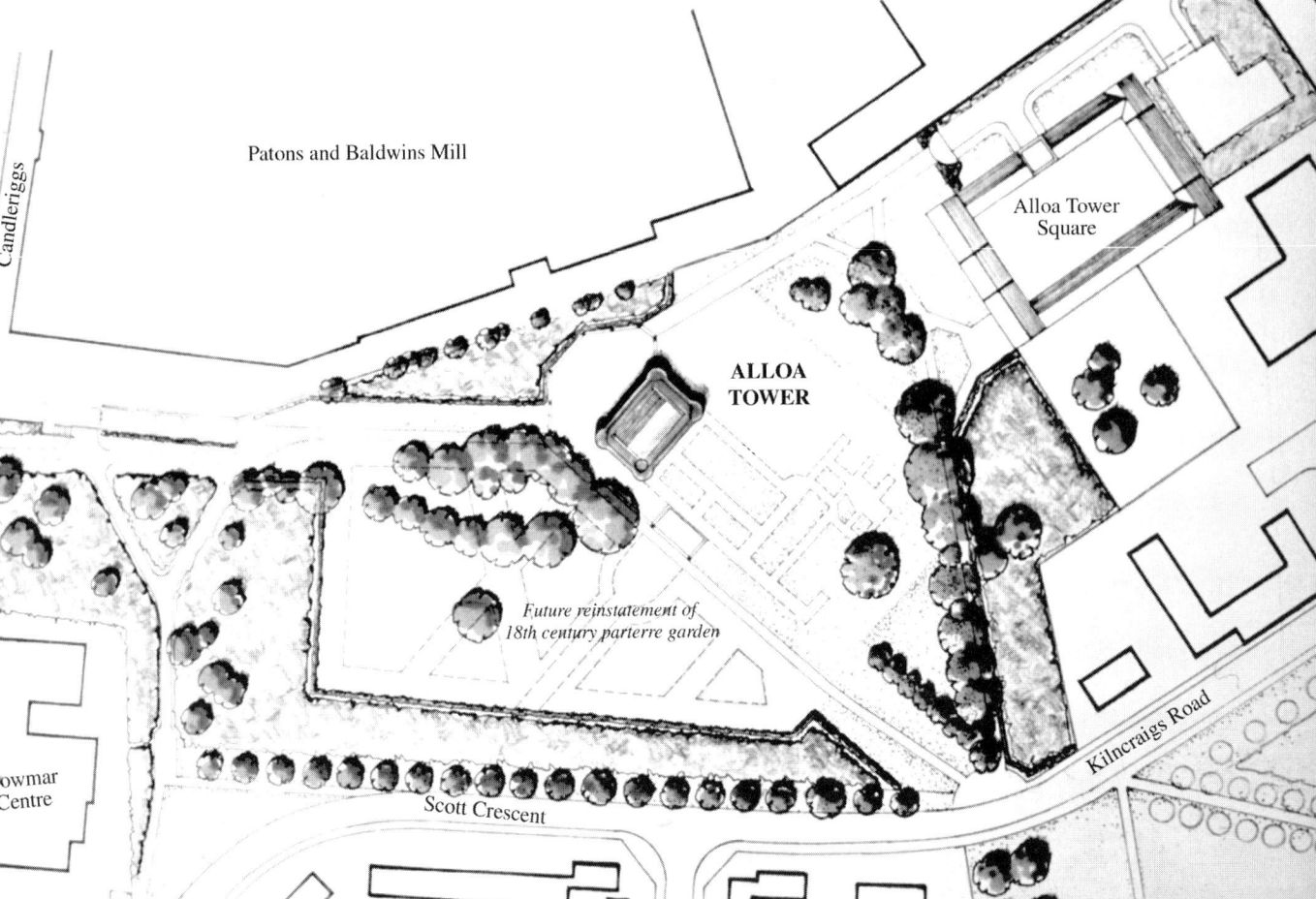

Fig. 7
Plans for enhancing the tower's setting.

Andrew Millar – **Alloa Tower**

The repair programme

I shall concentrate my comments on the Tower and not the Trust's wider involvement in Alloa. The choice of our design team was of paramount importance and I believe that the appointment of Bob Heath was crucial to the project's success. He had nursed the project for two years before I was appointed, provided a free survey (no mean feat) and generally brought expertise into how the system worked. Fortuitously in 1990, Martin Hadlington, a freelance architect, appeared, whose expertise was also to prove invaluable on the repair of the mediaeval roof, working together with Ted Ruddock, a conservation engineer, whose tolerance allowed minimum repair and disruption to fabric. Lastly, Gerry McQue and Eric Johnston, as quantity surveyors, brought a series of uncannily accurate cost estimates to bear and proved that this profession, much to my surprise, can have a sense of humour.

Apart from stone indenting, slating, leadwork and glazing, the two really interesting repair issues centred on the choice of slaked lime for the pointing and the repair of the mediaeval roof. It is quite galling to think that slaked lime, with all its by-products, used to be an every day material, witness the number of limekilns on old O.S. maps. Today, slaking is again being undertaken, but I believe that Alloa Tower was one of the first projects to use this traditional material on such an extensive scale. Over 70 tonnes of lime putty were used, often in less than ideal conditions, owing to the vagaries of finance. Three quarters of the building had to be pointed between November and February, to meet a quick spend target, and the contractor not only had to protect the work extremely well, but also had to look to factors such as orientation and wind chill in planning the work. The result is a building which has been washed with lime, progressively lessening as the mortar organically cures. The stonework is once again looking proud and surprisingly clean for a building that is located in the middle of an industrial town.

The second real point of fascination was the roof. Being very rare in Scotland, Bob Heath and Ted Ruddock saw it as a once in a lifetime opportunity. It really should be the subject of a detailed technical paper. The trusses were repaired in situ, using joiners who were given on-site training on dummy rigs, (Fig. 8). Each

Fig. 8
Finishing off a new ashlar post for the roof.

truss was individually assessed and only the minimum timber removed and replaced. This invariably had concentrated on the bottom triangle of the trusses, which had been saturated in pigeon droppings for twenty years, with obvious results. As we could not wait twenty years to do the work, a combination of green oak (from Loch Lomond - the Luss by-pass) was used, together with some seasoned oak from England, where the room for movement was more limited. Dowels were used if an original joint was being replicated and stainless steel bolts where an artificial joint was required. This, I believe, is called an honest repair. When the internal scaffolding was taken down, after three years in situ, the effect was (and still is) quite stunning, with only perhaps 10% of the roof having been replaced (Fig. 9).

Fig. 9
The mediaeval roof as restored,
cf. Fig. 4, p 116.

Crucial to this whole venture was the calculation by the engineer, which allowed apparently rotten timbers to remain, as long as there was a minimum core of 3 inches left, out of the original 8 inch section. This left sufficient strength in the timbers to allow the lighter load of slates to be transmitted onto the walls, as opposed to the weight of the original covering of sandstone slabs that required the 8 inch timbers.

The last point raised one issue, which I will mention only in passing. The exact form of the original mediaeval tower is not known but, in any event, much of the interest in the building lies in the works undertaken by the Sixth Earl, around 1700 - 1710. The external and internal remodelling is still extant and, therefore, the primacy date for repair was the early 18th century. This raised all sorts of interesting debates, some of which have been resolved, but some will undoubtedly continue to prove a focus for lively debate between the Trust and Historic Scotland.

Andrew Millar – **Alloa Tower**

Postscript

It is hoped that I have been able to give a flavour of the early years of this interesting and challenging project (Fig. 10). The project shows what a locally inspired initiative can do and, as with most successful projects, it has been dependant on a number of key players coming in at a number of specific points in the process. Specific thanks therefore have to go to the foresight and determination of Clackmannan District Council and to Lord Mar.

In 1996 the tower was opened as a historic property by the National Trust for Scotland. The support of the current Earl of Mar and Kellie, the Friends of Alloa Tower and the new Clackmannanshire Council are all crucial in maintaining this symbol of local pride and regeneration.

Fig. 10
The tower as restored in 1992, set in new "historic" landscaping.

Fig. 1
East elevation of Fawside Castle in 1976. The darker stonework on the right is the 14th century rectangular tower; the lighter coloured stonework to the south is the 15th/16th century L-plan tower.

Fawside Castle

by Tom Craig, BSc, MBA.

My family has been closely associated with the steelmaking industry in the West of Scotland for many years and it was there that I started my industrial career. I studied Mechanical Engineering at The Royal College of Science and Technology and graduated BSc at Glasgow University, followed later by an MBA from Edinburgh. After graduating I had a varied training. This included mass production of fasteners in Sweden, working in the shipbuilding industry with John Brown & Co. (Clydebank) Ltd., working with technical sales for SKF and as a design engineer, in Pittsburgh, with the United Engineering and Foundry Company. Currently, I am Technical Director of MacTaggart Scott & Co. Ltd., Engineers, Loanhead.

I have always been keenly interested in design and the relationship of art and engineering. Outside engineering, I am a director of the Richard Demarco Gallery in Edinburgh, in addition to being a trustee of the Scottish Sculpture Trust. With the latter body I initiated the Association of Sculpture and Engineering Technologies Programme. Under this banner the Trust co-ordinated a proposal for a monumental symbol of identity for Glasgow, entitled "The Flourish."

Why did my wife and I want to restore a tower house? Well, I am a passionately keen engineer, involved in designing and manufacturing a wide range of mechanical equipment. This ranges from the requirements of the world's navies, new machinery to operate Tower Bridge, to tracked vehicles and the aforementioned monumental sculpture for Glasgow. I find it offensive to come across bits of machinery that are not working, so I also restore clocks, cars, organs and anything that could work, if it is not in working order. This desire to repair, restore and to make things work is a strong motivating force. It therefore is logical that I might consider refurbishing a house, particularly if it was a ruin and, being romantics at heart, my wife Claire and I decided to restore a tower house. Murray Grigor, who has made films on the architects Frank Lloyd Wright and Charles Rennie Macintosh, once said to me, "Restoring a castle is a well known disease and the only way to overcome it is to go out and do it!" He was quite right but I haven't recovered from the disease, even yet.

I would like to describe the restoration of Fawside by going through the questions 'what?', 'where?' and 'who?' and, in so doing, I would hope to cover what we accomplished and how we did it. Having decided 'what' to do, the next question to concern us was that of 'where?'

Looking for a tower to restore

I work near Edinburgh, a city in which I might describe myself as a social misfit. Edinburgh is not happy with engineers and, in particular, engineers from Glasgow! My wife, who is English, is much better off in the local social circles.

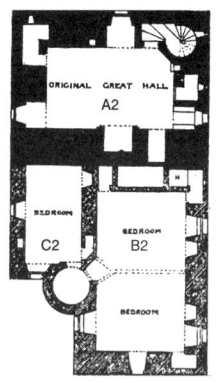

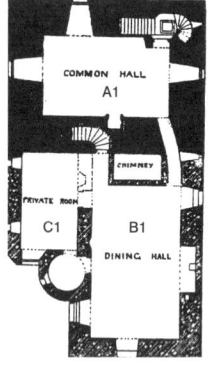

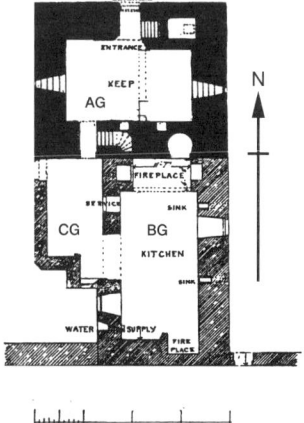

Fig. 4
MacGibbon & Ross's plans.

Fawside Castle – Tom Craig

We had to find somewhere near the City if we wanted to make our home near to my workplace. We studied Ordnance Survey maps, marked off each house recorded in historic writing and visited every castle we could find, starting within a radius of five to ten miles from Edinburgh, then fifteen, and so on, but to no avail. In desperation, we thought a good person to consult would be Nigel Tranter, whose name cropped up so often at the Castles Conference that he must be the father of many restorations. He, of course, was enthusiastic when he saw another romantic couple who wanted to restore a castle and immediately suggested we might consider Fawside. It was only about five miles distant from where I worked. It must have been a psychological blockage for, although nearby, we had never considered it. I went to school at a well-known institution in Musselburgh and when the weather was at its iciest worst we had to go for a run, rather than play games. The worst run, without doubt, was the Carberry-Fawside circuit. We had to run up to Carberry Tower, across the hill to Fawside and then return back to school, a distance of over six miles. With the bad memory of those freezing runs still scarring my mind, Claire and I went to have a look at Fawside. (Fig. 1). We saw that it was a big tower and would be a big, big project, much larger than we had anticipated. (Figs. 2 and 3, opposite). However, it was so attractive and had so much to offer that we decided to proceed. Fundamentally it was a friendly place, despite its ruined state, with spectacular views looking down on Edinburgh, over to the Kingdom of Fife and round to the old invasion route from the south, via Dunbar.

We undertook a lot of research to learn more about tower houses and Fawside, in particular. We toured a large part of Scotland, visiting other restorers, including some who had completed their work. In addition to other knowledgeable people, we also discussed the subject with David Walker of the Historic Buildings Council (HBC) who, at that time, was Chief Government Inspector of Buildings. Finally, we agreed that we would take the plunge and restore Fawside. We contacted the owner, a local farmer, who was thoroughly amenable to selling, as he had previously decided to demolish the building, not through vandalistic intent, but from a sense of responsibility, since it was a potential death trap to the local children who used it as an adventure playground. If there had been an accident then he might have been held to be responsible. Nigel Tranter heard of this impending demolition and managed to reverse the decision and even got the authorities to contribute to blocking up doors and windows to prevent entrance. The sum that we paid was very reasonable, being the value of two acres of ground around the castle. We now owned the castle on a spectacular site, in addition to a large 75 ft. long barn, plus the surrounding two acres.

The castle consisted of two towers - a late 14th century rectangular tower and a late 15th/early 16th century L-plan tower, added to the south. (Fig. 4, plans and cross section, left). It was an interesting structure in that it contained two periods of early Scottish domestic architecture, built in stone. It was modernised in the late 16th / early 17th century, perhaps as a result of its being set on fire by

Fig. 2 (left)
Looking up at the south gable of the L-tower and the two non-existent turret embrasures. Lower left is a mural chamber with a small window. The top floor with fireplace was termed B3.

Fig. 3 (below)
Floors C4 and C3 (with iron grilles) facing west. Floor levels were retained, using wooden wall-plates.

Fawside Castle – Tom Craig

the English at the Battle of Pinkie, in 1547. Now we are into the late 20th century and have completed its fourth phase of rebuilding or modernisation. I feel strongly that tower houses are working units, reflecting the contemporary needs of the owners, so we didn't slavishly restore it to a previous period. It does, in fact, have running water, up-to-date sanitation, central heating, electricity and LPG!

Rectangular 14th century tower

We were fortunate in finding that the 14th century tower, which we termed A block, was in pretty good condition. It had a vaulted roof, although the wallhead had crumbled away. The roof was covered by a foot of earth, which must have accumulated after the tower was uninhabited. We were not able to find out exactly why and when the tower was abandoned but it must have been before the Window Tax of the 18th century. It had four rectangular floors, approximately 25 ft x 15 ft. The walls were massively thick (about 6 ft) and, at the corner with the spiral stair, some 10 ft thick. There were two small windows high up in the walls of the ground floor, reached by steps hewn out on the inside of the wall, in order that they could not be readily assailed from the outside. Within the building, two fireplaces peered down. (Fig. 5, opposite). The Great Hall fireplace has similarities to that at Craigmillar Castle and has an interestingly joined two-piece lintel. (Fig. 6, opposite). The fireplace in the room below was obviously an addition in the 17th century and shared the Great Hall flue in such a way that part of the Great Hall fireplace had been blocked off to allow the flue to join the main chimney. An excellent garderobe was found within the east wall which led from the roof down to ground level. When clearing out the flue of the garderobe we came across some musket balls. They were imperfect and obviously someone, whilst sitting, answering the call of nature, was sifting through his collection and discarding those which might get jammed in his musket! The first flight of stairs is straight, within the thickness of the wall, starting from just inside the entrance door. There is a landing at first floor level from where the stair continued upwards in a spiral. At the landing there is a trap door leading to the pit - a very civilised pit in that it has a small rectangular vent high up in the wall, leading outside, plus what looked at first sight to be an Orkney chair back, gouged out of the wall. On closer examination the seat had a hole in it with a drain leading into the garderobe. During the 17th century conversion, the owners increased the size of the north and west facing windows to allow more light to get in. They left intact the original, much smaller, windows on the east side of the building.

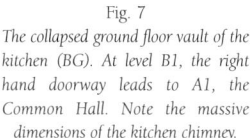

Fig. 7
The collapsed ground floor vault of the kitchen (BG). At level B1, the right hand doorway leads to A1, the Common Hall. Note the massive dimensions of the kitchen chimney.

L-plan tower

In contrast to the late 14th century rectangular building (A block), the L-plan tower (B and C blocks) was a jerry built affair, with rubble walls only 5 ft thick. It had suffered from the ravages of time, stone robbing and generations of vandalism. There was no sign of the roof and most of the vaulting on the ground floor had collapsed. (Fig. 7, opposite).

Using an L to be descriptive of the shape of the tower, the vertical part of the L (B block) consists of four floors 28 ft x 16ft in size, with the ground floor (BG) being vaulted. The horizontal part of the L (termed C block) consists of six floors within the same height, each floor being 18 ft x 11 ft (see Fig. 4). Initially it was thought that access to the first floor was by a narrow stair within the thickness of wall connecting the two towers. Obviously the original entrance had been in the re-entrant angle but this had been blocked up, presumably in the 17th century, and a new door formed in the west wall. However, upon excavation, we uncovered a scale and platt stair from this new entrance to the first floor. The barrel-vaulted kitchen contains an interesting water basin in the thickness of the west wall, which drains into the kitchen. Presumably the well was within the barmkin wall, close by, but we were unsuccessful in our search for it. In the east wall of the kitchen, two drains lead waste water outside. A massive fireplace with an oven to one side was built into the north wall abutting the old tower. The chimney is 11 ft wide by 5 ft deep.

Fig. 5 (left)
The fireplace in the original Great Hall of the old tower (A3). The opening had been reduced to accommodate the flue from the fire below, which must have been added later to the Common Hall (A2).

Fig. 6 (right)
The fireplace in Fig. 5, after restoration. Note the jagged lintel and the low doorway to the L-plan tower.

Fawside Castle – Tom Craig

Now for the "who?" factor. Obviously one of the most important people concerned with the restoration is the architect. Being an opinionated engineer, I find that I quite often have a conflict with architects - how can they design a building without fully knowing about the structural implications? I thought that finding a suitable person was going to be a problem, as no architect could afford the time to put up with my interference! As it turned out, we were extremely lucky. Ian Parsons was just finishing his Architecture degree at Edinburgh University and took on the restoration drawings as a final year project. It was quite an undertaking to have a project like this as his final year submission, rather than work on a hypothetical toilet for the Grassmarket.

When, not unexpectedly, he qualified, we invited him to carry on as our architect. I suggested he allow 60% of his time on Fawside and the remaining 40% on other projects, in case I had to stop for any reason. In fact he spent about 160% of his time and took us through, nearly to completion, before he joined a partnership in Edinburgh. At that stage Ben Tindall came along and put the final finishing touches to the work. The structural engineer, Ted Ruddock, was a tremendous success, too. He was a man after my own heart; not only were his charges modest, but also he had a very practical attitude. He stood beside the walls of the tower and said, "Look; if these walls have stayed upright for 600 years and are still absolutely plumb and square, the building must be structurally sound!" That was the sort of advice I wanted. I didn't wish to hear that he was unable to confirm the strength or life expectancy because of cracks here and there. The tradesmen came from the local area of Tranent and most were outstanding. We were extremely lucky with our builder who had been apprenticed as a stonemason. One rewarding aspect of the restoration was that he took on a new apprentice, who learnt in detail how to 'build' a castle. During the period he won several competitions for stone carving and represented Scotland in an international competition. The joiners were equally good, as was the electrician. Sadly, however, the plumbers, except for the first, were disappointingly poor. They were inept, incompetent and dishonest. If ever I am made redundant I am going to become a plumber!

Unfortunately it was the period when inflation had just started to take off, as already mentioned by Robert Clow. Unfortunately, too, my ability to pay for the work didn't match the rate of inflation, which rose in 1977-8 by about 27% in the building trade. However, the bank was supportive. It realised that there wasn't much point in forcing me to sell at an incomplete stage - it would have been similar to selling a car that only had three wheels - so they carried us right through to the end of the project. I am glad to say that they got all their money back, much to their relief, I suspect! Before the project had started I had seldom seen my bank manager; our meetings then became more frequent. However, the scale of this project was soon way above his head, so I had to deal with a Joint General Manager. In fact, over the period, three Joint General Managers passed through my hands! Such was the size of overdraft and their concern, that we had fortnightly meetings to review the situation. A parking space was specially made available for me within the Grassmarket and we started the meeting at 8.30am to suit my schedule! At one time one of the managers said to me, "Mr Craig, I don't know how you sleep at night". It was quite obvious that he wasn't, but I was. However, before I start to describe our work, I will touch briefly on the history of the building.

History

Fawside, like all Scottish castles and tower houses, is unique. It is a particularly interesting example in that it exhibits the needs and wishes of a mediaeval baron, after adapting an older building to his (modern) requirements. In addition, it provides a fascinating reflection of the social development that took place between the 14th and 17th centuries. It has a colourful, surprisingly well-documented history as the centre of fights, feuds, battles, murders and executions. Its coal mine was associated with some of the earliest mining in Scotland and perhaps for enslaving miners.

An early reference records that during the reign of David I (1124 - 1153) the lands of Fawside were held by Edmund of Fawside. Robert de Quency (whose forebears came from Normandy with Duke William) is reputed to have built a castle at Fawside. Four charters by the de Quencys survive. In the first, made around 1189, it is stated that Robert de Quency, Lord of Fawside and Tranent, granted land to the Cistercian Abbey of Newbattle. Seyer de Quency, son of Robert, enlarged the grant and assigned to the monks the exclusive right of digging coal. The monks, however, were not allowed to sell the coal and would have used it principally in their own establishments. In 1435, Aeneas Sylvius, an Italian travelling in Scotland, later to become Pope Pius II, wrote that as the Church was unable to sell the coal, it was distributed at the church door as alms. The "black stones" were received by the poor with as much joy as if the coal had been coin. Commenting on the lack of trees, he says "of wood for cooking and building they have none, for warmth the inhabitants burn stones".

In 1547 the Battle of Pinkie took place on the plain below the castle. This was the last 'official' battle between Scotland and England under separate sovereigns. Accompanying the English army was W. Patten as one of the first war correspondents. In "The Expedicioun into Scotlande" (published 1548) he describes the battle in detail, along with three sketches. Somerset had placed his heavy ordnance on the hill, within range of the castle;

"We had the Fryth on the north & this hil last remembered as I sayd, on the South (the west side whereof is called Fauxsyde Bray), whereupon standeth a sory castel and half a skore houses of lyke worthiness by yt, and had, westward before us, them lying in campe.

There was upon the Fauxside Bray (as I have before said) a castel or pile which was very bysy all the tyme of the battaile as ony of our men cam nye it to shoot at them with suche artillerie as they had, (which was one oother than of hand gunnes and hakbutes, and of them not a doosen neyther) little hurt did they; but as they sawe their fellos in the field thus driven and beaten away before their faces they pluct at ther peces, lyke a

Fawside Castle – Tom Craig

dog his taile and couched themselves within all muet but by and by the hous was set of fyre, an they, for their good will, brent an smoothered within".

The total destruction of the castle is said to have been averted "through its first floor and roofs being arched over with stone". MacGibbon and Ross deduce therefore that the addition of the L-tower had been made prior to the battle, since the rectangular keep is arched at the roof, whilst the former had arches only on the ground floor. The castle was obviously restored at some point after the battle and there are indications of 17th century modifications, where windows were enlarged in the old tower to admit more light.

Until 1364 workers in the monastic granges and houses were slaves, transferred with the land they worked on and brought back if they escaped. By the end of the 16th century, coal had become such an important commodity that causing damage to the mines was made a treasonable offence. Soon after this statute had been passed, John Henry, a former underground manager in Fawside Heugh, set fire to the mine in anger at being dismissed. He was duly hanged at the Mercat Cross in Edinburgh and his displaced head displayed on a pole above the mine "to mak siccar". This led directly to an act in 1606 which placed the miners under a severe bond of slavery - as severe as had existed up to 1346 in the monastic communities, which was not repealed until the Dundas law of 1799.

The family of Fawside was active throughout these years, playing a colourful part in local and state affairs. On 10th November, 1616, "Fawsyde's servitor, Robert Robertson, was delailit for the crewel slaughter of umquhile John Fawside in the barn of Fawside, with a knife or dagger. He paid for this on the Castle Hill of Edinburgh where he was beheaded."

In 1613 Robert of Fawside sold the estate to an Edinburgh merchant named Hamilton. Robert Fawside's younger brother, John of Fawside, accompanied James VI to England as a "Bowbearer" in 1603. We lose records of the Scottish family of Fawside in the latter part of the 17th century but John Fawside established his family near Robin Hood's Bay, in Yorkshire.

The work

The motto of the Fawside family who built the castle was most apposite: "Forth and fear nocht". To my mind that was the right way to start the restoration! We had planned to carry out the work, bit by bit, primarily out of concern for cash flow. We wouldn't have started had we known what the job was finally going to cost, but we decided to plunge into the unknown, slowly.

The first task was to measure the building. This was quite difficult since we could not get access to any height greater that the length of a ladder. We created 20 ft-long measuring poles and used photography to give us some idea of the vertical dimensions. An early requirement, to convert the barn into an office, workshop and bed-sit for the architect, necessitated services to be installed. Mains water was some 50 or more yards away but had insufficient head to reach the proposed header tank in the roof. We installed a 1000 litre fibreglass tank

Tom Craig – Fawside Castle

in the barn with a pump to force the water up to the roof in due course. Electricity was about 220 yards away and we were asked to make a nominal contribution to the cost of installation. The cost might have been 'nominal' to a small township but I thought it was excessive until I checked out the specification of the cable. Indeed, it turned out that my contribution was nominal! The cable was led underground across a field and terminated in the barn. We had to create an earth leakage trip, which was achieved by driving a heavy-duty copper pipe deep into the ground. No mains sewage was in the vicinity so we had to build a septic tank. We decided that a sixteen seater should be adequate! Soakaway tests which had to be carried out were successful. Telephone lines were led underground from half a mile away for a nominal connection charge. We decided that a pay phone would be a good idea, plus a separate line for the burglar alarm which contacted the local police station. At a later date we installed a primitive solid fuel boiler to provide hot water and central heating for the office, since in winter the temperature fell to mind and body-numbingly low levels. Having the office on site meant that Ian was able to draw there and act as Clerk of Works, which saved much travelling time and also gave us, and him, an element of tight control. It had the added advantage that an excellent relationship was built up between the architect and the trades people. Ian didn't think that he knew all there was to know about building, so the trades people assisted him considerably and willingly. It made a change from the normal situation where the trades people quite often fall out with the architect when they feel that they know more than the so-called 'professional'!

Inside the castle the first thing we had to do was to excavate the fallen stonework and debris that had accumulated from the collapsed vault and fallen internal wall, between B and C blocks. As stated above, the rubble was about five feet deep and removing it was a pick and shovel job, which took time and toned up the muscles. The doorway had insufficient width to allow the use of a dump truck, so everything had to be wheel barrowed outside. We found no interesting artefacts during the excavation except the discovery of the scale and platt stairway, which was architecturally important. Also interesting was unearthing an open gutter, cut in the floor of the kitchen, leading from one corner, through the kitchen door and out through the entrance. At the time we did not realise its use but when the weather changed and the temperature increased - lo and behold! Water began to trickle along the gutter and out of the house; obviously there was a spring in the vicinity.

We submitted drawings to the local authority for planning approval after having discussed all aspects of the restoration in detail with the HBC. By and large there were no major points of contention. On the whole we had few problems with the Building Regulations. Each room has adequate light, except for the ground floor of the old tower. This was classified as a store room. An interesting interpretation of the Fire Regulations was suggested by the authorities themselves. The old tower has a stone stair running from the roof to the entrance door, so there were no egress problems. The new tower has a stone scale and platt stair from the other entrance door to the first floor. You then have to walk through a room with a wooden floor before ascending the spiral stairs. One suggestion was to put a fireproof corridor connecting the two stairs. This would have ruined the dining hall (B1). The authorities then came up with the proposal that there was a safe exit from the first floor by going down the scale and platt stairs and that egress from any of the higher rooms would be to go up the spiral stairs, across the top room, onto the roof, then down the old tower stairs! This required that only the floor of the top room had to be made fire-proof.

The HBC was concerned lest the tower became a fairytale Disney castle. It was difficult to know what the original roof to the L-plan spiral stair had been. Unusually, the two roofs of B and C blocks were parallel, as opposed to being at right angles. The south gable of C block had collapsed, so we had to guess the original construction. We searched widely to find buildings having a similar roof structure but to no avail. This also involved tracking down old drawings, paintings and photographs of the castle, including an oil painting in the surgery of a Musselburgh doctor. We found one photograph in the library of the RCAHMS which showed the north gable of C block in a dilapidated state but clearly with a doorway leading to the roof of the old tower. In fact, the wallhead of the turret probably rose above the apex of the gable to permit a complete conical roof. If we had constructed it in this manner the roof would have been very prominent, so we compromised with the height to produce a visually satisfactory solution. This meant building in a reinforced lintel in the gable which certainly would not have been the original construction.

The HBC insisted that we harl the complete building, although there was no definite evidence that it had been harled originally. This decision suited us since it meant that we could restore the walls and cap house in brick and use stone lintels, jambs and crowsteps, as appropriate. We had intended to harl in the attractive buff colour that is a characteristic of many East Lothian houses and which blends so well with the harvest landscape but this wish was overruled by the Council who demanded that it should be white.

We sought grant assistance from every potentially interested organisation, be it a charity, trust, local authority or Council. The HBC made an initial offer for grant-related work. This was rather less than we had hoped for but as a result of developments they were able to make a greater contribution at a later stage. On applying to the local authority for a house improvement grant, we were bemused by their reply. Having considered our application they decided, with regret, that they were unable to help us, since the object of the improvement grant was to provide facilities for a house for the first time, or for a building that was being converted to a domestic dwelling. No matter how we looked at this, we thought that both of these criteria should apply to us! Other than a very kind personal gift of twenty-five pounds from a trustee of a charity, we received warm accolades for the project but no financial help. Overall, however, must be mentioned the facility that we received from the Bank. They persevered with us, through thick and thin, when others would have pulled the proverbial plug.

So much interest in the proposed restoration had been shown by the local population that we decided to mount an exhibition in the Brunton Hall, Musselburgh, with a polystyrene model of the castle and supporting drawings. We invited all interested societies and clubs to the reception since there had been certain mutterings of discontent arising from our submission for planning consent. Nigel Tranter opened the reception in robust style and invited those with any criticisms of the plans 'to raise them now or for ever to hold your peace'. This fairly took the wind from the sails of those who were happy to snipe from the protection of letters but who were not prepared to stand their ground in front of others.

At this stage I would like to mention some of the materials used: wood, stone, slate, nails, hinges and chandeliers. We were extremely fortunate regarding timber, which we managed to acquire locally from Lennoxlove Estate, after they had recently felled a forest of Douglas Fir. Second hand timber, in those days, cost £1.00 per cubic foot, with nails in it, or £1.50 if de-nailed. We were offered new timber at £2.00 per cubic foot. I thought that at this price the Duke must have been employing feudal serfs from his estate, who were laboriously using hand saws in pits! I therefore arranged a visit to the saw mill. I found it extremely well equipped with the most up to date machinery. The Manager was happy to cut the beams exactly to our specification. One in particular that I remember was the central beam for the Great Hall floor which was one foot square by seventeen feet long - a beautiful piece of wood. We also wanted planking to make broad floor boards, about an inch thick, which we were able to air-season as we had plenty of time. The fact that we didn't want the timber cut in specific widths, but wished it to be random, delighted him and made it easier and less costly to supply, due to the minimal wastage. We also used Douglas Fir for all doors and window frames.

We bought the roof from a maltings which was being demolished, nearby, at Joppa. The long timber rafters were in quite good condition and of a fair size, mainly 11 x 3 inches, but they contained hundreds of nails. We bought several claw hammers and employed local lads to extract the nails. The slates were laboriously loaded onto lorries and then unloaded into the barn for future use. The timber was used for fitting out the barn, staging and for temporary works. Any that was to be used in the restoration was treated by Rentokil. However, we did miss the opportunity of recycling the timber from Granton Pier, which was being dismantled at the time. The pier must have been constructed from Red Pine, at least a hundred years ago. We obtained a sample which looked well worn and dirty but when it was machined off the condition was virtually as new. The staining was only about one eighth of an inch deep and the wood emitted a wonderfully strong resinous smell.

There were no quarries currently working in East Lothian, so we were forced to go further afield to obtain supplies of stone. We bought freshly quarried sandstone from Watsons, which came from Doddington and Springwell quarries, both in Northumberland. The dressed stone in the old tower had a reddish colour, which was well matched by the Doddington stone. That from Springwell had a warm honey colour and was used for both inside and outside the L-tower. It was brought onto site in blocks, some of up to 10 ft. long x 3 ft. wide and 2 ft. high. The feat of moving these vast chunks of stone about the site was impressive, particularly since we did not have craneage. The Egyptians had an easier time, since they had thousands of slaves!

One of the advantages of having an engineering company at one's disposal was that most of the required metal components could be produced in the smiths' shop. This covered anything from fabricating doors for the barn, flame-cut door hinges, re-inforcing brackets and, finally, an impressive-looking chandelier for the Great Hall. We had fun in obtaining a supply of clench nails for the doors, a considerable number of which were required. One part of my post graduate training had been working with a firm in Sweden where they made a large range of nuts and bolts, using vast machines that thumped them out in a most efficient display of mass production. I sent over a sample of a hand forged nail to see if they could make a few hundred which, at one per second, did not represent a very long production run. The firm wrote back quoting some extraordinary (but no doubt realistic) price, which was far too high to accept. Following my refusal, they came back offering a substantial reduction and, after further negotiation, they decided to make them for us free of charge. And so they thumped out some 2,000 clench nails in high tensile bolt steel, which represented less than one hour's production. The head of the sample that I sent over was slightly eccentric with, of course, the distinctive marks from hammer blows. Back came the new nails, all identical, with perfectly reproduced hammer blows and, of course, an eccentric head!

With all the rubble cleared from the building and the necessary permissions granted, we started the restoration proper on the ground floor of block B (BG). This was the room with the collapsed vault and gutter which we planned to reinstate as the kitchen. Rebuilding the vault in traditional style, using stone and a semi-circular former, would have been prohibitively expensive, so we used a process similar to building ferro-concrete boats. Three eighths of an inch steel rods were bent to the correct radius and held vertically in place by stringers. Chicken wire mesh layers were then tied by wire to both the inside and outside of the rods, which created a rigid structure. Concrete was trowelled into and through this mesh to provide a very strong reinforced concrete vault, which was then plastered.

As the ground outside was quite a bit higher than the lowest internal floor level, we reckoned that we could have a serious damp problem, added to by the presence of the gutter crossing the floor and the water that trickled along it, from time to time. We therefore enlarged the gutter, improved its course, and infilled with stones to give free flow to any water that accumulated. The gutter plus an additional trench was used to bring services both into and out of the building. A damp-proof membrane covered the entire floor, on top of which concrete was poured in order to form the floor proper. We used a plaster called Devonite

Fig. 8
The new arch for the kitchen fireplace. The middle recess is a large salt aumbry. Behind this (in darkness) is the oven, which was left unrestored but covered. Some of the service drains, which can be seen, run inside the chimney.

(from Newton Abbot) on the vault, which proved particularly successful in combating damp. After the first layer, about ¹/₂ inch thick, roughly 90% of the damp was prevented. Further coats were applied on the remaining damp areas until we had eliminated any problem of dampness.

The fireplace arch in BG was 10 ft wide by 6 ft 6 ins high. This was reinstated with a beautiful Springwell stone arch. The oven, which is behind the rear right hand corner of the fireplace (see Fig. 4, p124), was left as we found it. We did not attempt to rebuild it since I felt that there was a limit to what one could take on at any one time, so it was left for a future generation to restore. Typical salt boxes were present in the sides of the fireplace. Within the fireplace we placed worktops, oven and hob and LPG fired boiler for domestic hot water and central heating. (We had a separate LPG system for the old tower). A ceiling with sunken lighting was placed above the sight line of the arch and blocked off the chimney. The chimney provided a perfect central route for all the services. Domestic hot and cold water, electricity, telephone, roof drainage, domestic drains, sewage plus the boiler flue, are all invisibly inserted and tapped off at the appropriate levels.

Once we had completed the ground floor we proceeded upwards and installed the next floor and worked on this basis until the wall head had been established

Fig. 9
Roofs on, turrets reinstated and chimneys rebuilt. Temporary wooden staging was cantilevered out from the wallhead. Barmkin wall repaired.

Fig. 10
Wooden staging was erected to allow the turret roof to be fabricated and slated. Turrets were rebuilt from the base, using brick, with dressed stone around the windows and wall head.

and the roof constructed. By this method we never needed to use external scaffolding until the harling was carried out. When we got to roof level we projected out temporary wooden staging to allow the roof to be built. (Fig. 9). Standing on the staging felt precarious, but it was stoutly built in wood, with substantial safety railings. (Fig. 10). All the tradesmen were very safety conscious and it is good to report that during the time of the restoration we had no accidents, other than minor cuts and grazes. Standing at the wall head level was unnerving, since the wind frequently blew with a vengeance. One does not need to go up to Ian Begg country in Plockton to experience wet and windy weather. Every time I was up on the walls I got colder and colder but that didn't appear to stop the builders, although one of the main hazards was getting cold and thus losing dexterity.

In an attempt to assuage the relentless wind, one of the earlier tasks had been to plant several hundred trees (a deciduous and coniferous chequerboard) in the field, and to surround the perimeter with a beech hedge For months, even years, no great growth was discernible. Perhaps they were so shocked by the wind that they retreated underground and put down roots for the future. Eventually they started to push their way up and now look quite substantial, having reduced the wind blow and chill factor considerably.

A major operation was restoring the spiral stairs, one in each tower. The treads were made of reinforced concrete with the visible surfaces being made of cast stone. A wooden female mould of the finished size was made and the internal

Fig. 11
Restoration of the east facing wall, finished and harled. The owner's initials under the rose, (with date of restoration under the thistle on the other dormer pediment).

surfaces coated with a suitable releasant. A half inch thick layer of suitably coloured sand and cement was rammed against the front (vertical) face of the mould. This was followed by a wire mesh armature with reinforcing rod being inserted into the void, with a 'Z' shaped piece of flat steel bar, one end of which projected outside the mould for tying into the stair wall, on assembly. A fairly coarse and dry concrete mixture was poured into the mould with the final top surface being a half inch thick sand and cement mixture. A steel sleeve was inserted, at the newel, to ease assembly in the stairwell and to provide repeatable accuracy. We cast about one tread per day and, when we had accumulated about five, installed them.

As Ian Cumming explained, 30% of the time on a building site is spent handling and moving materials. The prospect of manhandling everything up spiral staircases was daunting, so we cantilevered a beam out of the wall head and installed an electric hoist. This certainly eliminated much potentially wasted time.

Hunter Moran, our stonemason, was in his element and painstakingly carved some beautiful pieces which really were works of art. The two barley sugar water spouts were carved, with no drawings and taking guidance only from the very worn original spouts. On one occasion I thought I was going to upset him because he was laboriously chipping away at the blocks with a mell and chisel. I thought it would be more efficient to use some power, so I tentatively asked if he would like some pneumatic tools. His response, fortunately, was most enthusiastic, so I provided the machinery. That greatly speeded up the time-consuming roughing process. The quality of his dressed stonework, both inside and out, was excellent. This included some window and door surrounds and,

Fawside Castle – Tom Craig

in particular, two dormer windows, where a finely carved thistle and a rose each top one of the pediments. (Fig. 11). He also created a most impressive flat arch mantelpiece, about ten feet long and fifteen inches deep. (Fig. 12).

We decided that we would incorporate 4 inch thick insulation on all the exterior walls of the L-tower, purely for increased comfort and to reduce heat loss, using plasterboard for the internal surface. This was successful but, of course, did not have the solidity and deadness of plaster on stone. Ben Tindall designed a simple but heavy cornice which was run around the ceiling of B1, the dining hall, above the kitchen, which we always referred to as the cathedral, since it was my hope to install a pipe organ in it, one day.

We had to reinstate the dividing wall which had completely collapsed between B and C blocks. We rebuilt in brick and took the opportunity of incorporating a lift shaft, which might seem incongruous, but since my father and Claire's mother both suffered from arthritis, we decided to plan for the future. The HBC wasn't too keen on the idea but conceded that, provided we left three projecting stones from the collapsed wall untouched, we could go ahead. The lift shaft therefore starts about eighteen inches out from the wall. This gap proved a very useful space in which to run additional services and central heating. Due to the thickness of the original wall, we were able to build in a shaft of about 40 inches square, without outward intrusion. The lift shaft extended from the first floor to the top, servicing all the rooms and the machinery space was built into C block's roof.

As work progressed floor by floor, we found one or two interesting architectural features. At B2 level the space was turned into the laird's bedroom, with a large walk-in storage cupboard and a bathroom. In the bathroom there was a cupboard in the thickness of the wall, behind which we found a mural chamber

Fig. 12
A genuine 10 ft long flat arch in B1. The 4 inch thick insulation can be seen, plus an ash receptical/air vent in the hearth.

Fawside Castle – Tom Craig

with a sunken recess; perhaps it had served as a charter chest. For ease of maintenance and simplicity of installation, we decided to put the bathroom units on a plinth, some 15 inches above the floor.

At B3 we created another two bedrooms and a bathroom. The south facing room is particularly attractive, having additional windows to the east and west, quite a handsome fireplace and the two turrets. During the period of restoration we had three additions to the family and one of the turrets was often used for feeding the children; my mother-in-law thought it would be a most attractive space in which to die - this would have been most inconvenient! Behind the fireplace in the other bedroom is a deep recess, which might have been a priest's hole or another charter chest.

In spite of extensive research, we found little guidance as to what had been the pitch of the roof. The final solution was to erect a timber silhouette and walk down the road to judge the appearance for ourselves. By trial and error we achieved a well balanced assembly of the two roofs, in addition to those of the two turrets, plus the spiral stair which I have already mentioned. The roof structure was conventional, but we used plywood sheets in place of sarking boards. Handling the plywood sheets could only be undertaken in calm weather for fear of the board and the joiner both being blown overboard. Heavy-duty felt was laid under the slates. The plumber who carried out the lead work was excellent and the resulting roofs are very sound. We cast the rigging from reconstituted stone. Inside the roof area (or attic) we applied thick insulation and even put down flooring.

We were concerned about external drainage from the roof, both from the aesthetic point of view and from the practicality of maintenance. Most buildings deteriorate due to poorly designed and defective drainage, so I was determined to take extra care over this feature. I particularly dislike lots of vertical down pipes, which are ugly and require painting, so we decided that the majority of rain water from the roofs would be led to a central down pipe in the kitchen chimney. As a result, the valley gutter between B and C roofs runs to an open stone gutter in the parapet walk of A block. Moran Hunter carved an attractive stone spout which incorporated the lead flashing. The rain water from the outside slopes of the L-tower is led along cast iron gutters and through the wall head of A block. Water from the two turrets was discharged through the two barley sugar water spouts to which I referred earlier. The only less than ideal area was in the re-entrant angle, where we had to collect the water by gutter, and bring it down in an aluminium pipe. Because I also dislike the appearance of gutters passing across windows, I had considered using down pipes built into the wall. On reflection, however, we decided that the extra complexity and difficulty of maintenance were not justified, so gutters pass in front of three windows.

Having completed the L-tower, we then turned our attention to the rectangular tower, or A block. Nigel Tranter had suggested that we might consider leaving this section of the building as a ruin. Whereas this would have reduced the cost of restoration considerably, one of the major attractions for us was the

Fawside Castle – Tom Craig

combination of the two essentially different towers and how they had been integrated, to form a single building, for the needs of the occupants in the 17th century.

Communication between the towers had been made on the first three of the four levels and across the roof to C5. A doorway had been cut through the south wall of AG which leads to CG. On the first floor there is a wonderful passage of about 16 ft long, firstly through the 10 ft thickness of the south wall of A1 and then past the kitchen chimney in B block. It was very coarsely hewn with a large entrant radius and beautiful curve, no attempt being made to use dressed stone. Le Corbusier would have been proud to have executed such a design! (Fig. 13). Finally, one of the south facing windows on A2 had been enlarged to form a doorway to C3, with the other window being blocked up.

The amount of work required to restore A block was much less extensive than that for the L-tower. The spiral stair was reinstated as for the other stair, and it was interesting to note that the treads were higher and of a 'key-hole' shape. When first built, the tower had only one fireplace, in the Great Hall. The 17th century refurbishment suggested that the old tower was not used for the principal apartments, since the Great Hall fireplace had been crudely reduced in width to allow the flue from the new fireplace, below, to pass up and join the main chimney. By reducing the depth of the chimney with an artificial fire-back we were able to reinstate the Great Hall fireplace to its former size and lead the second flue and services behind. The floors were reinstated, which required some new stone corbels to be inserted to support the beams. The Great Hall floor had one massive beam dividing the length in two, with smaller beams laid at right angles from each end to the central beam. I checked by calculation that

Fig. 13
The long corridor between A1 and B1. Scotch plastered and irregular.

Fawside Castle – Tom Craig

it would take the dynamic loading of two sixteensome reels! We cleaned the walls of all the rooms as there still remained some of the old plaster which had been reinforced with horse hair. We 'scotch' plastered the walls, which involved trowelling plaster directly onto the stone, following the shapes of the stones, making no attempt to produce a flat surface. After the plaster had been applied, the surface was smoothed by sponge. The lack of flatness and straight lines was most refreshing.

The wall head or parapet had to be completely rebuilt and we opted for a simple crenellated wall, without a string course. The roof had a 3 ft wide walk inside the wall head, with gentle slopes to lead the water, in a gutter, round to the main down-pipe in the chimney. The vaulted roof was finished with two shallow pitches, covered by heavy duty roof felt. Over the felt we laid two-inch-thick dense polystyrene insulation, a thick screed of concrete and finally stone slabs. It is surprising the variation in temperature that occurs with the stone slabs. In winter the temperature obviously goes down to below freezing and in summer, with the sun beating down, the temperature might get as high as 40°C. This wide difference in temperature causes noticeable thermal expansion. The cap house is rectangular with a steeply pitched roof and stone crow steps. We provided a bird loft within the apex of the roof to accommodate a friendly kestrel, which stayed with us during most of the restoration.

SECTION LOOKING EAST

Windows are a fascinating subject and, metaphorically speaking, reflect the domestic requirements of the inhabitants. The original fenestration of the old tower was non-existent at ground level and only started at a safe height, indicating that security was more important than luxury. The windows were few and small, with a solid stone lintel. There was evidence of fixed glazing for the upper half and wooden shutters below. Not a great deal of light would have entered the rooms and there are stone seats in the window ingos. In the 17th century refurbishment, the windows which caught the sun were substantially enlarged and the stone seats removed. Those where the sun did not penetrate were left as originally built. We restored the enlarged openings with casement windows and the original small windows with fixed glazing and shutter boards. (Fig. 14).

WEST ELEVATION

EAST ELEVATION

In the L-tower the size of the windows was much greater, showing that times during the late 15th / early 16th century were perhaps more peaceful, although the windows still had iron grilles. Relieving arches were used to spread the weight of masonry. We decided on casement windows for simplicity and to allow maximum light to enter. To put in sash and casement windows would have been difficult, requiring expensive modification to the jambs, with a resultant reduction in area of glass. Whereas the casement windows can open for ventilation, they are of such a size that it would have been difficult to prevent excessive wind from entering the room. We planned therefore to have one pane capable of being swivelled, to provide ventilation. Another decision was to have the casement windows opening inwards, to allow easy and safe maintenance. This was a good idea in theory but it did make rainproofing and sealing more complex. I am not certain if, on balance, it was the best option.

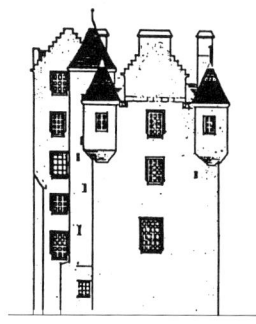
SOUTH ELEVATION

Fig. 14
Sections and elevations of the drawings submitted for planning consent.

Fawside Castle – Tom Craig

The woodwork throughout was skilfully carried out. The choice of Douglas fir, although a difficult wood to work, was most successful and it exuded a reddish golden warmth to the building. We had a most happy association with the joiners - Robertson and Thomson - one was small and typically Scots, the other a large cheerful local tradesman. They had a well equipped workshop some three miles away where they ran the timber and prefabricated the doors and windows. The electrical installation was another success story. It was carried out by one man on his own, who turned up as required and never held us back.

The final task was to harl the complete building. This was the only occasion when external scaffolding was required. A lot of preparatory work had to be undertaken in order to infill the effects of the wind and weather erosion that had occurred over many, many years. The team of harlers came on site and covered one face at a time. We were getting dangerously close to winter and heavy frosts, added to which high winds would sometimes prevent the work from being started.

We finally, finally finished! (Fig. 15).

In concluding, I would remark that, in reality, considering the scale of the restoration, we had very few problems. We progressed slowly, over a long period, with the result that few mistakes were made. The restoration was a team effort, with each member and craft dovetailing to produce a simple restoration of real quality. Hunter Moran has given me an assurance that the building, six hundred years old, will last for a further six hundred years, until it requires a further renovation! We have had tremendous satisfaction and enjoyment in bringing back to life what is now once again a solidly imposing tower house, doing justice to its spectacular situation. Having previously appeared as a sore and crumbling tooth on the hilltop, it now looks down commandingly over Edinburgh, the surrounding country and the Firth of Forth! It is interesting to reflect on the

Fig. 15
Fawside Castle after restoration in 1982. Spectacularly positioned on Fawside Hill, it has panoramic views over Edinburgh to the Pentland Hills, over the Forth to Fife, around East Lothian, the Lammermuir Hills and the Moorfoot Hills.

Fawside Castle – Tom Craig

changes that have taken place during its history - it is impossible even to dream of what the next six hundred years will bring - but Fawside Castle will bear witness.

Fig. 1
Mains Castle.
Photo: Robert McCallum.

Mains Castle

BY MIKE ROWAN, OWNER AND RESTORER.

When I was eight I crawled through a small hole in the walls of the ruins of Mearns Castle, Glasgow, and from that moment I began to dream that one day I would have a castle of my own! Mearns Castle was a real, no-compromise building, entirely of stone and extremely sound. I liked that a lot, but unfortunately by the time I was old enough even to contemplate its purchase, it had been bought. My first lesson, therefore, was to act fast, as there are many more dreamers that ruined castles.

My desire to build a house of my own spurred me on in the quest for a castle. It seemed to me that if the walls already existed, half the problem was already solved. I began to look for a small, simple shell of a building, in reasonable condition. To my great surprise I found one very quickly and easily. Buying it, however, proved to be a different kettle of fish altogether. The price slowly crept up and the terms became more and more difficult. It is far easier to sell than to buy, and in the end I was unable to purchase Caldwell Tower, but the experience did give me a much clearer idea of what I was looking for.

After that I have visited about five hundred towers or castles. Some were engulfed in huge Victorian mansions and others were nothing more than a site, with no visible trace of the building! There were a lot of near misses, but being a great believer in 'whatever will be, will be,' I finally found Mains Castle, (Fig. 1), near East Kilbride and negotiated its acquisition off the neighbouring farmer. Unfortunately for me, a slip up was made in acquiring the title and a new access which had been agreed was not incorporated into the title. This meant that all materials, vehicles and daily entry and exiting had to be past the farmer's front door and through the outflow from his midden. This triggered years of unpleasantness and strife. The final approach was then along a very rocky and muddy road. My second lesson, learnt too late, was to ensure one's own unhindered access! Fortunately, I eventually obtained that!

A bit of history

Seventy yards to the North of the castle is a Norman motte, believed to have been built by Roger de Valoins. One hundred and fifty yards to the South there is a crannog, probably created about 850 BC (along with the majority of Scottish crannogs). Three quarters of a mile further North there is an anti-aircraft battery, built in 1939. In a straight line, therefore, there are four generations of castles or fortifications, so to speak, ranging from 850 BC to 1939 AD.

The motte was taken over by the Red Comyn, who met his come-uppance in Dumfries. One of the Lindsays, the Lindsay of Dunrod (who went to "mak siccur" that the Red Comyn was really dead, having been mortally wounded by Bruce) got right in with the Bruces, for his troubles.

The lands of Kilbride, on which Mains Castle stands, were then given to John

Mains Castle – Mike Rowan

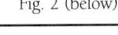

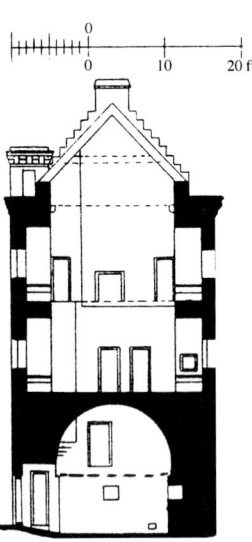

Fig. 2 (below)

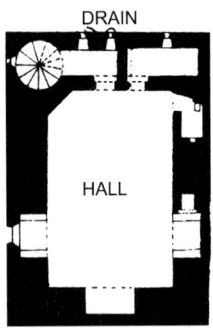

FIRST FLOOR

ENTRESOL

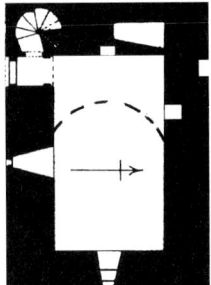

GROUND FLOOR

Lindsay of Dunrod by Robert II in 1384, the castle being built about 1450 on the site of the Mains Farm, to enhance the Old Kilbride Castle, which by then would have been rather delapidated.

In 1478 Princess Euphemia Stuart married David Lindsay (Provost of Glasgow) and they are believed to have stayed at Mains Castle, which remained in the family until Alexander Lindsay - the last of the Lindsays - was reduced to penury when legal costs and gambling considerably diminished the Lindsay fortune. Apparently, during the great Maxwell-Leckie feud, Alexander Lindsay fatally shot Alexander Leckie in the back, but was never brought to justice. However, he was forced to sell both Kilbride and Mains in 1619 and died in poverty in one of his former tenants' barns in 1630. We were invited to dinner by Bobby Younger, the restorer of Old Leckie, and were asked, before eating, if we knew that the last person to live in his house had been murdered by the last person to live in ours!

A brief description of the building in relation to use and defence

Mains Castle is a classic design for a 15th century keep. The outer dimensions measure 43 x 30 ft, with walls six feet thick on three sides and ten feet thick on the west. The inside space is relatively small but surprisingly cosy, and originally there were five floors. (Fig. 2, plans to the left). The ground floor (entresol) and the original first floor were enclosed in the stone barrel-vault, designed to protect the upper floors from fire attack at ground floor level. There animals, hay and grain (as rent) were stored. Rising through the height of the building in the thickness of the south-west corner is a spiral or turnpike stair, cunningly planned to turn in a clockwise direction, giving a right-handed swordsman the advantage over an intruder trying to fight his way up. The stair was kept very dark and the individual steps intentionally vary in height, so that in rushing up an unwitting invader would fall flat on his face! One castle in Dumfries, built for the Kerrs who were traditionally a left-handed family, actually has the spiral stair built anti-clockwise.

Above the barrel vault, effectively the old second floor, is the flagstoned Great Hall, which to-day still serves as a kitchen and general living quarters. Directly above that is the solar, where his lordship would have slept. It comprises two bedrooms, each with its own fireplace. There is a small recess in the furthest fireplace where the valuable salt would have been kept, dry and safe from thieving fingers.

The top floor or chamber would originally have been little more than a pigeon loft, but now it consists of an office-cum-bedroom, a further bedroom and the main bathroom. At each level there is also at least one mural chamber, a small vaulted room, contained in the thickness of the wall. From the ground floor up these are; the pit prison with access only from the guardroom above; the guardroom itself - now a loo, still with the original access to the pit; the pantry - currently the 'wet' kitchen; and two other garderobes, which were both mediaeval loos.

Oddly enough, within half a century of completion, Mains Castle almost became obsolete. Against bows and arrows as weapons it was a very strong house, for when firing down from the parapet there was a considerable better range for the defenders than for the attackers shooting up. However, the advent of artillery and hand guns around 1500 altered the whole emphasis of defence, which shifted from the parapet to the ground floor. Robert Clow has a theory that parapet walks went out of fashion in the 16th century because they always leaked. That might have been true at Aiket, but until the advent of guns one could appreciate the advantage of arrow firing or stone throwing from on high, down on the heads of adversaries below. An arrow, having a curved trajectory, is lethal even at the extreme limit of its range, as it falls on its target, each attacker being an individual target. However, a bullet has a straight trajectory (during its lethal phase) and it is much more effective at ground level. The attackers present a band of targets at ground level, so the bullet is likely to hit an attacker in the second or third row if it misses someone in the front. Seen from above, however, assailants still present themselves as individual targets, and if the bullet misses, it is more likely to hit the grass around about them, rather than anyone else. At that period there would also have been the problem of loosely fitting round bullets rolling out of downward-pointing barrels, when fired from a parapet walk!

Castle design therefore quickly forsook parapets in favour of gun loops at ground level. Scottish castles were still built to a considerable height, as this left a smaller area to defend at ground level and being built in the wilds, heavy artillery was not really a threat to them. To my delight, I discovered 25 bullet pockmarks on the stone around the south-facing loophole and after a considerable amount of research, deduced that this must have happened immediately after the Battle of Bothwell Brig. I reckoned that the famous Covenanters' standard which had flown at Bothwell Brig, the Kilbryde flag, had been carried from the field by the standard bearers, as they fled up the valley, on their way to Kittochside Farm, where it has remained ever since. The Standard party must have taken refuge in Mains Castle to escape the dragoons, who would have been 'mopping up' under the command of "Bloody Clavers" or "Bonny Dundee", the Episcopalian Royalist. I therefore dug a small section under the window and came up with two fragments of a lead bullet. With great anticipation, I sent them off to Strathclyde Police Ballistics Department. They turned out to be parts of a bullet from a First World War service revolver!

Whilst telling an Aberdeen mason about my theory, he advised me to look for sword sharpening marks on the lower walls. If you look around some of the ground-floor window ingoes and door jambs, it is possible to find that something sharp has been rubbed on the stone. The theory is that the owner's natural reaction, on looking out of the window and seeing a hostile party approaching, was to think, "Oh, Lord! Here they come and my sword's blunt!" When checked, I found several such marks.

On setting eyes on Mains Castle for the first time, I found it was a roofless ruin, without a splinter of wood in sight, but the walls were in good shape. Of course they needed repointing, but they were solid and upright, only one inch off the plumb in fifty feet, which is not bad after five hundred years! At the wallhead there was a great deal of restoration work to be done. The parapet walkway, its wall and the waterspouts all needed to be replaced, and one gable required to be rebuilt. I intended to do as much of the work as possible by myself, but a newly qualified architect-friend from Glasgow, John Wetten Brown, rashly agreed to work on site with me for a year. When working on the building his knowledge was invaluable and he was extremely useful in liaising with the architects I employed at the initial stage. But first, back to the beginning.

My work on Mains Castle

At the outstart, I would like to acknowledge my debt to Nigel Tranter for stimulating my interest in castles. It really was all his fault that I became involved in castle restoration in the first place. His books made everything appear to accessible and so possible. I poured through each of the five-volumed work and thereafter looked at about 500 towers! I ended up purchasing a 15th century ruin, but at least one that was fairly complete to the wallhead, right on my doorstep, then about one mile from East Kilbride.

To the south of the castle there used to be a loch, probably drained about 1750 as part of the agricultural improvements of the period. In it was a crannog, a piled dwelling built on the water, around which rubble and garbage slowly built up and eventually rose above the water level, to form an island.

When I first bought the castle off the local farmer, it was in the country. East Kilbride expanded to meet me but, thanks to the Secretary of State and a Public Enquiry, the Green Belt line has been drawn at Stewartfield Road, 500 yards to the South of Mains Castle. Now villas march over the skyline and down to the former edge of the loch, so I look out to suburbia, though the loch has subsequently been re-instated as a boating pond! Farewell to gravitas!

The present tower was built about 1450 and its silhouette hasn't altered since then, though the Victorians re-roofed the tower and consolidated the stonework, the north-west corner and the west gable. Fortunately, they hardly touched the few small windows, or formed new openings, so it was possible for me to perceive the original window detailing from the channels in the stone.

While we were restoring the castle, we lived in a beautiful Edwardian caravan, with cut-glass windows. Our friends and guests thought it was dead romantic, but it was a freezingly cold existence. After two extremely snowy winters, it was a blessing, but only a blessing in disguise, to move into an equally cold tower house! We were fortunate in our architects. I say architects, for initially my plans were drawn up by a firm called "Architectural Consultants Ltd.," whose office was in London, but their senior partner had a sympathetic feel for castle restoration.

As mentioned above, my on-site architect was local. Well, actually he was a final-year student at that time who was extremely helpful, practical, had style, and had dated my sister! Throughout the cold summer days of 1976 he worked with us on the scaffolding, mortaring, cutting, and re-building, as work progressed. He now specialises in castle restoration.

While clearing the ground floor barrel-vault, I found a hole in the floor. I struck a blade down a crevice and the pinchbar went down about three feet. "Wonderful", I thought. "I have found a well." So I persuaded an archaeologist to come out to excavate. He arrived with a hard hat, his miner's lamp and a ladder. I left him to it and went to work. Returning, I found him sitting in an old armchair, drinking whisky! It turned out that I had dug out a former pit about two feet down and, in prodding the bottom, my pinchbar had gone straight down a crack. He had cleared a further three inches and that was all there was to the hole. He thought it might have been some sort of cold store, perhaps filled with ice from the loch in winter and packed with straw.

At entresol level to the upper half of the castle's single barrel vault, there is a pit prison, or oubliette, accessed through the floor of a guardroom, off the spiral stair. Below, at ground floor, there is a large vaulted basement, with a timber floor at the guardroom level. The whole building is served by a single, narrow and worn turnpike stair, rising from ground level to the caphouse and parapet walk. Leading off the stairway, above the guardroom and its oubliette, is the Great Hall, some 16 ft wide by 27 ft long, which matches the area of the vaulted basement. Sadly, the fireplace in the hall had collapsed in the 17th century and had been replaced by an arched, fairly crude, Victorian substitute. (Fig. 3). Off the Hall are two deep window recesses, to the north and south, complete with 15th century stone window seats. To the west is a small lockable foodstore. To the north is a small garderobe with bifurcating chutes, one of which, being unrecognised by the Victorian restorers, petered out when they built over it.

As with other restorers, I was (mostly) extremely fortunate with my tradesmen. I took on masons and worked with them, getting them to teach me their various skills. The masons worked at weekends and I spent every weekend alongside

Fig. 3
The Great Hall: hand azed beams, Wigan pavement slabs reused and bare walls. A 'real Scot's feel' to the rooms. Photo: Robert McCallum, by kind permission of Ruth Cooper.

Mains Castle – Mike Rowan

them. The state of the upper wallheads and gables left me more than nervous. The joints were hungry for mortar and I was concerned that the next time a strong east wind blew, it would bring the gables down!

The joiner worked during the week, and again I worked alongside him when I wasn't collecting materials. In the evenings I worked on, late at night with John Brown, talking about the plans and discussing alterations necessary in the light of what the day's work turned up. It was somewhat demanding but, as I mentioned, the tradesmen were really good, interested and interesting. The first joiner, Bill, was outstanding, a great worker, now sadly deceased. After my wedding he went on a bender to celebrate and never quite recovered, so I had to take on a new joiner. I advertised in Glasgow's Evening Times. Ten men replied, but only one shone right out. He was a really good man from a nearby town. Called "Shug", he is now, happily, a millionaire, but at that time he just looked a great big bruiser, and was really clever. Thinking clearly, after working with him for a week, I said to him, "Shug. I never asked you. Why did you leave your last job?" "Oh, I hit the boss," said he. "You did what?" "Hit the boss." "Why?" "Well," he said, "he accused me of stealing." "Well, did you?" "Aye, but . . ." he replied. However, he turned out to be a really faithful and honest soul. Perhaps he realised that it was a poor man's castle on which he was working, and that I was not rich, and still am not. On that basis we established a certain sort of honour!

As I mentioned, the building was fairly complete to the parapet walk, but Robert Clow has already mentioned that parapet walks always leak, and should any restorer wish confirmation of this fact they only need to verify it with Graham Carson of Rusco Tower. Even he now spouts the water well clear of his castle walls. The original waterspouts at Mains were very long, four feet in the wallhead, projecting two and a half feet over it, into the void. To recut them would have been very expensive. I made up a plasticene model and balanced it on the edge of a table. This gave me an indication of the size of stone I would need in the wallhead to prevent the waterspout couping over. My plasticene model was drawn up and sent to Ogden Yorkstone Ltd., in Yorkshire, who cut the spouts in stone. I eventually had to cut a drip once they were in position, as the run-off water ran back, down the underside of the spout and onto the castle walls. Without scaffolding and held by friends and ropes, hanging way out over the walls, I cut the drip channels with a stone cutting saw! I used a two-part rubber paint to make a water barrier under the parapet stones. This was eventually breached by water, so I replaced it with a stronger, two-part resin on the stone's surface. This worked a treat, although I understand that three coats of a 50/50 mix of linseed oil and olive oil are equally effective.

I told the architect how I wished the roof to be designed and she obtained detailed structures from a firm of structural engineers. They provided a different design, based on the roof being hung from a large, laminated beam, running from chimney gable to chimney gable. The mason, when he saw the design, asked why we were putting the strain on the weakest wall, as there were only six inches of stone skin on the chimneys. It made me think and, when having a look at Provand's Lordship in Glasgow, I found that the same structural engineers were inspecting its roof. I asked if I could have a look. To my astonishment, there was the same solution that I had originally suggested. The structural engineer somewhat sheepishly admitted that my own original concept would, in fact, work, so as a consequence we went ahead with a structure similar to that of the 15th century prebend's house!

The roof had been a source of worry throughout the winter, but in fact it was much easier to construct than anticipated. The only difficult problems were getting the angles right at both ends of the rafters and cutting each piece to the correct length. It took four of us as many days to complete the woodwork and with two slaters it took about two weeks to sort, cut and hang the slates. At first I had intended to use grey West Highland slates, but while digging a drainage trench I discovered a 15th century blue Westmoreland slate from the original roof, so I decided to use them instead. Apparently at the time the castle was built the Lowland Scots were on much better terms with the English than they were with the Lord of the Isles.

Building Control insisted on both sarking and felting under the slates and as we were to use the attic as living space, we inserted cat-slide dormers. The Architectural Heritage Society of Scotland's local Strathclyde Group suggested pedimented windows, but with the Westmoreland slates, obtained from one of Glasgow's High Street goods yards (then being currently demolished), we felt cat-slide dormers (Fig. 4) would be less visually obstructive, when viewed from below if they protruded marginally over the parapet wall, or if seen from a distance.

I mentioned the reliability of the workmen. Well, that was true for most of the trades, but not for our slaters. It's strange. Robert Clow told me he had

Fig. 4
Dormers and parapet walk, off which the slater nearly spun before the parapet wall was re-instated. Victorian Caphouse and the overhanging waterspout in the background.
Photo: Robert McCallum.

Mains Castle – Mike Rowan

exactly the same problems and at Aiket his slaters had to employ someone outwith the firm to slate the turret and stair cap, as both tasks were beyond them. In fact, the slaters I used were terrible. At one stage we were working fairly far up the roof (and remember we hadn't rebuilt the parapet wall by then). One of the slaters was walking along the partially slated roof, one foot lower than the other, when suddenly he tripped. Now, these men could not work unless they had a pint in them. They would go out at lunch time and sometimes wouldn't come back. Alternatively, they would return with their carry-outs in a bag and work away at that height with their carry-outs nearby. Anyway, this lad tripped and ran straight down the roof. When his foot hit the edge of the wallhead, he just spun round and as he regained his balance he walked off, along the parapet at a right-angle, as if nothing had happened!

Whilst working on the roof we had to line the chimney, down to the Hall. I could easily climb down the chimney as its internal dimensions were six feet wide by two. We planned to put an 18 ft ladder down from the roof top and extended this at the bottom with a rope. This would meet a short ladder that we had inserted up the chimney from the fireplace in the Great Hall, at first floor level. Giving me the means of bolting the flue, made out of Selkirk metalbestos sections, all the way down, I should then be able to drill suitable plugholes, appropriately. One night, and by this time it was mid-December, I decided to start work, aided by a friend. When we got onto the roof we found it was somewhat windy. We laid the ladder along the roof ridge and the two of us slowly pushed it up until it was vertical, in order to give us access to the chimney. Suddenly the ladder slipped. We just caught it at the last minute before it shot over the parapet wall. Having fixed the flue, the ladder remained down the chimney for two further years!

The caphouse gives sole entry onto the parapet walk. However, its original construction at Mains has always proved a bit of a puzzle, for the Victorians rebuilt it in such a strange manner as almost to inhibit access onto the walkway. (See also Fig. 4). Now access onto the roof is somewhat restricted to all but the fairly agile who are prepared to bend and crawl under a very low lintel, whilst simultaneously climbing a very steep step.

In planning the internal use of the building, it was my intention to restore the castle without compromise, using traditional materials and finishes, wherever possible. However, there is an element of compromise in that I have electricity and plumbing, but the building has a very Scots feel, particularly the Great Hall, where bare stone walls, worn stone flags, timber window frames with oblong leaded lights, heavy timber beams and timber ceilings, don't exactly soften the appearance. If the Lindsays were rich, they undoubtedly would have hung tapestries and laid rushes on the floor, in order to soften the atmosphere. When dining by candlelight, particularly in winter as I often did, it was not hard to imagine the atmosphere of life at Mains in the 15th century.

At one time I had thought of using the ground floor as the kitchen and re-instating the entresol, entry to which was off the building's sole spiral stair. The side walls of the ground floor are two feet closer together than the springing of the vault, so there is a one foot ledge running along the base of the vaulting, to take the first floor joist. However, I didn't progress the thought and used the area instead as a store chamber. In MacGibbon and Ross, mention is made of the Lindsays' extensive outbuildings. Despite having cut several trenches I found no traces of these foundations, so the absence of any additional space therefore started to determine our use of what was available, within the castle walls

When we acquired the castle, the Great Hall had wall to wall grass, as the original flags no doubt floored several local farm kitchens. The slabs I laid used to form part of a pavement - in Wigan, of all places. We planned to lay them at the same level as the original floor. Everything had to be hauled up by hand and it has been estimated that we lifted some six hundred tons of materials, including the stone flags, into the castle! We cleared the earth infill on top of the vault, riddling the entire volume of soil to see what we could find, but only finding a fragment of mediaeval glass which showed, infuriatingly, that the original windows were diamond leaded. In the meantime I had already made most of the windows with rectangular panes! We re-filled the void above the vault with concrete on the day before we were married in the Great Hall, then laid the slabs when we came back from our honeymoon - in Gourock!

As already mentioned, there is a guardroom at first floor level on the west wall, just past the entrance to the entresol. As you enter the guardroom, you step over the trapdoor, the only access to the pit prison, which is a grim little room, 7 x 3 x 8 ft high. The only ventilation is provided by a tiny window, 1 x 3 inches, which opens immediately beside the base of the garderobe chute. I converted the guardroom into a garderobe, hiding all the modern plumbing in a chase in the stonework with a stone slab, in which I cut out a hole, so the stone acted as the toilet seat, following my policy of purity in finishes. (Fig. 5). At first it was so cold, that I couldn't concentrate when going to the loo! The next day I made a wee wooden seat, removable for aesthetes! But compromise was already to be seen, as I had put a flat cistern at the back, hidden behind the stone, and a toilet bowl, plus appropriate piping to the septic tank. These were installed underneath and behind the stone seat. I had also made and fitted a small copper

Fig. 5
Plumbing and toilet seat. The single stack drainage was cut into the wall on the right. I was particularly proud of the toilet-roll holder, also on the right, cut into the stone!
Photo: Robert McCallum.

Mains Castle – Mike Rowan

basin into the slit window ingo.

It was Robert Clow who put me onto a source for the 12 x 12 inch timber joists of the Great Hall which are also to be found at Aiket, but I used them in a different manner. At Mains the joist recesses were all there at three foot centres, so we decided to reinstate them exactly the way they had been built. As a consequence, they give a very pleasing ribbed effect to the ceiling. However, they were huge and each weighed eight hundredweight and were hauled up to the Great Hall floor by just two of us, with the aid of a truck and block and tackle, a somewhat exciting prospect as neither of us had ever tried anything like that before. The large timbers had previously formed the sides of one of the Scott Lithgow graving docks. I hand-adzed the joists clean, which gave them the feel and look of the original hand-finished timber. If you have never used an adze, then I must warn you that it will take more out of your hand than any other tool! It's the fastest blister-raiser in the building business! Leaving the palms blistered, the wrists and arms ache and using one is extremely hard work. One learns by experience and, given another opportunity, I would have floored in a different manner. To manhandle the beams into place I invited twelve hefty friends round, and even then it was quite a struggle to manoeuvre them into the first joist hole (which we had deepened) then slip them back into the other, opposite hole. I used second-hand timber for the flooring. We sanded one side and turned the planks over, laying them onto the heavy beams. Then we put 2 x 2 inch battens down and laid a further floor on top, sanding and varnishing to give the timber a clean finish. I'm now wiser after the event! Unfortunately all the noise travels through the floor, from above, and is magnified below. Then we discovered we had a problem with dust, which appeared able to filter through every crack between each floorboard. Undoubtedly, a sheet of polythene between floors would have sorted out the dust problem, and 2 x 2 inch battens, with a strip of polystyrene or similar sound deafening bonded onto the lower third, leaving a floating floor, would have provided a quieter castle.

Cooking is by an oil-fired Aga. You will have noticed that castle restorers tend to favour bright red Agas. In using the ground floor for storage, we were left with the necessity of cooking in the Great Hall which, after all, they did in mediaeval times. It had the advantage that the Hall would always be relatively warm. Fortunately for us, another garderobe chute ran down the wall behind the spot where we planned to position the Aga, which was ideal for bringing up the oil feed. In order to hide the flue behind the walls of the Great Hall, I numbered each one of the stones, removed them, cut off the backs, cut a chase up the back, inserted the flue pipework for the hot water tank, and replaced the stones in their original positions. It worked well, but that, too, was very hard work.

The channel cut in the window embrasures intrigued me and indicated how the windows worked. As a result, the windows are now detailed in almost the exact manner in which they were originally built. There was a slot in the rybats on either side for a transom and a glazing groove round the top of the window, above the transom. In addition, there was a glazing groove down the left-hand

Fig. 6
*Detail of window glazing. In the background: "Farewell to gravitas". The boating pond on the reinstated loch, with its crannog, from which trees still grow.
Photo: Robert McCallum.*

side, below the transom, but not on the right-hand side. This indicated that the left was fixed and the right-hand side opened. (Fig. 6). As so many of the speakers to-day have remarked, in particular Ian Begg and France Smoor, it is really wonderful to be able to have time to be in the building and let it talk to you, because you know that what it tells you is usually correct.

Inside all the windows in the Hall, eighteen inches above the centre of the window seat, there are some very interesting slots. (Figs. 7 and 8). The left side has a simple slot cut in the stone, about 4 x 3 x 2 inches deep. On the right-hand side, above the window seat, there is a groove which ends in a drop into a slot. This is the same size as that on the other side. It is clear that these were cut to take a wooden bar, one end being inserted in the left-handed slot and the other being slid through the groove and dropped into the slot opposite. They were a later addition to the castle, as the stonework is rough, but they seemed to

Fig. 7 (left) and Fig. 8 (right)
*Left hand slot is just below the Hall's windows and above the stone seals. Fig. 8 shows details of channel and drop slot, on the right
Photo: Robert McCallum.*

Mains Castle – Mike Rowan

be in the wrong position for gun mountings. However, a naval gun, discovered in Raasay Castle, Skye, showed that it was mounted in a kind of rowlock, 1' 3" high, which put the wooden bar at exactly this right position for the light artillery mounting.

On the next (third) floor I put two bedrooms, taking the one with the fine vaulted ingo for our own. Originally the walls were to be stone, as I had this feeling that stone was a wonderful material and everything should be finished in stone. Robert Clow rather charitably suggested that the bedrooms had a "genuine Scottish feel" - an euphemism for being stark, harsh and somewhat chilly! However, I changed my mind and plastered the bedroom, leaving the window surrounds with an exposed four inch margin of stone. (Fig. 9). It is a real treat to sit in the embrasure and I must admit that the rooms are so much better for being plastered. They feel so much more comfortable as well as being brighter and now the light reflected from the surface of the reinstated loch makes the bedroom, and the other rooms for that matter, even brighter still.

My ex-wife Pavla always delighted in the painted ceilings at Crathes, so much so that we couldn't resist the impluse to paint the beams and ceilings in the guest

Fig. 9
Bedroom now plastered. Photo: Robert McCallum by kind permission of Ruth Cooper.

and our bedrooms. She illustrated incidents and things from our experience and life at Mains. At first she lay on her back, a la Michaelangelo but, aches aside, she soon found paint dropped into her eyes, so she completed her work in a standing up position. I painted the beams with conundrums or aphorisms, such as "Do not sleep the whole night" over the bed, from Pinkie House, Musselburgh, where the recommendation included a painting of a stork and baby and "Who can kill time without injuring eternity," from David Henry Thoreau. My bagpipes are painted, as is the fox that ran away with our chickens. (Fig. 10). Pavla's puppies are also represented. It was principally Pavla's work and she was really skilled in the use of paints and brushes.

Fig. 10
Bagpipes, fox and flowers on a bedroom ceiling, based largely on the Culross ceilings with inspiration from Glastone's Land. Photo: Robert Clow.

The attic floor contains our daughter's room, my office and a bathroom. I panelled the walls with secondhand flooring. When that ran out, I purchased new and stained the timber to match. I don't know if I would do it again as I now prefer the appearance of bleached pine.

The bathroom. Yes. I have a horror of traditional bathrooms and 1970's avocado-coloured wash-basins and pans which one sometimes comes across in more luxurious restorations of that period. I felt they never looked right. Then I heard that Castle Menzies had a lead bath. That set me thinking on the use of different materials for our upstairs loo, basin and bath. At first I used slate with a hole cut in it over the toilet bowl, but that wasn't very successful, as the slate leaked when inadvertently peed upon, so I shaped a piece of plywood on top of the pan, and beat lead round it. There is now another compromise to comfort, in that now it, too, has a wooden seat! I had been to silversmithing evening classes at the Glasgow School of Art for some years, so I thought it would be a

Mains Castle – Mike Rowan

good idea to adapt my silversmithing experience to making a wash-basin and bath out of copper. As it happened, the materials cost less than a modern suite. I designed a hexagonal wash-hand basin (Fig. 11) and in designing an equally interestingly shaped bath I spent quite a lot of time sitting round in different positions, on the floor, just to make absolutely sure I got the shape right. (Fig. 12). The end products were somewhat original and bathing by candlelight in a copper bath, particularly with a picnic and a bottle of champagne, was quite a treat. But beware. If soaking in it for too long there is a tendency for the flesh that has come into contact with the copper to start turning green! Another snag arose in that we quickly discovered that it is very difficult to keep copper clean.

Fig. 11 and 12
The wash hand basin (left) and bath (right). The size of the taps indicate the different scale of the two illustrations. The basin is about 1 ft 6 ins in diameter. The bath takes two people, comfortably! Photos: Robert McCallum. Reproduced by kind permission of Ruth Cooper.

Apart from the stonework, it was the plumbing that took the most time. The drainage out of the building was desperate and a channel had to be cut in the stone, right down through the mural chambers, sometimes cutting through as much as four feet between them, all with hand tools. Fitting the four inch pipes was even worse, the only recompense being the enormous pleasure of designing and making the basins and bath.

Furnishing the castle was also quite a problem. I would have had to take most of the pieces of furniture apart in order to get them up the narrow turnpike stair, as they couldn't be craned in through the windows. I ended up making most of it myself, a quite satisfying feeling at first, but it became a time-consuming and an energy-sapping ogre, after a surprisingly short period. The two main beds were made with some reclaimed church panelling and I made the kitchen and workroom cupboards. Thereafter I downed tools as enough was enough!

So much for the interior. The exterior I left much as it was, repointing the stonework using a cement lime mix, whilst the scaffolding was up. A vast amount of repointing had to be undertaken, both externally and internally, in order to strengthen and waterproof the masonry. I decided not to harl, as the building didn't appear to have harling checks around the windows. Whether this was right or not, I do not know. I do have problems with damp penetration, but only when the prevailing west wind drives rain into the sandstone. In the turnpike, water can actually seep through the stone and run down the stair, usually when a gale is also driving the rain hard against the external wall, which is fairly thin at this point. What it might do for a prisoner in the oubliette, also on the west gable, goodness only knows. In the meantime the castle stands stark in its strong, square stone walls - both inside and out it has that uncompromising "genuine Scots feel."

People often said how brave we were to tackle such a project. In fact, closer to the truth, we had to be crazy to start in the first place and, once committed, we couldn't afford to stop! But should you still want to venture into the insanity of castle restoration, instead of buying one fully furnished, I have a further piece of wisdom to offer, once given to me by an excellent joiner, known around the West of Scotland as "Mad Danny"; "Even if you buy the b...... building, you don't own it. It has lasted generations and will last many more. You are only looking after it for your lifetime, so look after it well." I have never forgotten his advice.

Fig. 1
Rusco Tower.

Rusco Tower

BY GRAHAM CARSON OF RUSCO.

Long before my thirtieth birthday which, in case you are curious, was in 1966, I was extremely interested in archaeology, old buildings and, in particular, tower houses. Like many wee boys, I had been fascinated by castles, but unlike some, I had never grown out of this fascination and by my mid twenties I was day-dreaming about restoring one when I retired. I believe that Scottish tower houses have become an integral part of our landscape and heritage and as a result I have always felt that having a hand in the restoration of one would be a happy and rewarding privilege. Having this profound and enduring interest in castellated architecture, I was therefore more than prepared to compromise amenity in order to enjoy the pervasive atmosphere, the character and the charm of a most uncompromising form of house. Whether my wife was so prepared was another matter.

At this point in my life, I was hard working but not too well off, acting as the commercial traveller in my father's food importing business. I had had some limited experience of building work in the internal design of a house, the refurbishment of a small office building in Glasgow and the restoration of a 200 year old linen mill, minus its machinery, in Kirkcaldy. After my thirtieth birthday, I left my father's business, with a little success behind me and, although ambitious, I was keenly aware of the lack of fulfilment in the pursuit of material success. This gave me a determination to press ahead with my dream, there and then, rather than wait until I retired, yet accepting that it would probably take many years to realise. By 1970, therefore, I had decided that I had to restore a tower house, NOW.

Alas, I wasted many, many months, and longer, looking at maps, 'phoning people, making visits and so on and I drew a complete blank as far as finding one to restore was concerned. That was until a friendly fellow in The National Trust for Scotland, Bill Hanlon, said, "You must speak to Nigel Tranter, author of the five volumes on the *Fortalices and Fortified Houses in Scotland*". In actual fact when I spoke to him, Nigel Tranter only suggested going to a library and looking at his books, so it was no wonder his royalties remained modest. However, I bought all five books and out of the various volumes I picked eleven castles which might have met my requirement. Two of them were very special because they had originally been owned by members of the Carson family.

Down to Galloway I went, and the first visited was Hills Castle. It was no good at all, as it sat at the side of a farmyard. And then there was Rusco (Fig. 1). The building looked fine. It was almost complete to the wallhead. Internally all the timber had collapsed onto the vault, which was open to the Galloway skies. However, the situation was lovely. The ruin stood in a beautiful valley and had services of water, well - I presumed it did, for there is so much water in Galloway that I couldn't imagine there would be any shortage! Electricity was close by, telephone wires were near and the local minor road a mere 150 yards above, on the hillside.

I took Buffy, my wife, down to Galloway to see it. By the way, she was at the Castles Conference, so at it I had to be very careful in what I stated! Whilst I was quite taken with the prospect of something which needed lots of attention, but was not beyond redemption, my first problem was that I wasn't sure of her reaction! Having remained completely silent as we walked around the exterior, and having climbed to the first floor and looked straight up to the sky, her only comment was, "Oh, my God!"

The second difficulty was to acquire the castle, particularly when confronted by an agent who said, "Well, I'm sorry, but the building is not for sale." So I embarked on a series of white lies, like, "I'm going to be in the area, anyway." This was quite untrue, as I was 130 miles away, but I did see the agent, eventually, and by and by the owner, although the latter confirmed his reluctance to sell. Finally, I put myself in his shoes and realised that what he wanted was something that safeguarded him from having an awful mess in the middle of his estate. Therefore I wrote conditions into the offer, such as:- a target date for restoration, at the end of which, if I hadn't completed the work he would get the building back for nothing; that all the plans were subject to his approval and that he had a right of pre-emption, should we ever sell. This secured the deal, and in 1972 I bought the eleven acres round it, the castle itself (which, as I pointed out to him, was actually a liability) and the trees growing out of the upper walls - all for £3,500. It had taken five months between a Scottish lawyer and the estate's English lawyers to work out the legal details.

The history and ownership of Rusco

Rusco Tower is a very typical building of the end of the 15th century. It has several features which illustrate this, amongst which are the large numbers of mural chambers - seven in all, the corbelling which supports the parapet wall, very thick walls of up to seven feet and, perhaps more unusual, watersheds above the main windows.

Consisting of five floors, there is a stone vault above the second storey. This vault served the double purpose of preventing fire from spreading upwards and denying access through the building by any means other than by the one staircase that rises from the ground floor in the south east corner. Therefore the rest of the building could be defended fairly easily.

Like nearby Cardoness Castle, the main concept of defence was that it should be protected from the wall-head, from where missiles could be thrown down at anyone trying to gain entry. As gunpowder and cannons were only in limited use by the time Rusco was built, it was never meant to withstand this sort of siege, but merely to repel any attempt to reclaim stolen goods or gain revenge for a murder.

It seems possible that some of the men who were involved in the building of Cardoness Castle (Fig. 2) proceeded to Rusco, when the former was finished.

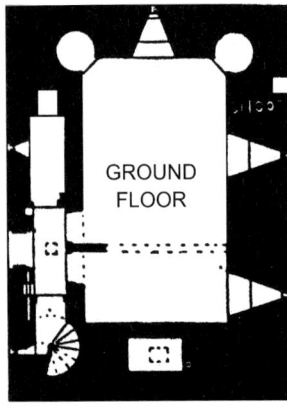

Fig. 2
The ground plan at Cardoness Castle. It has a not dissimilar detail of entrance to that of Rusco, only the position of the spiral stair is reversed.

Graham Carson – **Rusco Tower**

The land on which Rusco was built was given in 1494 by John Accarsane, jointly, to his daughter Mariota and her husband Robert Gordon, who was the second son of Sir John Gordon of Lochinvar.

Robert had a turbulent but, for that period, a regrettably common career, during which he was variously charged with complicity in murder, for which he was put to the horn. He was also accused of stealing a roof belonging to the Abbot of Kirkandrews and kidnapping the heiress-wife of a neighbour in order to secure her land, etc., etc. Despite all these interruptions, their marriage produced six sons and two daughters. From this power base the Galloway Gordons increased their power and wealth, latterly as the Viscounts Kenmure.

Mariota, the first Lady of Rusco, also had a rather eventful life. When her husband Robert died, she married Thomas McLellan of Bombie. This did not please her eldest son, so he seized her and sent her for safe-keeping to the Borders. When her new husband raised a court action in Edinburgh for her release, he was killed in the High Street by the son and his friends. She was released but, needless to say, did not remarry!

Not many years after being completed, it became a secondary home, for by then Robert Gordon and his family had become the heirs of Lochinvar, following the death of Robert's elder half-brother at Flodden, in 1513. This was a considerable blessing for it meant that no money was spent on developing or 'improving' the fabric of the building, although during the 17th century an extension of two floors was added on the north side.

Rusco has been owned by several families over the past five centuries. The Gordon ownership continued until about 1670, when it was bought by a family called McGuffog, from Wigtonshire. They sold it at the beginning of the 19th century to the first of two families called Hannay, who were not related. They, in turn, sold it to the Murrays who held it for a short time at the beginning of this century. Around this period it was the home of two farm labourers and their families, including a pig that lived on the parapet! Then the late Commander Cochrane purchased it. The present owners of the estate of Rusko, the Gilbeys, bought it in 1968 and, as previously mentioned, I acquired the castle and the adjoining land in 1972, thus bringing back the Carson name after nearly five hundred years.

Three years were spent working on the planning before we actually started the restoration in 1975 and, in spite of two periods when the work had to be stopped for lack of money, all the main reconstruction was finished by the end of 1979. That is not to say that all work was finished, for improvements have been carried out since and, of course, there is maintenance work, which is sometimes a problem and a great expense.

In 1982 the garden was started and has been expanding ever since - but I am jumping the gun.

The restoration work was assisted by grants from the Historic Buildings Council for Scotland, as were the driveway, cattlegrid and cobbling by the Manpower Services Commission, through the Community Enterprise

Rusco Tower – Graham Carson

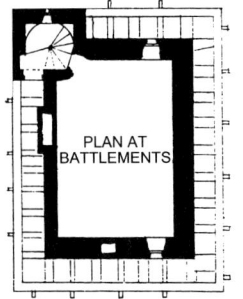

Fig. 3

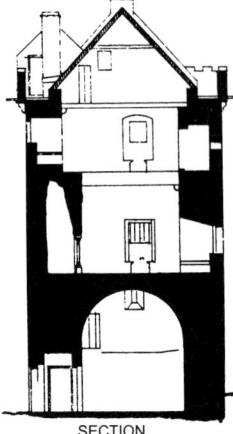

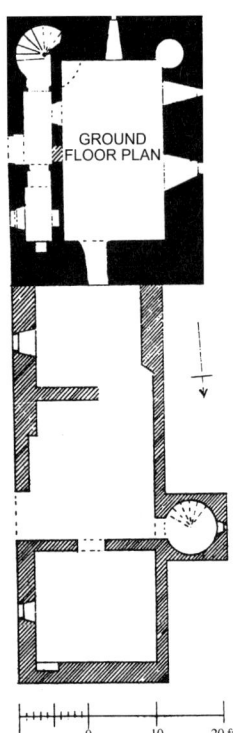

Programme. Wherever possible and practical, the building has been restored to its original state and this does apply to most, if not all, of the stonework. Most importantly, the tower has been returned to the purpose for which it was originally built, namely a home.

The external appearance

The armorial panel above the front door shows, in the top half, the arms of James IV of Scotland, signifying the direct ownership of the land from the Crown and, in the lower half, the arms of Gordon (three boars' heads) and Accarsane (three crescents) are quartered. Looking upwards, you will see imitation cannons which are the means of discharging the water from the roof and parapet walk. These are only to be found on the front of the building; round the sides and back semi-hexagonal spouts have been re-inserted exactly as they appeared originally. The pointing in the stone wall was carried out with a finish similar to the original, using shingle from the seashore. The pale pink stone, with which we replaced all the damaged stone dressings, came from Alnwick in Northumberland, the only quarry still open that produces a stone anything like the original, which came from either Turnberry or Ailsa Craig. It was transported round to the Solway by boat, not only for Rusco but also for Cardonness, where its 'dried blood' colouring can be clearly identified. The window on the ground floor level was inserted later, replacing arrow/gun slits like those at Cardoness, which we have copied elsewhere on the ground floor.

The extension to the north of the building, which many local people remember as a ruin, was added during the 150 years after the building of the tower. Unfortunately it was not built to the same standard, and by the time the recent restoration was carried out, the walls were literally crumbling away. The outline of the entire building is preserved in situ. In taking down its rear wall where it was joined to the tower, a garderobe chute was uncovered. This came from the parapet walk level and has been left open to show what the drainage system was like.

The interior

There are four doorways leading off the entrance lobby, in addition to the front door. (Fig. 3). The first, on the extreme right as one enters, leads to a small chamber which used to be a guardroom and is now the cloakroom. The second (now stoned up) was the entrance to the larger part of the undercroft, which was formerly a safe place for stock in time of danger and the third (a slightly smaller opening now the workshop) would possibly be for smaller animals. In its far corner is an oven or manger. The fourth door (a little further along, on the extreme left) opens to the stairway, which spirals up 75 steps to all floors and the parapet walk. The height of the doorways at this level is not an indication of the small stature of people in the 15th century. It was more a means of defence. The first doorway off the stair gives entry to the upper prison which has its own garderobe (still as it was) and a trap door that provides the only access to the pit, again with its own garderobe, but no window. In the narrow confined space the more dangerous malefactors (or valuable hostages) would be confined.

The next door up the stair opens into what would have been the servants' sleeping loft, now in use as a dining-room and kitchen. We do not know what the original purpose of the next little room was, but it makes a very useful store.

The doorway one floor further up leads to the Great Hall, which is and always was the heart of the Tower. In it were held the Barony Courts, when they were the means of enforcing law and order within the barony. Guests would have been entertained at this level, dining at long trestle tables and then sleeping on the floor. In the south-west corner is the garderobe chamber, now a 20th century w.c. The small recess there would have held a supply of damp moss before the invention of loo paper! There is a little study, the entry to which is at the level of the window seat in the west wall. When this doorway was covered with a tapestry, it would become a secret room and it has a small hole - a laird's lug - in the wall, for listening to any conversations between visitors or witnesses in the Great Hall, when they thought they were alone. Above the fireplace are the arms of the present Baron of Rusco. There are no less than four windows in the Great Hall, one in each elevation, although the north-facing one was originally a servery which was knocked out into the third storey of the 17th century extension, only to be changed to a window after that building fell down. The other three windows had glass in the top half and shutters in the lower section.

Immediately above the Great Hall and through the next doorway off the stair, is the solar or laird's private apartments. We do not know how this level was divided internally, but now it is partitioned into a bedroom and, at the back on the left-hand side, a bathroom. The old garderobe is reused as another w.c. and on the right there is a utility room for clothes washing, drying, sewing and for breakfast, etc. Sometimes the early morning sun streams in the east-facing window!

The top floor or garret contains two further bedrooms, one of which we call the doocot on account of the pigeon-hole beds, and a modern bathroom in between them. The final door leads onto the parapet walk, through a small caphouse. The walkway has heavy stone slabs. Large and chunky second hand stone Forfar slabs have been used for the roof, which are appropriately in scale with the tower.

The work at Rusco

We started work in 1975. The cows had been using the building as a house of ease for I don't know how long, and the floor was eighteen inches deep in rich manure. So my first job was to start clearing it. I hired an enormous great pump and it worked manfully for fully an hour and a half. I was standing up to my knees in rotting manure. Suddenly there was the most almighty bang, followed by a hissing noise. I rushed outside. Oh dear! There was what was left of the large pump, with its contents splattered everywhere! At that point I decided I

Rusco Tower – Graham Carson

needed an architect. It is surprising what motivates the human spirit in the moment of need. No matter what stonemasons stated about architectects at the Conference, I can assure you that a good one is essential. I was looking for someone with experience, compatibility, and preferably somebody who worked in a convenient place, as I worked in Kirkcaldy. The last thing I wanted was an architect who lived near my castle, for I wanted to be my own clerk of works. I had come across - and you have heard of him already from two people - Bill Jack of St Andrews, who had all the experience necessary. He was sufficiently far away, and we appeared to get on well at the first meeting. He did however say, "Where's your wife?" to which I replied, "Oh, she'll be at home doing the dishes and things like that". Latterly we discovered, after we had jointly gone to see him again, that Bill Jack had had an experience where a somewhat keen young man had tried to give him a castle-restoration commission, only to find that on their first meeting the wife said, "Not on your life!" and that was the end of that project!

Having been reassured by my wife that she was a fairly willing participant, everything went O.K. We agreed fees on an hourly basis. It seemed inappropriate to both of us to work in any other way, for bearing in mind the timescale I had planned, he wouldn't have been paid for a very long time! Anyway, it was much better from my point of view because I knew where I stood and I think it was probably cheaper in the long run. With a very good architect's survey behind us, which was vital, Bill Jack took us to see one or two towers, namely Pitcullo (restored by Mr and Mrs Roy Spence) and Inverquharity (for Mr and Mrs Sandy Grant). After that we planned furiously for a very long time, constantly aware of the need to design a home that would be comfortable, a home in which we would be very happy and one in which we would stay for the rest of our lives - all within a somewhat uncompromising surrounding - oblong, five storeys high, with walls ranging from five to eight feet thick and few windows piercing them. We were much helped by one factor which has been mentioned in other contexts by two of three speakers, namely the profusion of garderobe chutes within the walls. In fact, Rusco Tower had one from each floor, and they facilitated greatly the installation of the various services (phone and T.V. cables, water, electricity, soil pipes, etc.,) and in the planning of the layout of a comfortable home.

Clues to the former appearance of Rusco were discovered in a print of 1805 (Fig. 4). This was of immense value because some details were dissimilar to those contained in MacGibbon and Ross, or in Tranter, for that matter. The crenellations were quite different on the main tower. In the old print there had been crowsteps on both the tower and caphouse roof. These, too, had disappeared by the time we acquired the building. To the right of the tower there was also the afore-mentioned 17th century building which had, alas, almost completely collapsed by the time we came on the scene. The low wall in the foreground had completely gone, but the foundations of the higher wall behind, on the right-hand side, remain.

Fig. 4

On the subject of communications with the local authority and the powers that be, we attended an architectural summer school to educate us a bit with our plans. This we found very useful and at last, having agreed details between the architect and ourselves, they were eventually ready for submission. They went to the local authority and the (then) Department of the Environment, and bang, Bill Jack was not very popular with them, on my account, as some of my ideas for the interiors were considered to be insufficiently sympathetic. We arranged a meeting and I trotted off to the Department of the Environment, where, I must say, the officers were tremendously helpful. They compromised a bit. Quite correctly, I compromised an awful lot but we finally reached agreement. The Historic Buildings Council (to some extent consisting of the same people wearing different hats) was very, very helpful. In 1975 we were finally awarded our first grant of £10,000. That may not sound a lot in to-day's terms, but it was a tremendous amount in those days, representing 45% of the cost of grant-eligible work. We subsequently received a grant of a further £10,000 in 1977, on the same basis. The HBC had pushed hard for a fixed price contract, which we couldn't provide as nobody would give us one, due to the work being so open-ended, although we did have a detailed Bill of Quantities. Despite one major error, the Bill was nevertheless an extremely useful guide. We finished up agreeing to work on a basis of time and material, provided it was under Bill Jack's supervision. This consisted of his coming down to see us and examining what had been done, then putting in a requisition for payment of part of the grant relating to work completed. We fixed up a team of local men, a small joinery firm, a mason and labourer to work on the project. They remained working for us for most of the four years that it eventually took to restore the building. I have got a note in my book that the rates of pay, in those days, were joiner £3.00 per hour, masons £2.00 per hour and the labourer £1.50 per hour. I must apologise to Alistair Urquhart for having to pay the mason's wage below the level of that of the joiner, but that was the going practice! The actual work didn't take four years; it took only two and a half, but twice during that period I ran out of money, so we had to stop. We did have one very amusing labourer for a short time. His name was Cecil and he was as Irish as they come. We were debating how to excavate a hole in the rock for the water tank and Cecil, bearing in mind that this was very much at the time of the troubles in Northern Ireland, said, "Shure. I'll re-apply for my Explosives Licence."

Aided by the telephone every day of the week to keep in touch with the workforce, I was able to restrict actual site visits to once a week, whilst carrying on with my regular business.

On the question of sourcing stone, we've already had reference made to Doddington stone and that is from where most of our dressed stone came, but we also got some from Hopeman. We used York stone, which again has already been mentioned, for the parapet walk. Second-hand stone was obtained from the platform of Leuchars railway junction, which was used to form the crowsteps. Whenever oak was required we used new English oak, including six heart-boxed 12 x 8 inch beams (Fig. 5). I remember that they cost £460 and they went up, absolutely green, for being heart-boxed they didn't have to be seasoned. The six corbels on each side of the Great Hall carried the beams. This construction was not the original form, which consisted of beams lying along the wall, with a whole forest of little joists running across. The difference in construction didn't come

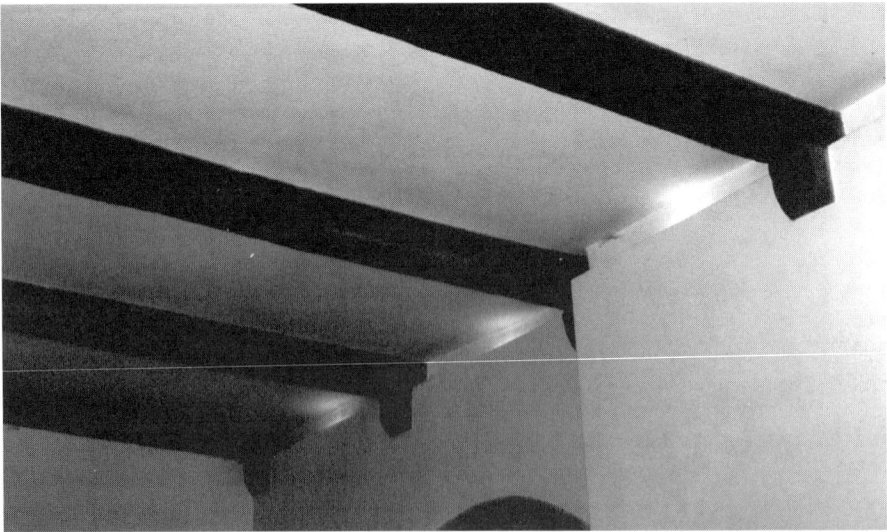

Fig. 5
Oak beams in the Great Hall.

to light until after we had installed the present structure, which was a blessing. Had it been otherwise, we would have had one of those awful floors that sag in perpetuity. Seasoned wood was obtained from a demolished church organ in Edinburgh. It was yellow pine, a great wood with which to work, once it has been de-nailed!

I have already referred to the god-send that the many garderobe chutes proved to be. We tried to keep a record of what we were going to cover up, so we photographed the work in progress as we installed the pipes. We ensured we also photographed the points at which we had to break into the walls, in order to support the soil pipes. You can imagine how impossible it might be to find these points at a later stage. In addition we recorded the vent holes for the w.c. and the kitchen cooker-hood. There are two stones, very thin, which have been thoroughly drilled with holes to act as a grille. Fortunately they are not really noticeable.

The only job at which the whole Carson family soiled their fair hands was that of de-slating a roof - and dirty work it really was! I had spent a whole day travelling round Forfar, looking for a suitable stone-flagged roof to purchase. Forfar slabs range in size from two feet (or more) wide to five or six inches, and from two inches thick to half an inch. They have a nice chunky appearance and their scale goes well with that of a tower roof. (Fig. 6). I finally bought slabs from a Forfar farmer that were still in situ on an abandoned farm building. They cost us £150. The whole family got together and, for the first time, all toiled as a

Fig. 6
East roof, looking towards the caphouse, showing the Forfar stone slates.

team. We manhandled them, but what no previous speaker has mentioned is their weight! The heaviest was about 3/4 of a hundredweight and they had to be handed down carefully, from person to person, from off the roof, using two ladders. There were eighteen tons of them and I can assure you that it was extremely hard work! Subsequently I discovered that if you are looking for second hand stone roofing, it is much easier to find it in the Yorkshire Dales. Undoubtedly, the slater found it equally hard work in re-laying the Forfar slabs at

Rusco Tower – Graham Carson

Rusco (as did the slater at Aiket) but at least he was only working off the parapet walk.

In the Great Hall there was a fine fireplace but, alas, it didn't work, as the distance between the hearth and lintel was far too great for the fire to draw up the chimney. (Fig. 7). Our solution was not dissimilar to that of Mike Rowan's at Mains Castle. We installed a canopy and flue liner that went right up to the top of the chimney and we built a plinth in the hearth, raising the level by one foot, in order to induce a better draw. However, the fireplace is used more for

Fig. 7
Fireplace in the Great Hall at the time of acquiring Rusco.

decorative purposes than to heat the Great Hall, as the main heating is provided by electric cables under the floor. This is most effective, if somewhat expensive to run.

Above the fireplace the Baronial arms are moulded in plaster (Fig. 8–opposite page). At the time of acquiring Rusco, we had no idea that there was a Barony associated with the building. About ten years later the previous owner said, "You know, Graham, I think there is a title connected to the building." So to cut a long story short, after a lot of legal wrangling, I became the Baron of Rusco and the arms up above the fireplace suggest I have literally plastered my achievement.

We had to repoint the external walls of the tower, which was quite a job. Initially, it was not awfully well done. It seemed that, driven by wind, the rainwater penetrated the walls and subsequently trickled downwards and inwards, only to arrive internally, further down the building. Thus, identification of the point of entry became somewhat difficult. We repointed one wall again, but still had problems and tried an application of silicon. Unfortunately, silicon breaks down under ultraviolet light and wasn't very satisfactory. In the end we had to use mastic where points of entry had been located, and had to replaster parts of the Great Hall and the solar as a result of water penetration.

The parapet walk also gave us similar problems Mike Rowan may joke at my expense, for parapet walks do not need to leak, but those at Rusco certainly did. On first inspection, everything appeared to be all right, so we merely repointed

Rusco Tower – Graham Carson

the flags on the south and west wall-walks. We had to lift them on the north and east wallheads, inserting a damp-proof course under them. But what troublewe had on the south and west! In 1987 we had to reconstruct the wallheads by taking down the parapet walls, lifting the flags, inserting a proper damp-proof course and putting the flags and wall back, coating them in a product

Fig. 9
Water damage at the entrance to the 'study', having percolated down through the thickness of the walls.

called Vandex, which claimed not to be affected by sunlight. To date it has proved its point, and we hope the problems of water damage are behind us.

Electric switch sockets had been set into the walls and the Quantity Surveyor had wrongly specified standard plasterwork. What with these and water penetration, we had burst pipes, due to electrolysis, stained plaster and all sorts of damp problems. In addition, there was condensation in the loft. I do not

Graham Carson – **Rusco Tower**

know if other castles have the same problem. Unfortunately, too, the joiner had forgotten to treat some of the timber, so we had an outbreak of dry rot that compounded our problems. We put in a dehumidifier, which drips into the loft cistern. Some of the other problems were eventually solved by changing the copper pipes to alkathene, where possible putting electric sockets onto the surface of the walls and treating the walls outside with the Vandex compound.

By the time we had finished in 1979, like Bill Cadell and his work at Linlithgow, we had received a Saltire Award. However, we realised we had made another mistake and that was over the construction of the approach road. We caused ourselves a lot of double-handling and lost time and money in bringing in everything along the old farm track at the lower level of the site. The intention was to cut a new approach road in from the minor public road above the castle, curving the new driveway down the hill and round to the front of Rusco. The great mistake was not to have undertaken its construction at the beginning of the restoration and this we only realised too late, once the new road had been built!

However, Rusco looks very handsome, standing as an inhabited landmark once again (Fig. 8), surveying the length of the valley from coast to the Galloway Hills, so we felt the Award, despite our problems, was well-deserved.

Fig. 10
Photo from the air, courtesy: Air Images.

Now that we have lived in the tower for a number of years and the 'snags' have been rectified, we have time to notice that there are one or two things that are hard to live with, but one gets used to them! Part of the deal with the Historic

Rusco Tower – Graham Carson

Buildings Council was to admit visitors. That is the formal reason why we have them, but morally one has a duty to show other people and to share with them what one has. Some ask strange questions, such as, "Do you really live here?" or "How do you manage the stairs?" There was one occasion when I had just finished showing fifteen innocent-looking young girl guides around, and was dressed, as usual, in my kilt. They had been camping on the other side of the valley. Having finished my spiel in parrot-like fashion, I said, "Now, would anybody like to ask a question?" The moment the words were out of my mouth, one little bright-eyed girl said "Yes; what do you wear under your kilt?"

The most rewarding part of having undertaken all the work has been the change in the quality of our life, despite the uncompromising nature of the building. In addition, we have had much happiness in watching the work progress and the memories of achievement in the completion of the restoration are still with us. However, we do feel very privileged to be custodians of something which stood for nearly five hundred years and we hope that, with a little help from us and our successors, it will do the same, again.

Tillycairn, Hatton and Forter Castles

by Ian Cumming

My interest in "ruined buildings" originated in the early sixties, from visiting dilapidated buildings. This was a period when, due to the combined effects of the rates, the cost of upkeep and general post-war impoverishment, many buildings were lost. Classic buildings which would now be considered of national importance were abandoned, vandalised, rifled, demolished and in some cases blown up. I was very struck by the wasteful destruction of such fine workmanship, aware that the scale of the loss was beyond replacement, in terms of both quality and sheer number of buildings. It seemed, at that time, that restoration was not affordable. The tragedy was that the skills that built these monuments, representing generations of accumulated knowledge, seemed destined to disappear. Modern buildings required the removal of the expense of those skills. My interest in this steered me towards a career in building.

My approach to restoration

There is a map currently available which lists about 1,250 'castles' in Scotland. These date from the 11th century through to the end of that of the 17th, when fortified buildings ceased to be built. For many of these buildings a description of 'tower house', 'fortalice' or 'manor place' would be more appropriate. This map includes a wide range of structures from mere vestiges of ruins to buildings that have been continuously occupied, from small fortalices, such as Benshie in Forfar, which has only three discernible rooms, to large and complex buildings, such as Edinburgh, Stirling or Kildrummie Castles.

In Glenisla, where I live, only two such buildings appear on the map, whereas 250 years ago there were five. If that ratio were to be applied over the country as a whole, there may well have been over 3,000 such buildings in Scotland. Looking through a list of the castles and tower houses, some 120 were built in the 15th century, 500 in the 16th and about 120 in the 17th century. The bulk of those of the 16th century were built in the latter half, which indicates a considerable amount of building activity throughout the country, within a very short period. Most of the building that remained in use were modified and altered to suit the domestic arrangements of the changing times. Those that fell into disuse, and a lot of them seemed to have suffered such a fate in the early 18th century, now present an opportunity for restoration to the period of abandonment, without the overlay of centuries of modification.

The castles and fortalices of this period represent the height of the master builder's skills, being built by craftsman rather than designed by architects and then built by builders. Although there are national and international influences, the vernacular influence on these buildings is paramount, making them very individual. They were largely built from local material, so their appearance owes a lot to the limitations of situation and material available, as well as to social

Fig. 1 (opposite)
Tillycairn Castle restored.
Photo: Ian Cumming.

factors. The form and decoration of these buildings were a cultural expression; they were meant to be aesthetically pleasing as well as convenient to use. The vernacular appearance of "belonging" to an area is wholesome and is what is generally missing in modern buildings. It is astonishing to think that out of the basic elements of stone and wood, with small amounts of lead, iron and glass, such varied, unique and fine forms could be built. It is for their asethetic and historical value that these ruins are worth preserving, whether as ruins, or by incorporating them into a building that can be used. I believe that the chances of these buildings surviving is enhanced by providing them with a use as a building. If left to the elements it is inevitable that they will eventually be lost. Questions arise as to the guiding principles and methods by which this can be achieved. The general principle for me is that the work done to a building should be reversible, in that, so far as reasonably possible, what you add to the ruin incorporates the existing fabric but can be removed at a later stage without detriment to it.

Before building or consolidation commences as much historical research as possible should be conducted. I have always found the most useful sources for this to be the Royal Commission of Ancient Monuments Library, local reference libraries and family records, not to mention the invaluable MacGibbon and Ross. Who built the building and who subsequently used it may also have a bearing on its internal arrangements and decoration. Parts of the building may have been altered and this frequently coincides with historical events, marriage, or change of ownership, where the new owners brought wealth and imposed their own ideas on the building. Archaeological investigation is an important part of the initial research. This falls into two parts - the upstanding archaeology and the below ground archaeology. In the past not enough of either (though especially the below ground archaeology) has taken place. The information gleaned from this work can be substantial and is important in the understanding of the building and its history. I firmly believe that the ruin should always be properly surveyed at the outstart and photographically recorded. This process should continue while work is in progress, as it is not often practical to scaffold the entire building specifically to do this work. The remains of the fabric of the building should be examined for a better understanding of the way it was constructed and the materials used. This means an examination of the mortar, the analysis of which can be undertaken by the Scottish Lime Centre in Edinburgh, assessment of the stone type and how it was crafted and an examination of the type of wood used, from remnants in the joist holes and other places. The archaeological work usually turns up slates and these will indicate details of roof construction. Further inspection of the ruin should indicate whether it had been harled and may reveal what type of plaster originally was used. Examination of the windows should also reveal the type of windows last used within the building. All this should be noted and recorded and should influence any planned work.

Personally I think that it is important to use compatible materials on a like for like basis and to avoid any temptation to use modern manufactured materials, such as cement mortars, concrete block and plaster board. These products are unsuitable and inappropriate. An analogy might be the approach of a furniture restorer to the repair of a Sheraton or other fine piece of furniture, where perhaps the leg is missing. The restorer does not replace the leg with white pine, for functional or aesthetic reasons. Furthermore, the pine has incompatible properties. The damaging effects of cement mortars and renders are now well known. There is also the wider concern that, although these products are comparatively cheap (thanks to the economies of large scale production) they will prove more expensive, in the long term, in terms of damage to the existing stone and possibly even to the environment.

Most of the evidence for the restoration is in the ruin itself, and parts which are missing are usually dictated by what is left. The areas which involve the most deliberation are often the wall-head and roof, and here nothing should be altered to fit a concept of what it ought to look like, or what 'logic dictates'. A solution should be sought which does not involve any removal or alteration of the remaining stonework, but accommodates what is left. At Tillycairn the solution of a 'bucket lid' over the main spiral stair was arrived at after lengthy discussion, and though there were conflicting opinions as to the correctness of this detail, it did include (and made sense of) all the existing masonry, whilst requiring the minimum amount of in-fill. If, in the light of subsequent discoveries, this solution proves incorrect, then nothing has been done to prohibit an alteration. The new build could simply be removed and returned to its pre-restoration state.

Having sourced suitable materials and carried out adequate surveying, archaeology and recording, the success of a given project depends crucially on how the work is pursued.

I believe it is best to undertake all work on the site, where it can be controlled in its minutiae. To this end I select, employ and work with a team, usually drawn from the locality, though this is not always possible. This team would typically consist of two stonecutters, two masons, two labourers and a joiner. All work is done on site; the stonecutters keep just ahead of the work in progress. Stones can be individually selected for cutting to blend in best, and 'sweetening' and 'snagging' can be done immediately. The joiner does all related woodwork from the laying of the roof through to making the windows, shutters, and panelling. This method is probably not too far removed from the way in which the building would originally have been built and, in restoration, it allows for a flexible, sympathetic and individually crafted approach.

Ideally the fabric of the building should be restored using matching stone, mortars, timbers, slates and plaster, where possible, and this is what I strive towards. In practice it is not always possible to do this, usually for financial reasons, and some compromises have to be made. For example, at Hatton Castle, in order not to irritate the purchase arrangements, the building had to be wind and weather tight by the end of the year (work only having started in March) and there was not the time, nor the finance available, to put the spiral stairways back in stone. We therefore cast on to the existing stubs of the principal stairway

Tillycairn, Hatton and Forter Castles – Ian Cumming

in matching composite stone. The secondary spiral stair was built in individually cast treads. Both were built in such a manner that in future they could be replaced in stone.

In all three castle restorations, I made efforts to use reclaimed matching stone from the locality. This is not always to the stonecutters' liking, as it is harder to work! However, there is only a limited amount to be found and at times I have had to resort to existing quarries for a suitable quantity of stone. At both Hatton and Forter the closest match in red sandstone was St Bees, which was passable, but not perfect. Ideally, I would like to have opened the original quarry that supplied the stone, which for a substantial building, such as a castle, should not be financially prohibitive. Frequently, matching timbers are also difficult to procure. Oak is fairly easily obtained, but the native scotch fir, with its distinctive honey colouring, that was once used extensively for both structural and finishing work, is very scarce. Slates, too, can be a problem, so those that remain in the second-hand market are frequently mean in terms of both thickness and size and are increasingly hard to come by, though there have been proposals in the recent past to re-open the odd slate quarry, which may relieve this problem to some degree.

I look forward to the day when I am landed with a project for which there is that little bit extra to cover the cost of obtaining these basic materials from their original sources.

In general, the final result should look to the casual eye as if no restoration has taken place. The integrity of the building should not have been compromised by concepts of restoration and design. I do not agree with the view, held in some circles, that modern materials such as brick, steel beams and concrete should be used in reinstatement work, in order that future generations can easily differentiate between the original structure and the new. Dating techniques are becoming increasingly sophisticated, accurate and cheap, and allied with proper recording of the work, it will be just as possible to tell the difference if the work is done to match, as if contrasting materials are used.

My career to-date

After various building projects in the south and east of England, culminating in the late seventies in the complete renovation of a house in Chelsea, I was invited to undertake the restoration of Tillycairn Castle, in Aberdeenshire. This project was completed by September 1981 and I remained in Aberdeenshire for the next few years, undertaking restoration and renovation works on many houses. After a further short spell working in London, I returned to Scotland to undertake the restoration works to Hatton Castle, Newtyle, and followed on from that with Forter Castle, Glenisla. Since then I have been working on Newmilns Tower and Dunure Castle for the Strathclyde Bulding Preservation Trust, and The Covenanters Inn, Newmilns, for the Glasgow-based St Vincent Crescent Preservation Trust - the recipients of an Historic Scotland Award, for which I and, no doubt Robert Clow, were most appreciative. I have also just completed

Liberton Tower for James Lumsden's Castles of Scotland Trust. However, work on the restoration of these buildings was undertaken after the Castles Conference in Glasgow.

The Work

At the time of the Castles Conference I had undertaken three castle restorations to-date. All were roofless ruins by the middle of the 18th century, and this presented me with a marvellous opportunity to restore in stone, thereby fulfilling my ambition to spend an early part of my working life using stone, in the restoration of these fascinating buildings. I'd therefore like to look at these three, briefly.

TILLYCAIRN The first was Tillycairn in Aberdeenshire, built by Matthew Lumsden in about 1544 to 1548. His father was responsible for building Provost Skene's House in Aberdeen. In 1979 the then owner was Mr David Lumsden, a direct descendant, who invited me to undertake the rebuilding. Work started in early 1980 and was completed by the following summer.

When I first examined the castle it seemed to me that it was rather a ruinous building (Fig. 2), but in retrospect, having undertaken the rebuilding of other castles, it was really in fairly good condition. Built of granite, it was largely complete to the wall-head, with the vaults still intact. It had well-dressed corbels supporting the caphouse, the parapet and roundels. The restoration entailed the reinstatement of the stairways, internal floors and walls, the reinstatement of turrets, the parapet walls and re-roofing the building.

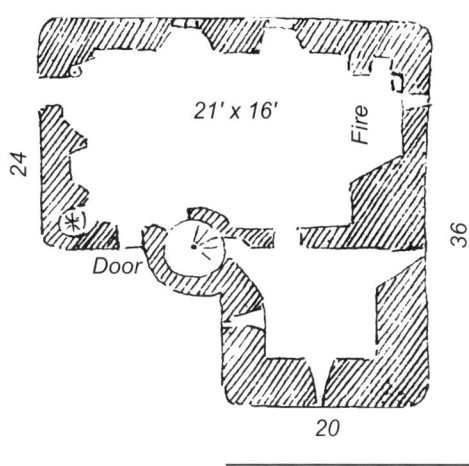

Fig. 2
Drawing of Tillycairn in its ruined condition by John Wetten Brown and a rather poor ground floor plan from MacGibbon & Ross.

Tillycairn, Hatton and Forter Castles – Ian Cumming

Although relatively straightforward to restore, the difficult area proved to be the roof. In its early form, the cap-house above the main stair had a conical roof. The drainage of rainwater from the rear of this was carried away by an unusual arrangement of a stone gully. A roof walkway with crenellated walls had been rebuilt at a later stage, probably around 1680, by re-arranging the chimney cope and raising the intersecting wall of the two wings. Access onto the roof was accommodated by providing a bucket lid roof to replace the earlier conical one, above the main stairway. The quality of this rebuilding work was poor and the result unsatisfactory. However, it did allow for an extra floor to be inserted at wall-head level, thereby increasing the usable space within the building.

Fig. 3
Shutters copied from Provost Skene's House, Aberdeen, as ownership extended to both buildings. Window details from nearby Kenmay House.

The detail of the windows' woodwork was copied from Kenmay House, just down the road, where I found some very old, thick, astragalled windows of almost the exact dimensions. The harling was a lime harl and it was interesting to learn that Alastair Urquhart, in his very amusing post-lunch entertainment, suggested a similar finish. Like him, our approach was similar in that I had to harl one whole face in a day and take the scaffolding down as the harl descended the wall, otherwise I would have left the marks of the lines of the transoms of the scaffolding, caused by the sun drying out the harl that wasn't in the shade of the scaffolding. When completed the building looked very handsome (see Fig. 1).

Ian Cumming – **Tillycairn, Hatton and Forter Castles**

HATTON CASTLE Hatton Castle, the second castle restoration I undertook, was a large Z-plan building, at Newtyle, built by the fourth Lord Oliphant in 1575. Situated near the village of Newtyle, Angus, it is a large building (Fig. 4).

Fig. 4
Hatton Castle in 1978, prior to restoration.
Photo: copyright: RCAHMS.

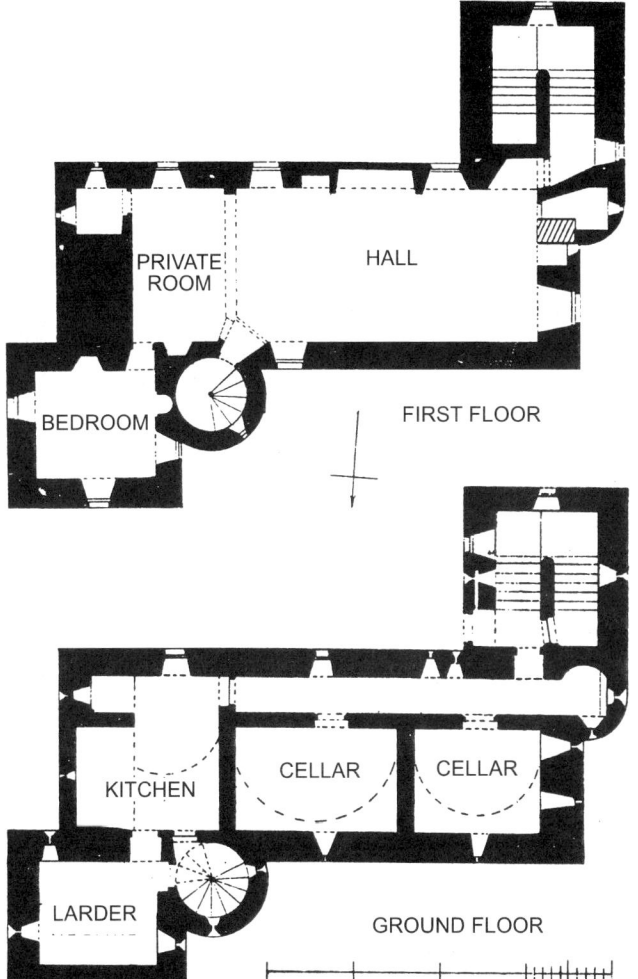

Fig. 5
Plans of ground and first floors by MacGibbon and Ross.

Tillycairn, Hatton and Forter Castles – Ian Cumming

the central part of which is over fifty feet long - the Great Hall measuring 35 by 20 feet! It was well built of local red sandstone and characterised by large rooms, well lit by big windows. There were few stone-work enrichments. The Oliphant Trust was set up specifically to purchase and restore the ruin which had been occupied until the early seventeen hundreds. Its restoration entailed the removal of the 19th century shoring up and reinstatement of missing walls, stairways, floors and roof.

Before commencing work on the castle, I set up a team of two stonemasons, two stone cutters and, in this case, when work started properly, three labourers. This was my normal practice in forming a team that would work together, on site, as I have already mentioned. We started building work in March 1987, having cut some of the required dressed stones the previous winter (Fig. 6), and work was largely completed by the following winter. Once on site, we erected a shed and, having discussed what was required with the masons, we selected the stones and prepared them for use, working two of three days in advance of requirements. The men would therefore come on site in the morning, knowing the precise stones that they were going to prepare that day. A bit later the joiner became part of the team and, of course, there was myself. I worked with them on a day to day basis, getting all the things that they needed, in terms of this and that, starting with teabags and ending up with the stone required for cutting and restoration.

Fig. 6
Dressed stones, cut during the winter months, awaiting use.

I scouted around the neighbouring countryside, although most of the farmers didn't know it, looking for demolished or derelict buildings, in order to find secondhand stone that matched the local reddish material that had been used at Hatton. But Hatton required nearly 650 stones to be cut and finding that sort of quantity lying about was very difficult, especially as much of the demolition work in the local area had already dried up. In the end I couldn't find sufficient stone and had to resort to using the ubiquitous block, internally, in spite of my real dislike for it. There wasn't much else I could do. Fortunately, when coloured, it was a near match to the stone.

All the chimney heads were missing, apart from that which served the Great Hall, so I copied the detailing as seen at a distance and rebuilt the chimney heads in stone. Needless to say, they were quite heavy and somewhat difficult to get up to such a height, but in the end it was well worth the effort.

At Hatton the joiner who joined the team was an excellent worker and good at his chosen profession. Following my policy, he was involved in doing all the joinery work in the project, in making the windows, the doors and even fitting out the kitchen! The decision was taken to make leaded lights for the upper half of the windows, with shutters below. Whether this was correct or not I do not know, for there was an argument in favour of re-installing sash and casement windows, but what was finally installed was certainly in the original form; so much for not putting back the clock! Oak was used (Fig. 7) and the joiner had it machined in a local workshop, just down the road, bringing it up to finish and fit in the castle. It was satisfying to organise and finish the work in such a manner, for had the work been put out to tender and made by a joinery firm, like it or not, when the windows arrived on site none of them would have fitted the irregular stone openings. In this manner I could double check his work on site, all the time.

Fig. 7
Rafter detail at wallhead, showing oak pegging on the "post and rail" structure, supporting rafters, prior to beam "filling", between rafters and posts

Oak was also used for the flooring. This had been previously kiln dried. A double skin was installed in order to hold the sound deafening, so we cut the boards and sank them between joists to give a space of about four inches. Into this space ash and sand were mixed to provide the deafening. Above, the oak flooring was straight forwardly butt-jointed. Incidentally, there seemed to be little purpose in kiln-drying the oak. It had been dried to about 10% to 12%

Tillycairn, Hatton and Forter Castles – Ian Cumming

moisture content, but by the time the floors were down and the walls had been plastered the oak had soaked in so much moisture that it expanded quite considerably. When the castle was heated, the oak tended to contract again, so one was left with the problem of either filling in the gaps or lifting and relaying some of the planks. Of such is one of the penalties of restoring these buildings too quickly and minor (or major) problems inevitably arise. If in fact the building had been left for a year one might have been faced with less of a problem.

It had been decided to install underfloor heating at Hatton and, by large, I remain doubtful as to the success of this form of heating. I was left with a number of physical problems. On the ground floor I had to dig out six to eight inches below the ground level, in order to be able to install the system and its associated insulation. The latter was essential to ensure that the head was reflected upwards, and not lost in the bedrock. This caused problems with damp, as the excavations were almost as deep as the footings of the building, so I wasn't very happy with it. However, that was what the Trust wished, so that was what was undertaken.

By the beginning of 1988 the upper areas of the building were beginning to take shape. I was interested to hear that other speakers at the Conference had used brick or block. Except in unusual circumstances (like the one I had already experienced at Hatton) I didn't and still don't see the need for it, as in most cases one can build just as quickly in stone and the feel to the building is authentic. The north face of Hatton was quickly rebuilt from the level of the Great Hall, upwards, including the main spiral staircase (to the rear), as was the north-east tower. As work had only commenced in March of the previous year, one can appreciate the speed at which the stone rebuilding took place.

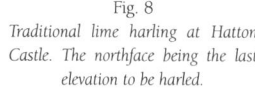
Fig. 8
Traditional lime harling at Hatton Castle. The northface being the last elevation to be harled.

The building was re-harled within twelve working days (Fig. 8). I gave it one coat, just of lime harl, which met Historic Scotland's specification, at that time.

I was under considerable pressure to complete it well before Christmas, as I wished to beat the frosts. In the event we were extremely lucky as, even though we were working for the fortnight during the month of November, there were no frosts for the whole fortnight. The result was reasonably successful, though we have a lot to re-learn over the use of lime and since that time much has already been learnt. The lime used was supplied by Chards of Bristol. At a later stage it started to peel off the crowsteps, which were very porous, and in this state the subsequent frosts tended to burst it off. In retrospect I should have given the lime more time to set or, alternatively, the answer might have been to leave the crowsteps unharled. We also had a rather disheartening experience, in that we had worked extremely hard, in one day, to complete the harling on one whole elevation. It had just been completed when the wind got up and cracked it, so it had all to be scraped off, next day, and re-harled again - fortunately that was the only disaster of that nature we experienced.

In finishing the interiors, I have always found that plastering gives me one of the greatest problems. At Tillycairn I had used a plaster made by Tilcon, a renovating plaster, evidently also used in hospitals. Although fairly satisfactory, it was expensive, so at Hatton I decided to use Thistle renovating plaster. This was quite successful, except on the ground floor where chickens had been reared in the past and their droppings had seeped into the walls, over the years. This had a disastrous effect on the plaster and it burst off at the lower levels. In future buildings I will revert to using lime and I suspect that that will sort out some of the problems.

FORTER CASTLE The third castle on which I wish to talk briefly is in my home glen. It was built about 1560 by the Ogilvie family (Fig. 9). A little later they

Fig. 9
View of Forter Castle from the NE –
"dumpty and aggressive looking".

Tillycairn, Hatton and Forter Castles – Ian Cumming

acquired Airlie Castle and also owned Craig Castle, nearby. Forter is a dumpy, aggressive-looking building, lying in a commanding position at the upper end of Glenisla, about twelve miles from Alyth, at the foot of the Balloch Pass. It was burnt down in 1640 by the Duke of Argyll, along with Airlie and Craig Castles. Airlie was rebuilt a hundred years later, but there is nothing left of Craig Castle. Forter survived as a ruin, which, considering its exposed position and the passing of three hundred and fifty years, is a fitting tribute to its builders. I don't know if there are many buildings that were ruined and abandoned in 1640 and restored in the twentieth century.

It was built on the L-plan, with four floors (Fig. 10). The ground floor comprised of three vaults, above which was the Great Hall, measuring about 32 ft x 19 ft. The main stair in the wing rises to the first floor, which was vaulted. Access to the upper storeys was by a spiral stair in the re-entrant angle, although the Laird's private room was only reached by a mural stair from the Great Hall. It was a very exciting building on which to work, being unusual in that it was built of random rubble whinstone, probably taken from the scree on the lower slopes of nearby Mount Blair. It had somewhat unusual dressed stone windows, made of granite, but some of the other dressed stone was a mixture of sandstone, granite and limestone. This uncommon mix might be explained by the close proximity of quarries for all three stones. The limestone quarry, about a quarter of a mile away, must have provided the lime for mortar, as well, for nearby, between the old quarry and the castle, there was a large kiln.

Fig. 10
MacGibbon and Ross's view of Forter's re-entrant angle on the ruined western elevation and their plans of basement and first floor.

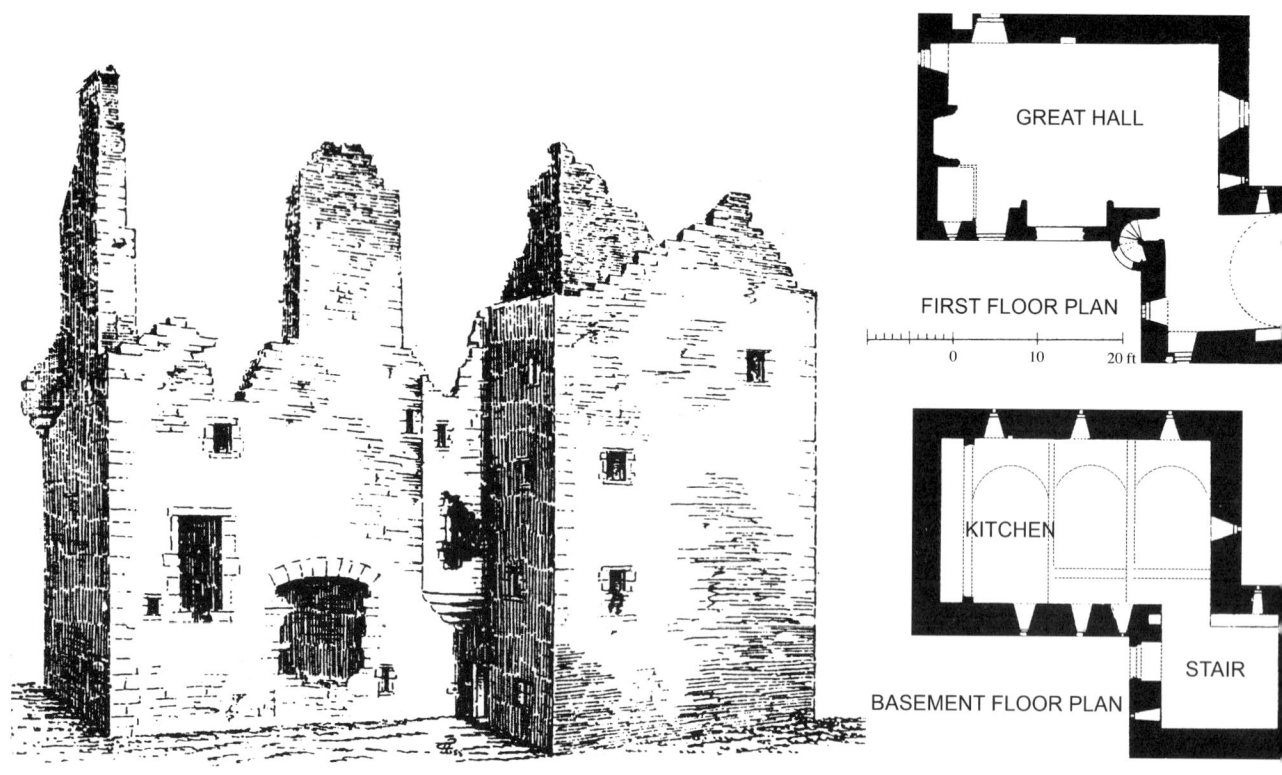

A previous attempt to re-inhabit Forter has been recorded, but there was no evidence of restoration in the building itself. My first job was to clear out the inside and rebuild the vaults. I was interested to see Alastair Urquhart re-instating the vaults at Muckrach, with Ian Begg, as I had to undertake a similar sort of exercise here. The middle walls of the vaults were missing. As there was no vestige of where they had been and no clear indent in the ground to indicate where the doorways were, I arranged for an archaeologist to identify where the middle walls had run. However, having built up the walls, I framed out a base in scaffolding, up to the height where the arches sprung, and then covered it with a platform, laying polystyrene on top of the platform, in the shape of an arch. This was then covered in wooden planks and I built the vaults over this structure. I was interested to hear Ian Begg talk about some of the vaults having had the frame lined with lime, in order to smooth out the finished vault. However, I have seen and worked on a number of castles where the lines of the timber framing are still visible, as the timber grain has marked the mortar that oozed out between the stones, when first mortared into place to form the vault.

The stairway was quite complicated, but it was great fun to re-vault it. It had been a scale and plat stair on the ground floor, which turned, eventually, in a full square. In other words it went up and round a corner, up and round another

Fig. 11
Rebuilding of the vaults above the principal stairway. Doorway (at first floor level) forms a little passageway into the Great Hall.

corner, and so on, so I had four arches above each of the four rising stairways of the four sections of the stair. We reinstated this in stone, which was a luxury I enjoyed undertaking, but the other stairways, due to lack of time and lack of finance, were cast in situ, onto existing stubs. I had to build the first three or four steps in, blind, and rebuild part of the staircase wall, before I could take down the shoring that supported a large area of crumbling wall, above. I was very pleased to find that the next part of the old steps, when located, tied in exactly with the other four treads that I had put in blind!.

Fig. 12
Rebuilding of the spiral staircase to gain access to the upper floors.

From the Great Hall a mural stairway had to be built up to the Laird's private room (Fig. 12) which, rather unusually, didn't appear to have had an access doorway between the two rooms, although a similar detail is to be found at Breakie Castle, near Friocheim. We also built a garderobe chamber off the Great Hall. I suppose that was a bit of a licence, but it did take the weight off the corridor, below.

The north gable of Forter had fallen down in about 1900, and had to be completely rebuilt and on the floor above the Great Hall the chimney from the kitchen on the ground floor had also to be rebuilt in stone. If one bears in mind that we started rebuilding the vaults at the beginning of June, and that by the beginning of September I was working on the third floor, I hope that I have demonstrated once again that, provided one puts one mind to it, the rebuilding in stone is not necessarily a slow process! By the end of October we were laying the roof but, sadly, by November my involvement with Forter ceased. This was a great pity, as I would have liked to be involved in the timber work and plastering, but that was not to be.

In concluding what I have to say, may I state that I strongly believe that anyone who undertakes the restoration or rebuilding of one of these towers is doing this country a great favour. As already mentioned, there is only a limited number of these buildings left standing in Scotland. When one considers the numbers left, and compares these with the vast numbers of castles and manor houses in a country like France, it is very important to save as many of these castles, tower houses and fortalices as possible. Unless taken into care and restored by private owners or trusts The State will certainly never have the financial resources in the future to stabilise, let alone restore, even a token number, so unless taken into care and restored by private owners or trusts they will disintegrate eventually, and sometimes extremely rapidly. In my relatively brief lifetime, I have seen, in addition to the effects of rain, wind and frost, the effect of vandals, an activity that is on a dramatic increase. I have witnessed the wanton destruction of three or four feet of a five foot thick wall, back in March 1991, by a vandal who couldn't think of a better way to spend a Saturday afternoon. It is futile to believe that these towers will still remain for future generations to see or to excavate, should they be left unrestored as a matter of policy or fail to be professionally stabilized. Furthermore, the promotion of a leave-them-alone-view only serves to undermine all the good work undertaken by the Historic Buildings Council, over more than half a century. It also invites the inevitable destruction and loss of many of the castles that still stand, in some form or other, despite weather, stone-robbers, vandals or well intentioned (but purist) architectural historians.

Fig. 13
Rebuilding of the wall between the tower and the wing, incorporating a recessed circular aumbry, and the laird's private stair (bottom right in the photograph) rising from the Great Hall below.

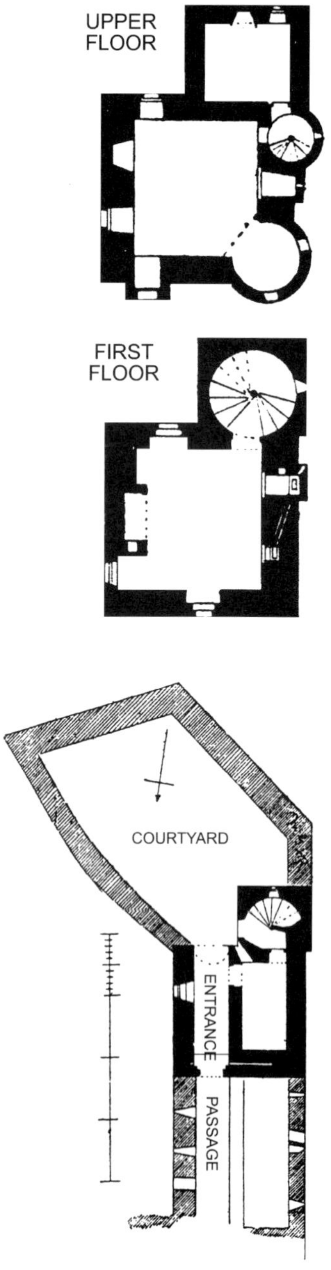

Fig. 1
Gylen Castle, Kerrara. NW elevations and plans. MacGibbon & Ross.

In Concluding - Castle Tioram and the like . . .
BY MICHAEL C. DAVIS.

Michael Davis, an architectural historian and conservationist, concluded the Castles Conference with a short speech, but nine years later the castle restoration debate that warmed in the City Chambers, during the Civic Reception, has continued and moved on. The latest round has been triggered by the possibility that the new owner of Castle Tioram, in Moidart, may wish to resurrect it from romantic ruin to something of its former architectural drama. Rather than repeat what was briefly said at the Conference, Michael Davis's paper, printed here, was given originally at a discussion arranged by the Society of Antiquaries of Scotland in late 1998. As his message is to try to inject a sense of proportion and breath of vision into the clash of archaeological and architectural culture, it forms a suitable conclusion to this volume.

In the Seventies, restorers might well have been seen as one of many products of the new democratic age: romantic enthusiasts paradoxically saving and adapting against a background of large scale town centre redevelopment and wholesale demolition of country houses. Since then, the honing of conservation theory and practice, together with privatisation fears and new assumptions about the commercial value of property, has made professionals and public more wary: witness the Portencross Association's recent well aired fears of loss of access to the vicinity of Portencross Castle and the shore beyond, should the tower be restored. What may to one man be a question of archaeological, architectural or conservation philosophy, may to another be coloured by wider perceptions and beliefs, not least by political standpoints and sympathies regarding ownership of property and heritage.

I offer you not a single narrow doctrine (and burn all heretics) but an argument that the controversy surrounding possible proposals for the restoration of Castle Tioram (the present cause celebre of castle restoration) exists not in the clash of absolutes, but in the collision of partial and varied views. Tioram might, indeed, at first seem like a two-cornered fight between "purists" and "restorers"; the encapsulation, in fact, of a widening public suspicion of the castle restoration trend (in so far, at least, as the public cares at all).

To display the breadth of viewpoints on how to treat a ruined historic structure, I propose not to take you to controversial Tioram, but to Gylen, near Oban. (Fig. 1). Here, in this beautiful spot above rugged cliffs on Kerrara, Miss Hope MacDougall of Dunollie has set out to consolidate Gylen Castle, a ruined but complete shell, using Martin Hadlington as her architect. Hadlington even proposes to replace the turf on the wallhead, when the consolidation scheme is complete.

Surely, there can be little to argue about here, except for those who would prefer a gradual structural collapse (or even demolition of safety grounds) to any treatment of a ruin. It is safe to say that very few feel that a modern consolidation scheme run along SPAB lines would threaten the integrity of a structure or its

In Concluding – Michael C. Davis

archaeological and architectural evidence to an extent which would make decay and ultimate loss of the structure preferable.

However, there may be concern that repairing but not re-roofing a ruin - and it is certainly not the first time that Gylen has been repaired - makes a similar repair inevitable to a later generation. How soon will it be before the new lime mortar is washed out? Will another restorer of Hope MacDougall's mettle, or an architect of Martin Hadlington's discernment, be at hand? Will there even be funds to complete the current repair? And will consolidation alone solve the problem of the saturation and erosion of sculptured detail over time? It is an often overlooked point that even romantic ruins do not stand up on their own and that both Tioram and Gylen have been subject to consolidation work in the past. At Tioram, (Fig. 2), in fact, a large section of wall was manifestly rebuilt in the 19th century.

And what if.....? What if the client at Gylen had been of a different mettle? What if she had been more concerned with restoring "as was" than with conserving "as is"? What if she felt that this *"architectural* gem" had not been built as a ruin, had survived complete to the wallhead, and that a re-constructed roof could be very close to the original, could provide long-term protection to the structure and could recreate fairly exactly he original appearance? And by inserting floors into the sockets once more, the spatial qualities of the rooms could again be understood and enjoyed and the lines of sight and views from the windows appreciated once more.

Rightly, one must point out that new work, however close to the original and however self-effacing it might be, is always of its own time. How much reconstruction is permitted by SPAB doctrine should perhaps represent a dilemma for SPAB-ites, rather than the rest of us. How carefully William Morris

Fig. 2
Castle Tioram.
Photo: Michael C. Davis

Michael C. Davis – **In Concluding**

weighed the impassioned phrases of his manifesto and how, through the years, practising SPAB members have adapted to the spirit rather than the letter is open to debate. The Third Marquis of Bute, latterly one of the most spabby of all architectural patrons, was not above reconstructing Wester Kames on Bute, inserting a thin red line of tiles to distinguish old from new. If, to-day, one architect refused to re-roof a renaissance building, there would be little difficulty in finding a leading conservation architect to take his or her place.

And *what if* the proposals for Gylen had involved the implementation of a scheme, devised years ago, by the late Leslie Graham MacDougall (rather in the manner of Lorimer's Dunderave) but with, of course, modern conservation specifications - a full restoration in the modern sense, yet respecting the archaeological evidence and the integrity of the existing structure, drawing a line between conservation of the old and the contemporary revivalist creativity seen in the lush excitement of bellcast roof forms?

This approach, too, is a point of view, with its own integrity and with conviction in its own terms. History has not actually stopped. We are not standing at the end of time. We feel the duty to preserve and the desire to create. After all, though Lorimer's restoration of Dunderave may not please the archaeological "fundamentalist", he created a new chapter in the history of the building, making it far more, rather than less, significant to architectural historians of the future. However self-effacing or otherwise we may be, our present day treatment of ruins cannot represent a scientific reconstruction of the past, detached from the march of time. Instead - whatever we do - it represents a creative revivalist conceit and therein may lie the significance of such work for the future.

Beyond such approaches lie a good few more. Not all are beyond the serious regard of architectural conservation. Building a modern castle of steel and glass above the ruin of a consolidated vault or within a fragmented but stabilised shell has some considerable appeal, not least because it has scarcely been done. Nor are all such possible approaches necessarily without their own artistic integrity: to a modern architect of imagination and calibre, the design of the new work - tomorrow's heritage - may, of course, figure more importantly that the preservation of the old; and so it may too, alas, to an architect or client of less enlightened interest, or of less talent.

All of this may give an impression of a neat sorting out of many allegiances. Nothing could be further from the truth. Most of us react instinctively; few of us trouble to plot our precise standpoint. Dilemmas therefore abound. Should respect for the past interpose a museum doorway between the past and present, or is the point of conservation to live with the past, sensitively preserving and altering it? Is architectural conservation about aesthetic value judgement or about historic significance? Is the present to be the life support machine for past relics, or is the present part of a continuation of artistic development? Do we live with the past, or with the past in a glass box?

If any form of consensus is to be reached, we all have to acknowledge that a

In Concluding – Michael C. Davis

wider world exists out there. For most, there is little difficulty in recognising this, for we naturally find our feet in different camps. I can see the validity in almost every point of view. For me, choosing one and one approach alone would be repugnant. I take pleasure in diversity of approach, within limits. But for some, the blinkers are on. I want to probe a few related issues before I conclude.

Firstly, the term "archaeology" is increasingly invoked to describe actual objects and structures which have archaeological interest or value; hence a cairn or limekiln might today be described as "archaeology". In part, this is simply a sloppy use of English, for archaeology is really a process, a method, a discipline, a means of learning about the past, rather than the object or thing itself. Such usage is acceptable when applied to prehistoric objects, for the fact of their constituting archaeological evidence of a pre-historic period is usually the most important thing about them. Not so, historic architecture. An historic building, ruined or whole, may contain archaeological evidence, and evidence of different phases of its occupation, but such evidence is only one strand of its significance to us and only one line of exploration in understanding its history. To describe a tower house or fortified house as "standing archaeology", that absurd modern buzz-word (or words), is to use a term loaded with persuasive and partisan imagery. It tends to reduce a building to only one facet of its relevance, swaddling it metaphorically in the tissue paper of a museum archive box, like some prehistoric pot (but in practice not necessarily doing anything to protect the above-ground structure). Coming with the worthy vibes which "archaeology" has, the term seems to provide a compelling message to regard a building not so much as architecture, but as an object for a museum case, the security of which it is unlikely ever to be afforded.

It is also a term which holds too much water. Does Craigievar require to be burnt out before it becomes "standing archaeology"? Presumably not: you don't need to torch a building to find archaeological evidence! And if a tower house or Scots renaissance chateau can be thus described, what of more recent historic structures? What of the Glasgow tenement? Is this "inhabited standing archaeology", perhaps? By so widely applying a word not intended for objects at all, but for one method of exploring and understanding the past, we lose definition. Let us stick to "archaeological evidence" please, rather than investing entire buildings in the proprietorial embrace of archaeological imperialism!

Secondly, there is the curious interface within architectural conservation between historic significance and aesthetic value. Is historic significance alone sufficient reason to wish to preserve (rather than record) a building? "Surely you wouldn't only want to save attractive buildings?" ran a question, when I showed little enthusiasm for a campaign to save the Leith Fort tower-blocks. The question was apposite, caustically pointing up the equally subjective alternative view of rating on aesthetic merit. Yet, surely both approaches have to be squared in any reasonable conservation stance.

In order to inject a sense of proportion into the castle restoration debate, it is worth stating that, to an architectural conservationist, the loss of features and character on humble historic buildings, very much in the public face, might be as significant as major alterations to a 16th century castle which is hidden away on private land. Similarly, discussion over the propriety of using blockwork under harl may seem almost irrelevant to many, when the setting of the restored structure has been adversely affected by a neighbouring development. Awareness of such differing priorities is essential if we are to grasp the problem as a whole, seeing dimensions we may not have known existed.

Of all the protagonists, the castle restorer seems to be the current bogeyman. Restorers may be well intentioned enthusiasts, knowledgeable and scholarly, with a firm grasp of conservation theory and practice. Or, then again, they may not be so. If the 1991 AHSS conference revealed anything, it was simply that restorers, whatever their intentions, were not necessarily either archaeologists, architectural historians, architectural conservationists, revivalists or even among those attempting to forge a new architectural synthesis.

But why should we be surprised? Why should we expect more of those tackling fortified houses, for example, than any other historic building? My own expectations of alterations proposed for listed buildings, in general, are pretty low. We accept astonishing levels of interference with listed buildings and buildings within conservation areas. Nor has there been much agitation to the effect that derelict 18th century tenement facades in our streets should be cases for consolidation or "standing archaeology" alone.

And what of Historic Scotland? In the forthcoming 'siege of Tioram', after all, many will look to their war engines. But I would wish to propose an alternative view to that of Historic Scotland as a principal protagonist; I would view the whole planning process, Historic Scotland included, as the battlefield itself.

Outwith our concerns, so far, lie two key matters highly significant to the future of Tioram, namely access and scenic value. I say outwith our concerns, for neither issue is necessarily in line with the protection of archaeological evidence or with historical integrity, though they may well be of greater real importance than any matters we have discussed so far. Since we do not yet know exactly what Anta Estates (the new owners of Tioram) intend, we cannot comment in specific terms on the former. After all, restoration might, in a real way, increase potential access to the structure by making it safe and opening up the upper floors. Scenic value, however, is a curiously double edged sword, and I shall effectively deflate any use of it by pointing out that probably the most widely appreciated scenic building in Britain is Eilean Donan Castle in Wester Ross, the 20th century reconstruction of which has been condemned as twee by aesthetes and as false by archaeologists. Even so, it is bloody good scenery. Turning Tioram's aspect back to its original spectacular architectural appearance would not necessarily harm and may well enhance its scenic power.

How, to conclude; do we apply breadth of vision to Tioram and the like? How do we reach a working consensus? My answer is that we look at Tioram not in isolation as a castle - a very artificial approach - but as we would any ruined historic building. Just as there is more than one way to skin a rabbit, I argue for

In Concluding – Michael C. Davis

a degree of diversity of approach in castle restoration and for, within the limits of respect for archaeology and architectural conviction, a broad church. It is, in any case, what the planning system gives us with listed buildings. A recent article in *The Herald* paraphrased the views of one Historic Scotland official to the effect that "the aim of listing is not to preserve buildings in aspic, merely to protect them from insensitive assault: buildings have to move on. They have to be alive". If buildings had in the past been kept without alteration, "Edinburgh Castle would have remained as the tiny St Margaret's chapel on top of the hill".

So, as my parting shot, think of Tioram (Fig. 3 below), but look at Alexander "Greek" Thomson's Caledonia Road Church in Glasgow which, in terms of Scottish and European architectural history, is *far* more important than Tioram. Each represents a potential case for conservation. Do we really want to let these buildings fall, or help them down on safety grounds? Would such an extreme approach be culturally unforgivable?

Should we consider consolidation or rebuilding missing portions, or even re-roofing, if someone offers to pay the bill? Should we be more concerned with a general principle than with assessing the actual nitty-gritty of *how* it is to be done? Should we consider restoration in a good, congruous revivalist scheme, allowing a degree of creativity in new work, if that is what is on offer? Should we say 'no' to exciting, avant-garde introductions in steel and glass, if they are of high design quality and do not compromise the old... if that is what is on offer?

Should we, on the other extreme, simply allow any form of alteration and addition, congruous or not, artistic or not, well specified or not? At the end of the day, we must each of us make up our own minds, based on what we consider to be important in the treatment of historic ruins.

If I have opened a few formerly closed minds to the evaluation of other viewpoints, then this paper has served its purpose.

Fig. 3
NW building within the courtyard at Tioram, showing successive additions.
Are we at the end of history?
Photo: copyright: RCAHMS.